PR IN PRACTICE SERIES

Evaluat Public Relations

A Best Practice Guide to Public Relations Planning, Research and Evaluation

Second Edition

Tom Watson and
Paul Noble

CHARTERED INSTITUTE OF PUBLIC RELATIONS

KOGAN
PAGE

London and Philadelphia

Publisher's note

Every possible effort has been made to ensure that the information contained in this book is accurate at the time of going to press, and the publishers and authors cannot accept responsibility for any errors or omissions, however caused. No responsibility for loss or damage occasioned to any person acting, or refraining from action, as a result of the material in this publication can be accepted by the editor, the publisher or either of the authors.

First published in Great Britain and the United States in 2005 by Kogan Page Limited
Second edition 2007

120 Pentonville Road
London N1 9JN
United Kingdom
www.kogan-page.co.uk

525 South 4th Street, #241
Philadelphia PA 19147
USA

ISBN-13   978 0 7494 4979 7

British Library Cataloguing-in-Publication Data

A CIP record for this book is available from the British Library.

Library of Congress Cataloging-in-Publication Data

Watson, Tom, 1950–
   Evaluating public relations : a best practice guide to public relations planning, research & evaluation / Tom Watson & Paul Noble. -- 2nd ed.
      p. cm.
   Includes bibliographical references and index.
   ISBN-13: 978-0-7494-4979-7
   ISBN-10: 0-7494-4979-9
   1. Public relations--Evaluation. 2. Public relations--Evaluation--Case studies. I. Noble, Paul, 1955– II. Title.
   HD59.W325 2007
   659.2--dc22

                                                        2007026140

Typeset by Jean Cussons Typesetting, Diss, Norfolk
Printed and bound in India by Replika Press Ptv Ltd

Contents

1

Principles of public relations practice

In this chapter, evaluation is introduced and set in the historical perspectives of public relations' evolving practice. The nature and extent of public relations theory are explored and definitions of public relations are discussed. Definitions of evaluation and description of key practices complete the chapter.

Ask any group of PR practitioners around the world to list the major issues facing their discipline, and it is almost certain that evaluation of PR activity will be ranked very highly, if not the number one topic. The measurement of activity and outcomes has many facets which will be described throughout this book. To set the context of evaluation, the theory and debate over the discipline of public relations need to be explored. For some practitioners, theory is 'stuff' that gets in the way of 'doing PR'. Yet theory is developed from observed practice and helps predict outcomes. This, in turn, gives greater strength to practitioners in developing robust campaigns. Evaluation helps them define campaigns, monitor their progress and provide evidence of outcomes. So theory and sound evaluation practices can and should go hand-in-hand.

THE ROLE OF THEORY

Public relations is a relatively new professional activity that is still developing its body of knowledge and theoretical approaches. At present, the role that theory plays in public relations practice is limited. As practice expands worldwide, the demand for greater agreement on concepts, embodied in models and theory, is expected to grow, if only for reasons of clarity of communication from one nation to another.

The adoption of the scientific research process for the study of public relations issues and problems offers many advantages to practitioners in the creation of effective campaigns and other public relations activities. Robustly researched theories offer prediction, understanding and replication. Prediction gives greater assurance to planning and execution of activities and a practitioner could, therefore, buttress his or her professional experience with the application of relevant theory to explain that, if a certain course of action is followed, it is likely that certain consequences may follow. That a practitioner can apply proven theory will help in the making of 'intelligent practical decisions'. When there is a lack of theory, it is exceedingly difficult to create a consistent decision-making methodology for use in planning and evaluation, let alone make predictions on outcomes of public relations activities.

Public relations practice is in the humanistic, social science framework and therefore unlike the more precisely measured natural sciences. Because public relations activity uses a multiplicity of communications techniques, it does not operate in isolation (as would a natural science experiment in a laboratory) from other communications influences and so concepts and theories are likely to be based on observed practice. However, predictive understanding has already been identified as an important value of theory for use by the practitioner. Whether objective knowledge can be obtained, in the style of natural science, is a challenge for future research programmes. At present, it is most probable that understanding based on observation is likely to create the path forward for public relations theory as it has done for much of social science (see, in particular, the discussion of action research in Chapter 4).

Practitioners are often closely involved in the mechanics of their activities and need to develop a structured understanding of the issues they are influencing in order to understand the attitudes of others. They also need the rigour of predictive understanding to verify logically the phenomena (such as publics, communities and media) with which they plan to communicate.

Replication is another attribute of theory that has value for planning of public relations programmes. If theory provides clear guidance to 'explain and predict phenomena of interest to us', the theory should be applicable in many similar situations. It can thus be replicated in practice and in future research activities.

For public relations, the methodology of the scientific research process in its social sciences form offers the opportunity to create model theory that can be applied to current practice. Practitioners of public relations are active in an industry that has evolved rapidly by borrowing concepts from a wide range of other disciplines. There is an increasing opportunity to develop theory that is relevant to practice.

THE EVOLUTION OF PUBLIC RELATIONS

Public relations practice, as it is observed today, has developed from press agentry and publicity since the turn of the last century. The US academics James Grunig and Todd Hunt consider that 'public relations-like activity' can be traced back to 1800 BC among Greek rhetoricians, but the direct line of descent from the Aegean to today's public relations industry is difficult to detect (Grunig and Hunt, 1984).

It is seen by many as having evolved from the United States and practitioners there claim descent from Phineas T Barnum (of Barnum and Bailey Circus fame). More likely, it comes from a governmental base in the major combatant nations during the First World War. The need to control information and to motivate the populations of Great Britain, France and the United States led to the formation of government propaganda organizations. An example given is the US Committee on Public Information, which conducted informational communication programmes to induce changes in public opinion.

This one-way informational concept of public relations as the practice of persuasive publicity continued as the dominant mode throughout the 20th century. It was epitomized in the United States and the UK by the role undertaken by press agents who offered to get clients' names in the press in return for payment based on the lineage that appeared.

A significant contribution to the development of public relations came from Edward Bernays in the 1920s. He promoted a more sophisticated one-way approach to communications by contending that public relations attempts to engineer public support through the use of information, persuasion and adjustment.

For many public relations practitioners, persuasion is the desired outcome of their activities, whether it is to change the attitude of government towards a client, promote an employer's point of view or create awareness of a product or service and thus support sales. It is also the judgement applied by clients who ask whether the 'PR effort' made changes that were both beneficial and made an impact on profits. Yet Bernays did not simplistically advocate crude, one-way communications. His aim was to apply social science methods first to research the situation and then to create the most effective methods of communication.

Absent from these early approaches was a developed concept of two-way communication, of strategy and of feedback applied to the programme of activity (as discussed later, very much evaluation in a formative role). Bernays and other leading US practitioners, some working closely with advertising agencies, were more methodical in their research and strategy, but press agents and publicity people remained short term in their approach. They concentrated on gaining column inches of copy in newspapers and magazines, not defining strategies to meet client objectives.

From the 1950s onwards, notions such as 'mutual benefit' and 'goodwill' became more widespread and public relations began to move away from its roots in publicity towards a more planned approach. While significant progress has been made, this issue remains a major concern. In 2004, a research study conducted for the UK's IPR (Institute of Public Relations) and CDF (The Director's Forum) concluded with a series of recommendations including: 'The PR industry should place more emphasis on the technical understanding required to conduct proper planning, research and evaluation (PRE).' Chapter 11 discusses this study in more detail.

PRACTICE PARADIGM

James Grunig has defined four descriptors of public relations activity: press agentry/publicity, public information, two-way asymmetric and two-way symmetric. Press agentry/publicity has already been described. Public information is the distribution of positive information undertaken by 'journalists in residence'. These are both one-way models in which the practitioner does not seek information from the public through informal feedback or research.

His two-way asymmetrical model uses research to identify messages most likely to produce the support of publics without the organization's behaviour changing. Grunig says 'the effects are asymmetrical because the hoped-for behavioural change benefits the organization and not publics'. This model is closest to the Bernays mindset defined many decades before and remains the epitome of modern, sophisticated public relations practice.

One of Grunig's main contributions to public relations theory is the symmetrical model of public relations. He described it as 'benefiting both organization and publics'. It is public relations with a social conscience and is closely linked with some of the more altruistic of public relations. Indeed, in 2003 a report jointly funded by the UK's Department of Trade and Industry and the IPR identified one of the current issues in UK public relations practice as: 'Public relations must increasingly be seen in the context of longer-term strategic relationship management and engagement on emerging trends such as corporate social responsibility.' (See Chapter 11.)

DEFINING PUBLIC RELATIONS

What is public relations? For many, the simplistic answer is getting their name (company, client, self) into newsprint or on air in a report or article; for others it is publicity that attracts response through name recognition or rising sales. Governments see it as dispersal of information, for example in a health promotion campaign.

Measuring the results of these one-way (outward only) processes is usually done by accumulating press cuttings and broadcast transcripts and giving a value to the mentions (such as advertising equivalent cost), column inches and airtime. These may be descriptions of some everyday public relations activities, but they do not define the public relations process nor explain the meaning of the term 'public relations'.

The management function of public relations is most frequently expressed in definitions. One of the most widely taught, especially in the United States, is that of Cutlip, Center and Broom (2006: 5): 'Public relations is the management function that establishes and maintains mutually beneficial relationships between an organization and the publics on whom its success or failure depends.'

There are several phrases to note in this well-known definition. They first describe public relations as a 'management function', which implies it is a deliberate, planned action that has an outcome in mind. This is reinforced by 'identifies, establishes and maintains', which demonstrates research and a continuum of activity. 'Mutually beneficial relationships' relates to a two-way communication process through which the organization will act in the interests of both itself and the groups or publics with which it interacts. This definition goes one stage further than others do by defining publics as those 'on whom its success or failure depends'. This verges on tautology as publics by their very nature are of central importance to an organization by giving it a reputation and a commercial, governmental or other organizational raison d'être. However, this is a comment that queries an aspect of this definition, not its central thrust of being a managed process of two-way communications.

In the UK, the common definition is that proposed by the Chartered Institute of Public Relations (CIPR). It embodies many of the aspects of the US definitions but notably omits the management function and says: '[Public relations] is the planned and sustained effort to establish and maintain goodwill and mutual understanding between an organization and its publics' (www.cipr.co.uk).

It does share the continuum element of 'planned and sustained effort' with objectives of establishing and maintaining goodwill and understanding, also an aspiration for two-way communications. As in the Cutlip, Center and Broom definition, there is a strong aspirational element that presupposes there is a nirvana of perfect communications which could be reached, if only 'goodwill and understanding' were established.

By contrast, in an earlier era Bernays emphasized the persuasive element in his definition that 'Public relations attempts to engineer public support.' This is a one-way definition and is probably closest to commonly found practitioner attitudes. Bernays developed his theories of public relations from his interpretation of social sciences and psychology, in particular. He considered that knowledge of psychology was important because practitioners had to understand the diversity of human behaviour. By understanding behaviour, public relations programmes could be designed to meet the needs of both client and the target publics. There is no aspirational element offered because Bernays' definition is action-oriented. Not surprisingly, his contribution to public relations theory has been strongly criticized as encouraging the manipulative and being anti-democratic.

US academics Botan and Hazleton (1989) observed that: '[Public relations] serves as the definitional label for the process of attempting to exert symbolic control over the evaluative dispositions (attitudes, images) and subsequent behaviours of relevant publics or clienteles.' This is one of the few definitions that offer a conceptual approach to the process as opposed to the majority which describe the objectives of public relations practice. It also firmly places public relations in the persuasive, asymmetric model because of its emphasis on controlling communications to meet an organization's objectives.

Two conclusions can be drawn from these many definitions of public relations. One is that there is a clear gap between the two-way communication models advocated by academics, such as Grunig, and the reality of one-way models adopted by practitioners. This is a divergence that runs parallel throughout comparisons of academic research and actual practitioner behaviour. The second, referred to above, is the debate between the managerial view of public relations practice, which is not confined to one-way or two-way definitions, and the altruistic approach that is exemplified by many two-way definitions. This separation is not as clearly reflected in the theory of public relations, although an important challenge to the primacy of the symmetrical model is currently being mounted. With the emphasis on promoting altruistic values or at least those that are of mutual benefit, public relations theory appears to have taken a different path from other communication and marketing disciplines by emphasizing legitimacy at the expense of applied functional research.

PUBLIC RELATIONS THEORY

There is considerable debate as to whether there is a broad base to public relations theory. Theory is a term loosely applied by many commentators on public relations issues to a wide range of professional axioms or, to use the summary offered by American writer Ray Simon, 'the broad range of "how to" skills with which it [public relations] is practised' (Simon, 1984).

Despite a welter of text, theoretical development is limited. Most research and writing is concerned with the management and methodology of public relations and observation on the culture of public relations. US academic Jim VanLeuven has acidly commented: 'Much of what passes for theory in public relations comprises a loose collection of professional axioms that pull together divergent perspectives in public relations practice to further establish public relations as a necessary management function' (VanLeuven *et al*, 1988).

Grunig and Hunt commented more than 20 years ago that 'public relations is an infant scholarly field'. James Grunig in a more recent article says of the nature of public relations theory: 'One can think of many theories that apply to public relations but it is more difficult to think of a public relations theory (one that has not been borrowed from another discipline). Public relations as a scholarly discipline, therefore, appears to be fragmented and not unique as a discipline.'

GRUNIG'S PRIMACY

Grunig's four models of practice and his situational theory of public relations have been in development for over two decades (Grunig, 1984). In that time, there has been little competition to these models, although some elements, notably his reliance on the symmetrical model as the 'excellent' form of public relations practice, are increasingly debated. Grunig's four models do not in themselves add up to a theory of public relations because they are essentially observations which have been processed into a classification of practitioner behaviour and attitudes.

From this base, however, Grunig has developed his situational theory, using the symmetrical model of public relations (Grunig, 1994). This theory seeks to explain why people communicate and when they are most likely to communicate. He says it explains how predicted communication behaviour can be used to analyse the mass population into publics. Grunig says this theory provides a means of segmenting publics in a manner similar to theories of market segmentation. It aims to predict the differential responses which are most relevant to the planning of public relations activity: namely, responsiveness to issues; amount of and nature of communication behaviour; effects of communication on cognition, attitudes and behaviour; and the likelihood of participation in collective behaviour to pressure organizations. Grunig continues to develop this theory and it is also used by others to study other concepts such as the interaction of publics, the media and public relations practitioners.

EUROPEAN PERSPECTIVES

The European approach to public relations research differs strongly from the anglophone tradition. It is more sociological and rhetorical in nature, unlike the US research which is rooted in managerial theory as well as borrowing from concepts of communication and public opinion. The Europeans are thus more distant from public relations practice and management. British academics Toby MacManus and Danny Moss, commenting on Europe's first PR research symposium in 1994, noted: 'The contrast between different research traditions was marked. The Dutch and German contributions emphasized theoretical and normative issues, whereas the UK and US papers were more empirically based' (MacManus and Moss, 1994).

European approaches have made little impact on mainstream public relations practice and the internationalization of public relations through the expansion of major US- and UK-owned consultancy networks throughout Europe may reduce their influence further. The reverse case of US-sourced theory's influence on European researchers is demonstrable by the broad acceptance in academic writing of Grunig's four models of practice and his situational theory. The primacy of American theory has been admitted by the Dutch academic Betteke van Ruler who commented: 'Most of the thinking about public relations theory comes from the United States' (van Ruler, 1992).

European scholars have interpreted sociologists and communications theorists such as Weber, Habermas, Foucault and Bourdieu when setting public relations in a social perspective. German academic Manfred Ruhl says that the failure to appreciate the potential role of public relations by practitioners and their clients/ employers is due to lack of interest in constructing concepts, especially of public relations' 'social dimensions' (Ruhl, 1992). The theoretical and historical evolution of public relations described in this chapter shows that public relations has moved in a mainly managerial direction. By its very nature, management has demands for reporting, measurement and planned outcomes, and so evaluation should be an integral part of public relations practice which mainly follows informational one-way or asymmetric two-way models, as described by James Grunig.

QUESTIONNAIRE RESPONSES

Evaluation questionnaire for industry leaders

To get a worldwide view of attitudes to public relations evaluation, industry leaders around the world were surveyed on key questions.

Q: Typically, how do you or your organization evaluate public relations activity?

There is no one typical way: evaluation depends on types of programmes – appropriateness, clients – their needs and means, time – availability, and imagination – how to go beyond tradition. **Dejan Verčič, PhD, partner, Pristop Communications, Slovenia**

Using a suite of tools that might include internal reviews, surveys and external procurement of media evaluation. **Alison Clarke, Group Business Development Director, Huntsworth plc, UK**

1. In-house media monitoring, external service for TV, radio.
2. Evaluation team evaluates all organizational programme areas. These all (seven in total) have communication strategies.

3. For short campaigns, external pre and post surveys. Mid-campaign surveys for those longer than 12 months. **Fran Hagon, Senior Manager, Corporate Public Affairs and Marketing, National Prescribing Service Ltd (NPS), Australia**

We prefer to evaluate our outputs against pre-determined business and communications objectives agreed with the client. So if a client wants to move from number 2 to number 1 in the market the measurement criteria are clear to all. Some clients invest in media analysis services – which have some value if share of voice in a small press community is important. However, we find these tools lack the sophistication to be tailored to individual client needs and therefore can give a false picture of achievement and definitely have limited value in the broader PR remit. **Crispin Manners, Chief Executive, Kaizo, UK**

There isn't a typical approach. We sit down with clients at the start of every campaign and decide what the best way to evaluate is. It ranges from outside research for a government department to coverage analysis and the estimated advertising equivalent for a manufacturer. Every report is different but we have some standard templates. **Loretta Tobin, Deputy Chief Executive, Harrison Cowley, UK**

Mainly through media monitoring and assessment of the level of interest and focus on the client company. **Ray Mawerera, Managing Consultant, Words & Images Corporate Communications, Zimbabwe**

The answer is very simple. 'We achieved our targets, or x per cent of the target.' Of course, this relies on having clear targets in the first place. These come back to the inputs, outputs and outcomes elements, which can be measured in various ways. Measuring inputs/outputs provides clients with interim confidence in the programme, while measuring outcomes is the only measure of effect. **Annabelle Warren, Chairman, Primary Communication, Australia**

Various ways are used – media use of key messages, placement, desirable publication, etc. Functions – analysing attendance by 'right' audience and outcomes thereof, depending on the aim of the function. Clara Zawawi, Director – **Client Relationships, Professional Public Relations, Australia**

Ideally by conducting pre and post research to measure changes in opinion, perception, knowledge base; factual accuracy and tone of news stories; modified public behaviour, or altered position of the opposition. **Tom O'Donoghue, President, O'Donoghue & Associates, Canada**

A software package is used to evaluate the volume, quality and value of coverage (equivalent advertising value × 3). It also measures the penetration of key messages against those set at the beginning of the campaign. **Laurna O'Donnell, Board Director, Beattie Communications, UK**

Mostly it is at a basic level of measuring media hits and undertaking some basic analysis – linked to messages, audiences, volume of coverage, etc. **Mike Copland, Chairman, Brodeur Worldwide UK**

On a variety of levels, but the best ones start with established benchmarks up-front and well-defined objectives. That's easier said than done. From there, it really depends on the nature of the programme. **Matt Kucharski, Senior Vice President, Padilla Speer Beardsley Public Relations, USA**

Evaluation has been the actual, not media coverage or attitudinal, outcomes of this organization's activities. **Richard Offer, Head of Publicity, Police Complaints Authority, UK**

Throughout our policy-making and communication processes, evaluation takes place. This includes evaluating our member needs, developing the Association's policy stance, implementing the PR campaign, and following the completion of the campaign, evaluating the results, which entails monitoring legislative change, media coverage and subsequent membership levels. **Adam Connolly, (formerly) General Manager – Government Relations, NSW Farmers' Association, Australia**

Clients like advertising equivalency. **John Bliss, Principal, Bliss, Gouverneur & Associates, USA**

2

Evaluation and communication psychology

As early as 1920, US public relations practitioners were discussing the role of evaluation of public relations activity. Forty years ago, writers predicted that evaluation practices would move from informal judgement to scientifically derived knowledge. At the beginning of the next century, evaluation is still earnestly discussed. This chapter looks at evaluation theory and its link with psychology.

Like most studies of humans, there is considerable and continuing debate among psychologists on behaviour. The causes and responses are never simple and often unpredictable. Yet for the purposes of communication public relations practitioners seek some characteristics or certainly something upon which they can base their campaigns.

Because of the continuing discussion of behavioural and mass communication theory, it is not possible to offer simple verities. However, this chapter will review the main themes among theorists and then link them with evaluation theories.

In the 1930s, there were studies that argued that the mass media had a powerful and continuing ability to influence public behaviour. The reasons put forward were based on rising literacy, the immediate impact of radio broadcasting and the rise of mass movements in many European countries. An example often cited was the 'War of the Worlds' radio broadcast by Orson Welles, which convinced many thousands of listeners that Martians had attacked the east coast of the United States, whereas Welles had enhanced a well-known story by the science fiction writer HG Wells.

During the next two decades, there was a swing to the reverse argument that mass media did not have a persuasive impact, the so-called 'minimal effects' theories. From these theories, the genesis of many current attitudes and public relations practices can be found.

Some of the key concepts, outlined by McCoy and Hargie (2003), are:

- Interpersonal influence is very strong and opinion leaders play a vital role in spreading and interpreting information (Lazarsfeld *et al*, 1948).
- Among the barriers that limit campaign effectiveness are: *selective exposure* – the tendency to attend to messages that are consistent with prior attitudes and experience; *selective perception* – the tendency to interpret a message in terms of prior attitudes and experiences; and *selective retention* – the tendency to remember messages that are consistent with prior attitudes and experience (Hyman and Sheatsley, 1947).
- Contrasting with this 'cognitive consistency' was Festinger's theory of cognitive dissonance, which said that attitudes can be changed if they are contrasted with a dissonant attitude that is inconsistent with the existing viewpoint (Festinger, 1957).
- While Festinger's theory said that changes in attitudes could come via dissonance, it has become evident over time that people select information because it is relevant to them, rather than because it reinforces existing attitudes (McCoy and Hargie, 2003).
- Over time, discussion moved from the impact of mass media to the influence of interpersonal networks. Social learning theorists have pointed out that we create, modify and retain attitudes in discussion with other people in all the social networks. For example, we may see a story in the media but our attitudes towards an issue, ethical stance or product may be formed when discussing it with others in our family, workplace or other social environment.

There have been many theories and models to explain attitude and the ways in which we receive, retain and act upon information. There are domino models that show that step A leads to step B and so on until the message recipient acts in a predictable way. The domino model is often found in communication strategy documents which propose that a particular approach will almost certainly result in a specific outcome. However, we humans don't think and act in a mechanistic manner. If we accept that models are only illustrative and not predictive, they can be of assistance for the development of public relations campaigns.

The dominant paradigm of practice is the equation of public relations with persuasion. In order to discuss models of evaluation, the nature of persuasion should be reviewed. From communications psychology, there are schemata and models that offer processes which public relations practitioners can apply to the evaluation of their own models. Among the frameworks that have been proposed, McGuire's Output Analysis of the Communication/Persuasion process has attributes that can be considered for persuasion-based public relations evaluation (McGuire, 1984). It can be summarized in six steps as:

PRESENTATION	Getting the message to the target.
ATTENTION	Target pays attention.
COMPREHENSION	Target processes messages. [The target does not necessarily understand the message or understand it correctly or as intended, but does acquire an understanding.]
ACCEPTANCE	Target incorporates message as understood and cognitive/affective state is changed as a result. [This can include boomerang effects.]
RETENTION	Target retains message for a specified time. [The message may, however, be changed as a result of retention and is not therefore the same as acceptance.]
ACTION	Target behaves in the manner desired by the originating communicator.

McGuire's model is not a domino model, as he outlines the likely problems at each stage that may result in attitudes that are not the ones sought. However, it does show that distribution of information, the most evaluated element of public relations activity, is only the first Presentation step in a communication process. To concentrate on that step only is of little value to monitoring the campaign's progress and judging its outcomes.

This six-step process of the model can be further condensed into three major stages of OUTPUT (Presentation), IMPACT (Attention, Comprehension, Acceptance and Retention) and EFFECT (Action). The implication for public relations evaluation arising from this stepped process is that judgements should encompass the full range of the communication process from OUTPUT to EFFECT.

It can be argued that models or evaluation actions which measure Output are ignoring the full (and sometimes difficult to judge) persuasion process. They view only the first major stage and omit Impact and Effect. Yet it is in the interest of the client/employer to assess whether public relations effort (expressed in terms of time, budget and staff resources) has been effective in attaining the desired goals of Acceptance or Action.

In the discussion of current public relation practice by academics, there is often criticism that campaigns propose unattainable behavioural change. McCoy and Hargie (2003: 309–10) argue that 'PR practitioners must first break away from reliance on behaviouristic domino models, secondly accept more conservative expectations of effects and, thirdly, aim for alternative potential outcome. Event researchers who have investigated the communications effects of campaigns and have found positive results acknowledged it is simplistic to believe that PR creates awareness which in turn leads to knowledge, which in turn leads to the formation of a favourable attitude, which result in a behaviour change.'

US researchers Dozier and Ehling (1992) have written that PR campaigns have a 0.04 per cent chance of achieving behaviour change. So McCoy and Hargie (2003: 311) propose that practitioners should set alternative and more realistic objectives which could include agenda setting and the stimulation of interpersonal discussion, which as we note earlier is one of the most likely sources of attitudinal and behavioural change.

As Australian commentator Jim Macnamara (1992) says: 'This... does not imply that communication has no effect. But it does indicate that it is dangerous to make assumptions about (behavioural) communication outcomes.'

NUMBER ONE PRACTITIONER TOPIC

In Delphi studies among UK and US practitioners and academics of research priorities conducted by White and Blamphin (1994) and McElreath and Blamphin (1994), the topic of evaluation was ranked at number one in the development of public relations practice and research. It was important for self-esteem and reputation that methods of evaluation were devised to measure the effectiveness of campaigns.

Yet what is evaluation of public relations? Is it measuring output or monitoring progress against defined objectives? Is it giving a numerical value to the results of programmes and campaigns? Is it the final step in the public relations process or a continuing activity?

When discussing the topic of evaluation, there is considerable confusion as to what it means. For budget-holders, whether employers or clients, the judgements have a 'bottom line' profit-related significance. Grunig and Hunt have written of a practitioner who justified the budgetary expenditure on public relations by the large volume of press coverage generated. He was flummoxed by a senior executive's question: 'What's all this worth to us?' In the UK, articles in the public relations and marketing press refer to evaluation in terms of 'justifying expenditure', which is similar to Grunig and Hunt's example. White (1991) suggests that company managers have a special interest in the evaluation of public relations: 'Evaluation helps to answer the questions about the time, effort and resources to be invested in public relations activities: can the investment, and the costs involved, be justified?'

The definitions by many experts emphasize effectiveness, for example: Cutlip, Center and Broom (2006) – 'systematic measures of program effectiveness', Pavlik (1987) – 'evaluation research is used to determine effectiveness', Blissland (cited in Wilcox *et al*, 2000) – 'the systematic assessment of a program and its results' and Lindenmann (1993) – 'measure public relations effectiveness'. Developments of these definitions are those which are related to programme or campaign objectives, a reflection on the management-by-objectives influence on public relations practice in the United States. Wylie (cited in Wilcox *et al*, 2000) says, 'we are talking about an orderly evaluation of progress in attaining the specific objectives of our public relations plan'.

The term evaluation is a broad one and this breadth gives the potential for confusion. Cutlip, Center and Broom (2006: 364) both illustrate the scope of evaluation and argue that evaluation is a research-based activity: 'The process of evaluating program planning, implementation, and impact is called "evaluation research".' Public relations uses research for a variety of purposes. Dozier and Repper (1992: 186) argue that a distinction needs to be drawn between research designed to analyse the situation at the beginning of the planning process and research designed to evaluate the planning, implementation and impact of the programme. However, they themselves blur this distinction by stressing that the first type of research acts as the benchmark for programme evaluation. In short, a research-based culture is an evaluative culture and vice versa.

If evaluation is an integral part of programme planning (rather than a separate and optional extra activity tacked on to the end), which is itself a circular process with outputs continually feeding back to fine-tune implementation, then the distinction between research to assist implementation and research to measure results becomes increasingly hazy.

OBJECTIVES OF EVALUATION

For effective evaluation to be undertaken, starting points have to be set out, a basis of comparison researched, and specific objectives established. Dozier (1985) has commented that 'measurement of programs without goals is form without substance; true evaluation is impossible'. Weiss (1977) says the 'purpose [of evaluation] should be clearly stated and measurable goals must be formulated before the questions can be devised and the evaluation design chosen'. This is an argument endorsed by many commentators.

The start point and the objective must be defined as part of the programme design, then waypoints can be measured and the effectiveness or impact assessed. White (1991) argues that 'setting precise and measurable objectives at the outset of a programme is a prerequisite for later evaluation'. This is often easier said than done, but Swinehart (1979) says that the objectives of a campaign or programme should be closely related to the research design and data collection as well as the campaign methods and strategy used.

He says that there are five areas of questioning that should be applied to objectives:

1. What is the content of the objective?
2. What is the target population?
3. When should the intended change occur?
4. Are the intended changes unitary or multiple?
5. How much effect is desired?

By posing these questions, it can be seen that simplistic media measurement or reader response analysis only considers output – volume of mentions – and not effects. Objectives of, say, more mentions in the *Financial Times*, which may be sought by a quoted industrial company, are little more than a stick with which to beat the public relations (more correctly, press relations) practitioner. Dozier (1985) refers to this approach as 'pseudo-planning' and 'pseudo-evaluation'. Pseudo-planning is the allocation of resources to communications activities, where the goal is communication itself, and pseudo-evaluation is 'simply counting news release placements, and other communications'.

Swinehart (1979) divides evaluation into four categories: process, quality, intermediate objectives and ultimate objectives. He suggests that there is more to evaluation than impact. He also paves the way for effects-based planning theories:

1. Process is 'the nature of the activities involved in the preparation and dissemination of material'.
2. Quality is 'the assessment of materials or programs in terms of accuracy, clarity, design, production values'.
3. Intermediate objectives which are 'sub-objectives necessary for a goal to be achieved', eg placement of news.
4. Ultimate objectives which are 'changes in the target audience's knowledge, attitudes and behaviour'.

This analysis points out the need for planning and evaluation to be linked. The simpler approaches such as those undertaken by 'media-mentions' calculators separate planning from the campaign and subsequent evaluation.

COMPLEXITY OF EVALUATION

Patton (1982: 17) makes the same point in the context of evaluation in general when he describes the move towards situational evaluation which requires that evaluators have to deal with different people operating in different situations. This is challenging because: 'in most areas of decision-making and judgement, when faced with complex choices and multiple possibilities, we fall back on a set of deeply embedded rules and standard operating procedures that predetermine what we do, thereby effectively short circuiting situational adaptability'. The natural inclination of the human mind is to make sense of new experiences and situations by focusing on those aspects that are familiar, and selectively ignoring evidence that does not fit stereotypes. Thus the tendency is to use existing techniques and explanations, selectively ignoring evidence that indicates a fresh approach might be required.

Situational evaluation not only takes into account the environment in which the programme to be evaluated is operating, but also considers the audience for whom the evaluation is being undertaken. FitzGibbon and Morris (1978: 13–14) explain: 'The critical characteristic of any one evaluation study is that it provides the best possible information that could have been collected under the circumstances, and that this information *meets the credibility requirements of its evaluation audience*' [italics added]. Evaluation is not undertaken for its own sake, but for a purpose, and that purpose requires the audience for whom the evaluation is being undertaken to regard the evaluation process and methodology as relevant and reasonable.

Another aspect of the complexity associated with public relations evaluation is the large number of variables with which public relations practice is concerned. White (1991: 106) explains the point when comparing the disciplines of public relations and marketing: 'Marketing is a more precise practice, which is able to draw on research as it manipulates a small number of variables to aim for predicted results, such as sales targets and measurable market share.' However, public relations remains a more complex activity: 'Public relations is concerned with a far larger number of variables.'

A further dimension of public relations' complexity, which is associated with all forms of mediated communication, is the introduction of an additional step and/or a third party. 'But appraising communication becomes more complicated as soon as the media steps in' (Tixier, 1995: 17). However, when public relations is used in its principal tactical incarnation of media relations, then the lack of control over this mediated communication muddies the waters even further. For example, when comparing publicity-generating media relations with advertising, one market researcher (Sennott, 1990: 63) explains:

> I just saw a press kit from which nobody wrote a story. Good kit. Looked good. Nothing happened. So in public relations we have an extra phase to look at. That leads to some interesting problems in trying to determine how what we do is linked to our success in getting placements.

METHODOLOGY PROBLEMS

There are some intrinsic methodological problems that make the evaluation process difficult. These include:

1. Campaigns are unique and are planned for very specific purposes. It is therefore difficult to evaluate the reliability of a unique event or process.
2. Comparison groups are difficult. A client would not be sympathetic to leaving out half of the target population so that one could compare 'intentions' with control groups.
3. Control of other variables, such as those outside the control of the public relations practitioner. These may impact on the campaign's target publics and may include campaigns run by competitors, the clutter of messages on the same subject from advertising, direct mail, word of mouth etc.
4. Timescale can affect the process and the results. For methodologically sound evaluation, a 'before' sample is needed as 'after' data. This, however, means implementing the evaluation process before the campaign.
5. The probity of the person or organization managing the campaign also being responsible for audit or evaluation. There is a danger of subjective judgement or distortion of result.
6. The plethora of techniques for evaluation of varying effectiveness.

EFFECTS-BASED PLANNING

To develop a more complete approach to planning (and subsequent evaluation) is the purpose of the 'effects-based planning' theories put forward by VanLeuven *et al* (1988). These are closely associated with management-by-objectives techniques used widely in industry and government. Underlying VanLeuven's approach is the premise that a programme's intended communication and behavioural effects serve as the basis from which all other planning decisions can be made.

The process involves setting separate objectives and sub-objectives for each public. He argues that the planning becomes more consistent by having to justify programme and creative decisions on the basis of their intended communication and behavioural effects. It also acts as a continuing evaluation process because the search for consistency means that monitoring is continuous and the process of discussion needs evidence on which to reach decisions. Effects-based planning, says VanLeuven, means that programmes can be compared without the need for isolated case studies.

The search for consistency is one of the most difficult practical issues faced by the public relations professional. A more disciplined approach will allow the parameters of the programme to be more closely defined and for continuous monitoring to replace a single post-intervention evaluation. It will also bolster the objectivity of the evaluation process.

DEFINING EVALUATION

In contrast, evaluation as a practice is firmly rooted in social scientific research methods. As Noble (1994) points out: 'Evaluation as a means of assessing communications effectiveness is nothing new.' Rossi and Freeman (1982: 23) traced the origins of evaluation as a social scientific practice back to attempts in the 1930s to evaluate Roosevelt's New Deal social programmes. However, Patton (1982: 15) argues that evaluation did not emerge as a 'distinctive field of professional social scientific practice' until the late 1960s, about the same time as evaluation began to emerge as an issue in public relations. Public relations evaluation and evaluation as an identifiable social scientific activity have – separately – come under scrutiny over about the same timescale and can learn lessons from each other.

For example, Patton (1982: 15) confirms the broad nature of evaluation with his definition:

> The practice of evaluation involves the systematic collection of information about the activities, characteristics, and outcomes of programs, personnel, and products for use by specific people to reduce uncertainties, improve effectiveness, and make decisions with regard to what those programs, personnel, or products are doing and affecting.

In commenting on this rather convoluted definition Patton makes the important point that: 'the central focus is on evaluation studies and consulting processes that aim to improve program effectiveness'. This places emphasis on evaluation as a formative activity: that is, obtaining feedback to enhance programme management.

Public relations, in particular, frequently embraces evaluation in a defensive, summative guise: assessing final programme outcome. For example, Blissland (cited in Wilcox *et al*, 2000: 191) defines evaluation in summative terms: 'the systematic assessment of a programme and its results. It is a means for practitioners to offer accountability to clients – and to themselves.' Broom and Dozier (1990: 17) criticize this style of public relations evaluation (which they confusingly describe as an 'evaluation-only' approach) because research is not seen as essential for planning, but limited to tracking and assessing impact. It encourages the view of evaluation as a separate activity undertaken at a distinct, late stage in the programme. The implication, frequently made, is therefore that programmes can be implemented without evaluation.

In contrast, Wylie (as cited in Wilcox et al, 2000: 192) presents a more balanced view. He reverts to Patton's emphasis on formative evaluation, but without excluding summative thinking:

> We are talking about an orderly evaluation of our progress in attaining the specific objectives of our public relations plan. We are learning what we did right, what we did wrong, how much progress we've made and, most importantly, how we can do it better next time.

After a short review of what the term evaluation means in public relations, Watson (1997: 284) confirms that there is indeed 'considerable confusion'. He asserts that definitions of evaluation fall into three groups: 'the *commercial*, which is a justification of budget spend; *simple-effectiveness*, which asks whether the programme has worked in terms of output; and *objectives-effectiveness*, which judges programmes in terms of meeting objectives and creation of desired effects'.

While all these three groups of definitions display a summative ('evaluation only') focus, at least the third group introduces the concept of relating evaluation to the objectives set and therefore – by integrating evaluation into the planning process – at least establishes a formative foundation. It is also possible to argue that an evaluation process that establishes that the public relations programme has achieved the objective(s) set, by definition justifies the budget spent.

The most recent and authoritative definition comes from the Commission on Measurement and Evaluation of Public Relations, whose *Dictionary of Public Relations Measurement and Research* defines evaluation research as:

> A form of research that determines the relative effectiveness of a public relations campaign or program by measuring program outcomes (changes in the level of awareness, understanding, attitudes, opinions and/or behaviours of a targeted audience of public) against a predetermined set of objectives that initially established the level or degree of change desired. (Stacks, 2007: 7)

This clearly states that PR evaluation is about measuring outcomes against the set objectives in a robustly organized manner. It rejects the defensive justification reasoning for evaluation and makes the emphasis on programme effectiveness that is judged by outcomes and not output.

PRINCIPLES OF EVALUATION

In summarizing current thinking on public relations evaluation, Noble (1999: 19–20) has set out seven principles of evaluation:

1. **Evaluation is research.** Evaluation is a research-based discipline. Its purpose is to inform and clarify and it operates to high standards of rigour and logic. As the orbit of public relations extends from publicity-seeking media relations to issues management and corporate reputation, research will play an increasingly important role in the planning, execution and measurement of public relations programmes.

2. **Evaluation looks both ways.** Evaluation is a proactive, forward-looking and formative activity that provides feedback to enhance programme management. It is also a reviewing, backward-looking summative activity that assesses the final outcome of the campaign/programme. By so doing it proves public relations' worth to the organization and justifies the budget allocated to it. Formative evaluation is an integral part of day-to-day professional public relations practice and aids the achievement of the ultimate impact with which summative evaluation is concerned. However, public relations loses credibility – and evaluation loses value – if formative techniques are substituted for measurement and assessment of the ultimate impact of public relations programmes.

3. **Evaluation is user and situation dependent.** Evaluation should be undertaken according to the objectives and criteria that are relevant to the organization and campaign concerned. It is a function of public relations management to understand the organization's expectations of public relations activity. Having managed those expectations, the activity then needs to be evaluated in the context of them. It is also a management function to assess the objectives level appropriate to the campaign concerned and to implement it accordingly.

4. **Evaluation is short term.** Short-term evaluation is usually campaign or project based. Such campaigns are frequently concerned with raising awareness through the use of media relations techniques. There is not usually sufficient time for results to feedback and fine-tune the current project. They will, however, add to the pool of experience to enhance the effectiveness of

future campaigns. Short term in this context definitely means less than 12 months.

5. **Evaluation is long term.** Long-term evaluation operates at a broader, strategic level and usually concerns issues management, corporate reputation, and/or brand positioning. It is here that there is maximum opportunity for (or threat of) the substitution of impact evaluation methodologies with process evaluation. The key issue is to ensure that evaluation is undertaken against the criteria established in the objectives. Direct measurement, possibly in the form of market research, is likely to form part of the range of evaluation methodologies employed. Because the communications programme is continuous and long term, regular feedback from evaluation research can help fine-tune planning and implementation as well as measuring results.

6. **Evaluation is comparative.** Evaluation frequently makes no absolute judgements but instead draws comparative conclusions. For example, media evaluation frequently makes historical and/or competitive comparisons, as well as comparing the messages transmitted by the media against those directed at journalists. The purpose of process evaluation is frequently to encourage a positive trend rather than hit arbitrary – and therefore meaningless – targets.

7. **Evaluation is multifaceted.** Public relations has been established as a multi-step process, if only because of the additional stepping stone represented by the media. A range of different evaluation methodologies are required at each step (or level), with process evaluation, for example, being used to enhance the effectiveness of impact effects. The concept of using a selection of different techniques in different circumstances has prompted the use of the term toolkit to describe the range of methodologies available to the communications practitioner.

The reaction of practitioners to the evaluation debate has included emphasis on the role that the setting of appropriate objectives plays in enabling effective evaluation. In the UK, a *PR Week* campaign has called for at least 10 per cent of public relations budgets to be assigned to research and evaluation. Theorists who have long argued in favour of careful objective setting echo these exhortations. Similarly, they have called for public relations to become more of a research-based discipline.

In an ideal world, the setting of specific, quantified and measurable objectives would indeed be the panacea for effective evaluation. However, public relations is rarely – if ever – able to achieve substantive objectives by itself, certainly in the marketing environment where the evaluation spotlight shines brightest. Evaluating public relations by comparing outcomes with objectives set then becomes meaningless if public relations is only one element of the mix, however important. Similarly, allocating 10 per cent of public relations budgets to research and evaluation, however laudable at first sight, implies both that research and evaluation are separate (if closely connected) entities, and that evaluation is a highly desirable added extra rather than an integral part of professional public relations practice. There is a seductive argument that public relations activity which cannot (or will not) be evaluated should not form part of professional practice. (This issue is explored in detail in Chapter 8.)

Interview

David Gallagher has an air of resignation when the subject of evaluation is raised. 'I am not sure whether we know what we are looking for, why we are looking for it, and what its significance might be.' He argues that evaluation (of public relations) is frequently discussed in a marketing context, often using an advertising model. He accepts that it might (at least in theory) be possible to develop a model that would give some idea of the ROI from public relations as a marketing discipline, but that is a limited view of public relations leading to an evaluation system that would not give the user much predictive value.

Predictive value is a point that Gallagher comes back to. 'In theory, it would be nice if you were looking at evaluation to do some mid-course adjustments or maybe at the end of the campaign or programme to assess its efficacy. But I see now the shift for evaluation programmes to be predictive in terms of the type of yield you are likely to get from the investment.'

A related theme for Gallagher is the need for public relations to establish its own data set. 'I would feel better about PR evaluation in almost any application if there was PR-specific baseline or benchmarking data available.' Rather than 'borrowing' data from the advertising department, market research agency or public policy group, he would like to see data specifically derived to test certain hypotheses about the effectiveness of the PR programme. 'Starting from that point, then set your objectives, set your strategy, set your creative elements against that baseline data,' he continues.

But overall Gallagher is sceptical about most evaluation systems and unconvinced that they do much more than help obtain a larger slice of the marketing budget. He recognizes that the theory is all very well, but it is likely to take a significant investment in both upfront research and back-end evaluation to result in a highly correlated set of data. 'And in PR, budgets are generally relatively small so that the investment required to measure at the beginning and the end would, in some cases, offset the amount you spend on the programme.'

Ruth Yearley focuses on the public relations process. 'Understand the business opportunity or problem that your client is faced with, and what role public relations can play in that. Get specific PR objectives and don't over-promise. Make sure that your PR objectives are communications objectives not business objectives. Understand the latter, but don't promise things that are not within your gift.' Gallagher picks up on the discussion of objectives by stressing the importance of the linkage between PR and business objectives. 'If you can't make the link you should question why you are doing it. I am surprised by how tenuous the link is sometimes between PR objectives and stated business goals.'

Both Gallagher and Yearley argue strongly for softer measures to assess the value of the public relations function in general and public relations programmes in particular. In a telling aside, Gallagher points out that other professional functions within the organization are not subjected to the same type of scrutiny. 'I've yet to see the legal department called in to justify themselves on the basis of the ROI it provides.'

Yearley puts the evaluation debate into a consultancy context by stressing the use of the term 'evaluation' rather than 'measurement'. 'Increasingly, our clients take a qualitative, emotional approach to evaluating our outputs. A piece on BBC Radio's agenda-setting *Today* programme in the UK carries a lot of weight, irrespective of reach and target audience. Public relations seems to evoke a different reaction from other disciplines: there's a lot more kudos in editorial publicity, than briefing good creativity or buying media well. It's quite an emotional and amorphous evaluation as opposed to a metric.'

Gallagher adds that although many clients do not understand the public relations process, they know good public relations when they see it and they know bad public relations. So, in defiance of a research-based evaluation programme, gut feel (or professional judgement) has a role to play. He concludes: 'I haven't seen an evaluation programme that wasn't mostly based on gut feel and then retro-fitted to accommodate some sort of statistical analysis. That's not to say I would not prefer some sort of analytical model, it's just I have not seen one that is truly analytically based.'

David Gallagher is chief executive of Ketchum, London and Ruth Yearley is planning director.

3

Practitioner culture – why we do what we do

There is a considerable gap between the academic desire for a social science-based approach to public relations evaluation and the 'seat of the pants' methods used by the vast majority of practitioners. Although some researchers claim that practitioners are becoming more sophisticated, the evidence is that there are barriers to widespread acceptance of systematic evaluation and its techniques across the world.

HOLY GRAIL OR REINVENTING THE WHEEL

The discussion of the evaluation of public relations activity and the application of methodologies is long-standing, with Phillips (2005) identifying discussion as early as 1929 (Thurstone and Chave) that was concerned with the measurement of attitudes. Much of the North American heritage of public relations is based on psychological studies into attitude and public opinion. This followed through strongly after the Second World War with a prominent example being

Hyman and Sheatsley's (1947) article on 'Some reasons why public information campaigns fail,' exemplifying the evaluative trend with an emphasis on psychological barriers to campaign effectiveness. McCoy and Hargie (2003) have tracked the linkage between mass communication theory, with its psychology antecedents and influences, and the evaluation of public relations activity, and linked it to prominent public relations researchers and theorists such as Grunig and Hunt (1984), Dozier and Ehling (1992) and Pavlik (1987).

John Pavlik (1987) has commented that measuring the effectiveness of public relations has proved almost as elusive as finding the Holy Grail. Until the mid-1990s, most studies found that public relations practitioners and their employers/clients had ignored evaluation. Tom Watson's studies of UK practitioners in the 1990s showed many areas of movement on attitudes. By the latter part of the decade, the attitude in the profession towards evaluation and its integration into campaign and programme planning had changed. Nonetheless, there remains work to be done. The IPR/CDF (2004) study included this statement among its recommendations: 'A significant change in the culture of the PR industry is required towards more sophisticated PR measurement as opposed to the "magic bullet" approach that so many PR practitioners appear to desire.'

The culture of public relations practitioners is a fundamental issue when considering attitudes towards evaluation and the methodology used. In textbooks and articles about public relations, writers and academics are almost unanimous in their advice that programmes must be researched during preparation and evaluated during and after implementation. Many researchers, however, have found that a minority of practitioners used scientific evaluation methods. Only recently have methodical studies been undertaken in other countries to explore the experience of practitioners and attitudes of different nationalities and cultures. James Grunig (1984) has a celebrated *cri de coeur* on the subject:

> I have begun to feel more and more like a fundamentalist preacher railing against sin; the difference being that I have railed for evaluation in public relations practice; just as everyone is against sin, so most public relations people I talk to are for evaluation. People keep on sinning, however, and PR people continue not to do evaluation research.

Glen Broom and David Dozier's research on evaluation over a 20-year period in the United States encompassed local (San Diego), national (PRSA) and international (IABC) samples. A consistent finding of their studies was that evaluation of programmes increases as the practitioner's management function develops, whereas it either plateaus or falls away if he or she has a technician role (writing, media relations, production of communication tools). Dozier (1985) says:

> Some practitioners do not engage in any program research, others conduct extensive research. Practitioners vary in the kinds of research methods they use from intuitive, informal 'seat-of-the-pants' research to rigorous scientific studies. Although little longitudinal scholarly research is available, the best evidence is that – over time – more practitioners are doing research more frequently.

There have long been indications of the lack of self-confidence in the UK public relations profession, with some commentators arguing that the need of some practitioners to evaluate activities was 'partly a matter of professional insecurity'. Taking a different tack, another prominent practitioner, Quentin Bell, a former chairman of the UK's Public Relations Consultants Association, said: 'Unless we can get clients to insist on evaluation, there will not be a PR consultancy business in 25 years' time' (Bell, 1992).

'BEAN COUNTERS' V CREATIVITY

At the heart of the debate is the belief among some practitioners that evaluation is stripping away 'creativity' and replacing it with a 'bean counter's mentality'. The argument goes that evaluation is an accountant's attitude that is not forward looking, only historical. Buttressing this, typically among older practitioners and those from a journalistic background, is that public relations is not a profession or a science but is an art or a craft that defies definition or measurement. Evaluation is thus perceived as potentially threatening because it may transform this 'black art'.

The US public relations pioneer Ivy Lee believed that his work was not definable because it was an extension of his personality. It had no existence other than through him. A common attitude found by all research was that output in terms of media coverage and anecdotal evidence would pass for evaluation. Two examples quoted in an article in *Public Relations Journal* are: 'there are still plenty of clients who are satisfied with the warm fuzzy feeling they get from counting their media clips' and 'Memories! Two or three months after the program, the PR practitioner notices there is still talk about the program. It's one of the best gauges.'

Other writers have argued that the desire for evaluation could restrict practitioners to doing that which can be measured at the expense of that which is 'best'. A failing in this argument, and in the practitioner comments above, is that there is no way of knowing whether the 'warm fuzzy feeling', the 'memories!' and the 'unique and excellent' are effective in reaching the objectives of the programme or campaign. All public relations campaigns need 'bright ideas', but they can be a disaster if they don't work.

LARGE-SCALE STUDIES

Although there have been many small sample studies, the main extensive national and international studies have been conducted by David Dozier among PRSA and IABC members, Walter Lindenmann among a selected group of targets in the United States (Lindenmann, 1990) and Tom Watson among Institute of Public Relations members in the UK (Watson, 1994 and 1996). In Australia, Gael Walker in the mid-1990s (Walker, 1994 and 1997) and Tom Watson and Peter Simmons (2004, 2005) have conducted extensive studies.

Table 3.1 *Evaluation methods found by Dozier in US national survey*

Method	Mean rate (1–7 scale)
Informal 'seat of the pants' observation	5.0
Clip file evaluation	4.4
'Scientific' evaluation	2.4

In early work, David Dozier (1984) found that practitioners in San Diego were using quantitative measures in documenting programme activities and media placements (ie output measurements). By comparison there was little empirical research used in planning programmes or evaluating impact.

Because of their educational background, practitioners whom Dozier studied did not generally have a good knowledge of research techniques that can be applied to evaluation of public relations programmes. Dozier found there was a correlation between the practitioners' college education and their use of techniques. Most had little exposure to social science statistical techniques and many (43 per cent in one study) had come to public relations practice after initial experience in journalism (an average of 3.5 years), which left them predisposed to measurement by media coverage. At the time of this study, objective, scientific evaluations of public relations programmes were the least frequent method of analysis. On a seven-point 'never to always' Likert differential scale, 22 per cent said they never used a scientific approach while none said they always used it. The median score of 2.4/7 indicated that 'scientific' evaluation was infrequently undertaken. The most popular technique was 'seat of the pants' informal observational methods that had a median of 5.0/7 and were closely followed by clip file evaluation at 4.4/7. Said Dozier, 'the more scientific the style, the less frequently it is used'.

In his third international study, Dozier (1988) reported on a study of members of the International Association of Business Communicators (IABC) in the United States, Canada and the UK (Table 3.2). It found again that the most common approaches were informal (median of 4.3 on a seven-point scale), mixed 4.1/7 and scientific 2.9/7. The samples were different in the IABC study (in that there were non-US practitioners and the population was largely in-house practitioners, whereas the US sample had been nationals from all areas of practice) but the gap between informal and scientific remained large.

Table 3.2   *Evaluation methods found by Dozier in an international (IABC) sample*

Method	Mean rate (1–7 scale)
Informal 'seat of the pants' observation	4.3
Clip file evaluation	4.1
'Scientific' evaluation	2.9

An earlier long-term study by Dozier with Glen Broom had found that managers of public relations activity who had expanded their role over a six-year period were more likely to take a more scientific approach, whereas those whose job content had remained static were less inclined to do so. The implication was that managers who aspire to a greater involvement in their organization are likely to use more advanced planning and measurement techniques. Technicians appeared to use little or no evaluation techniques for judging their output and its impact.

LINDENMANN'S RESEARCH

One of the most prominent US non-academic commentators on evaluation has been Walter Lindenmann. In the late 1980s, Lindenmann undertook a nationwide survey 'among public relations practitioners in the country as a whole' on public relations research, measurement and evaluation (Lindenmann, 1990). The survey methodology was a mailed self-administered questionnaire comprising 53 items. It was sent to 945 potential respondents. The sample was created from five categories: major corporations, large trade and professional associations, large non-profit organizations, the 20 largest public relations consultancies and academics. The key findings were:

- 57.4 per cent believed that outcomes of public relations programmes can be measured; 41.8 per cent disagreed;
- 75.9 per cent agreed that research is widely accepted by most public relations professionals as a necessary part of planning programmes;
- 94.3 per cent agreed that research is still more talked about than done (54.2 per cent strongly agreed with this);
- research was undertaken for the purposes of planning (74.7 per cent), monitoring or tracking activities (58.1 per cent), evaluating outcomes (55.7 per cent), publicity polls (41.1 per cent) and tracking of crisis issues (36.4 per cent). (Multiple responses were sought for this question.)

The expenditure on research and evaluation showed wide variations. Many respondents, principally in large corporations, utilities, trade associations and non-profit bodies, claimed that it was included in budgets, but they were almost equally balanced by those who claimed not to have budgets for this activity.

Lindenmann found that the 89 respondents who did allocate funds for research indicated that the sums were small: 22.5 per cent said it was less than 1 per cent of the total PR budget; 31.5 per cent said it was between 1 and 3 per cent; 21.3 per cent between 4 and 6 per cent and 12.3 per cent said it was 7 per cent or above. Many respondents complained of a lack of money as the main reason they were not carrying out as much research as they wished. Among the verbatim reasons given by respondents were 'tight budgets mean that the dollars go for "bread and butter" programmes'; 'to do it right is expensive and it isn't a top priority when you are working in a down market'.

As for future developments, three issues had strong support. Some 54.2 per cent believed that evaluation would grow in importance; 50.2 per cent agreed that public relations research needed to become more sophisticated; and 58.5 per cent said that public relations professionals needed to be educated in research techniques and applications. Lindenmann says that more than nine out of ten respondents showed some level of agreement that the importance of evaluation would grow. The issues that he considered negative were:

> the acknowledgment by better than nine out of every ten PR professionals that research is still talked about in PR than is actually being done. Also of concern was the finding that, in the view of seven out of every ten respondents, most PR research that is done today is still casual and informal, rather than scientific or precise.

Lindenmann's conclusion was that the public relations field has made considerable progress in adopting research and evaluation techniques, but that it still has 'a considerable distance to travel'. He added: 'It is very encouraging that those in the field feel strongly that PR research, measurement and evaluation projects will almost certainly grow in importance... .'

When Lindenmann's research can be compared with Dozier's studies, it seems that there is a common thread of greater acceptance of research and measurement and a desire to play down the 'seat of the pants' approach that Dozier has found prevalent. The Lindenmann study sample was made up of practitioners in large organizations who would be expected to have better access to resources and who may be playing a leading role in their organization's policy development.

The word 'may' is chosen deliberately because it was not obvious as to the job titles of those to whom the surveys were sent. The responses came from public relations executives (74 per cent), public relations counsellors or suppliers (15 per cent) and academics (7 per cent). The term 'public relations executive' covers a multitude of responsibilities and job titles, ranging from those who are policy-makers in the dominant power coalitions of their organization through to communications technicians to whom the survey may have been passed by a superior.

An indicator that Lindenmann's observations of higher standards in research and measurement may be over-stated lies in the response to two statements – the 94.3 per cent who agreed that research is still more talked about than done (with echoes of James Grunig's cri de coeur above) and the 41.8 per cent who agreed that trying to measure public relations outcomes in precise terms is 'next to impossible'. Interestingly, 63.7 per cent of the small sample of academics (18 only) agreed with this but, more importantly, so did 49.3 per cent of the largest sample, which was corporate executives.

Other data which also questions claims of higher evaluation standards is that most research, when undertaken, is done by individuals trained in public relations and not in research techniques (61.8 per cent) and that most research is 'casual and informal' (72.7 per cent). This is a picture of 'seat of the pants' research, possibly undertaken because of budgetary limits, lack of knowledge, personal preferences and habit.

Lindenmann's research did not reach out to all levels of public relations practice, especially small regional consultancies and industrial companies where the typical unit is of five people or less. Thus it is not possible to apply his conclusions to the breadth of practice in the United States or to similar anglophone countries. It is, however, of value in establishing attitudes to evaluation and measurement among larger US organizations.

Dr Lindenmann continues to write extensively on evaluation, and in 2005 published a paper on the historical perspective of public relations research and evaluation. This and other papers can be found at www.instituteforpr.org.

WATSON'S STUDIES

The first survey by Tom Watson was conducted among UK-based full members of the IPR in 1992 (Watson, 1994). Among the key results were:

- Practitioners viewed evaluation very narrowly and lacked confidence in promoting evaluation methods to employers and clients.
- Most relied on output measurement of media coverage. Few undertook research or pre-testing when preparing campaigns.
- Evaluation was not undertaken because of a lack of time, budget and knowledge of methods.
- Evaluation was feared because it could challenge the logic of practitioners' advice and activities.
- Seventy-five per cent claimed to undertake some form of evaluation, with 61.6 per cent of programmes being evaluated, mainly by the project manager.
- Little was spent on evaluation, with 74.3 per cent (who answered this question) indicating that the total proportion of budget was zero to 5 per cent.
- The picture that emerged was of the practitioner as a 'doer' rather than an adviser.

Watson summarized practitioner standards on evaluation and planning as 'basic'. He added that 'the culture of public relation practice appears largely concerned with functional communications (ie communications for the sake of it) and not with planning to meet agreed objectives and creation of desired effects'.

In 1996, many aspects of the study were repeated in a UK sample, again taken randomly from the UK-based full members of the IPR. Comparing the results of the two studies, Watson found there had been a sea change in attitudes towards evaluation and an increased respect among practitioners for the topic (Watson, 1996).

Many benefits were perceived from using evaluation techniques and there was little rejection. During the four-year period, many practitioners had set up evaluation systems. These were mostly informal and self-assessment, but they had begun to undertake regular activity.

Evaluation was seen by 63.9 per cent as increasing respect from clients and employers and 67.7 per cent indicated that these groups accepted evaluation results. By 1996, 15 per cent more practitioners were undertaking evaluation, with 21.8 per cent doing it systematically and 39.1 per cent 'often'.

Budgets, however, had not moved markedly. In 1992, those allocating 0–5 per cent totalled 74.3 per cent and four years later it had risen to 80.2 per cent. Watson commented that 'we are evaluating more, but we aren't spending more'.

The importance of evaluation was indicated by 85.1 per cent who ranked it as 'very important' or 'important'. Only 4.5 per cent said it was 'unimportant' or 'irrelevant'. There was no similar question in the 1992 survey, but written comments were often trenchantly doubtful about evaluation, eg: 'PR is not a science; most practitioners are inadequate; clients are too thick.'

Watson concluded that because information on evaluation was more easily available and the subject was regularly covered in trade publications, the topic had risen up the profession's agenda and had become 'less difficult to sell as a concept and practice to clients and employers'.

AUSTRALIAN STUDIES

Australian evaluation expert Jim Macnamara refers to a 'philosophical consensus' on its importance, but says application of evaluation has been low in public relations. Two 1993 surveys in Australia found a substantial gulf between attitudes and practices among practitioners. Consistent with public relations best practice credo, academic

Gael Walker found there was 90 per cent agreement or strong agreement that research is widely accepted 'as a necessary and integral part of the planning, program development and evaluation process' (Walker, 1997). Only 55 per cent, however, reported very frequently or occasionally 'measuring or evaluating the outcomes, impact or effectiveness of PR programs or activities'. A worldwide study by the International Public Relations Association found that 90 per cent of Australian public relations practitioners believed evaluation was necessary, but just 14 per cent 'frequently undertook research aimed at evaluating' (IPRA, 1994). Australia's figure was slightly lower than the United States, South Africa and the average for the whole sample.

A recent president of the Public Relations Institute of Australia said in 2002 that there 'is little evidence that the use of research has increased significantly in public relations since 1994, and some surveys suggest that even if more research is being used, there is still a long way to go' (Macnamara, 2002). In 2003, Mercer Consulting reported that more than 50 per cent of an Australian sample reported that communications effectiveness was measured either on an ad hoc basis or not at all (Mercer, 2003).

The most recent survey of Australian public relations practitioners' evaluation practices and attitudes was undertaken among members of the Public Relations Institute of Australia by Tom Watson and Peter Simmons. A picture of a media relations-centric approach was found (Watson and Simmons, 2004; Simmons and Watson, 2005).

It also found there was an increase in research and evaluation activity, but the focus remained on outputs, not outcomes, of communication. Media coverage monitoring and media content analysis dominated research methods used to plan, monitor and evaluate PR communication. Some 89 per cent of practitioners reported often or always measuring the volume of communication, but just 32 per cent often or always measure resulting changes in behaviour.

The data show that UK and Australian attitudes are broadly similar, although Australian practitioners indicated that cost is much less of a barrier to evaluation than a lack of time and knowledge. Analysis of attitudes and responses to an open-ended question suggests that lack of research skills and confidence, longing to show bottom-line results, and frustration at decision makers' misunderstanding of public relations has made evaluation a cause of anguish for many practitioners.

SMALL SAMPLE RESEARCH

Silver Anvil study

An indicator of attitudes that may be slowly changing was the analysis undertaken by Blissland (1990) of entries in the Public Relations Society of America's (PRSA) annual Silver Anvil case study competition. This is a competition open to all members of the PRSA and is a highly prized professional award.

Blissland compared entries from the end of the 1980s with those at the beginning of the decade to see if there were changes in attitude to evaluation methods over the period. All Silver Anvil winners in the years in question were reviewed and Blissland identified three groups of evaluation methods, namely: measures of communication output, measures of intermediate effect and measures of organization achievement. He also created sub-groups in each of the groups.

The main findings were that of the 12 evaluation sub-groups, two were strongly preferred – media coverage and inferred goal achievement. Contacts from the media and financial measures were the least used. The preferred categories fall into Dozier's 'seat of the pants' definitions.

A cosmetic change of nomenclature was that, in the early part of the decade, only one entrant used the term 'evaluation' but 88 per cent used 'results'. By the end, 83 per cent were using 'evaluation' as the term to describe their outcomes section. They also used more evaluation methods, too. This rose from a mean of 3.6 methods/winner to 4.57 methods/winner.

The statistically significant changes were the use of behavioural science measures, and two measures of organizational goal achievement: inferred achievement and substantiated achievement. Blissland concluded that by the end of the decade there was marginally greater reliance on the output measure of media coverage, which rose from 70.0 per cent to 79.2 per cent. However, when this is linked to the inferred (that is, unsubstantiated) achievement claims, which rose in winning entries from 53.3 to 87.5 per cent, it is hard to agree with Blissland's conclusion that 'Clearly, progress has been made.' In a chameleon-like manner, the Silver Anvil entrants have learned the new buzz-words, but have remained even more attached to output measures and unsubstantiated claims. Blissland admits that the entries do have some sizeable gaps in methodology:

> However, much remains to be done. The rigour of behavioural science methodology was still missing from the evaluation of more than half (55.6 per cent) of the most recent Silver Anvil winners...

And while most winners claimed organizational goal achievement from only circumstantial evidence, more than half of the winners – 56.7 per cent – did not bother to substantiate such claims with behavioural science methods. Thus, unsubstantiated claims of goal achievement outstripped substantiated ones by about two to one.

Blissland's study is a snapshot of award entries that may contain *ex post facto* thinking to justify actions. To gain a prize or pass the test does not indicate best practice. Blissland claims that Silver Anvil winners 'may well represent the leading edge in evaluation practice', but this could be an over-statement of the quality of the entries.

A recent study of Australian practitioners, which looked at several years of winning entries in that nation's Golden Target PR awards, has found that lip service has been given to evaluation, with most winners using very limited media analysis to support claims of success or effectiveness (Xavier, Patel and Johnston, 2004).

German practitioners' attitudes

European research on evaluation has been undertaken mainly in Germany. Barbara Baerns studied attitudes among German in-house public relations managers in the 1990s and found similar results to Dozier's studies (Baerns, 1993).

A postal survey was undertaken among 216 managers who were members of the German Public Relations Association (DPRG). It had a response level of 69 per cent and led Baerns to a conclusion similar to that of Grunig's 'evaluation and sin' analogy:

> Almost all West German public relations experts in managerial positions regarded analytical work as important in the context of public relations. However, almost all of them rarely analysed and controlled what they had accomplished irregularly or never. If controlling occurred, then [it was] mostly as press analyses. With regard to possible contribution by science (*ie social science methods*), PR experts showed themselves to be uncertain – or said that it was not in demand at all.

Baerns questioned the managers on three aspects of public relations activity – planning, analysis and control and their view of whether their work met the US descriptions (such as Dozier's analysis) of communications manager or communication technician. Although Baerns' data is largely concerned with attitudes to planning of public relations activity, the results link with Watson's UK studies that also viewed this subject.

She found that the majority of respondents (55 per cent) regarded long-term public relations planning as 'indispensable', while 39 per cent referred to the priority of day-to-day events. A small number (7 per cent) regarded planning in public relations as 'impossible'. Baerns then explored the ways in which planning took place and found a considerable gap between the reported attitudes towards planning and the reality of what took place. In her paper, she asks the reader to 'draw your own conclusion' from data which was difficult for her to assess. Analysis of the data illustrates the gap between the practitioners' claims and their normal behaviour (Table 3.3).

Table 3.3   *German PR practitioners' attitudes*

Attitudinal statement	%
Could name phases in the planning of public relations	49
Gave no answer to the question	17
Could not distinguish between planning and phases of operation	14
Listed public relations goals	14
Gave meaningless answers	6

Her conclusion was that the majority said public relations planning was indispensable, but the majority did without it. As for analysis and control, Baerns found 88 per cent of managers regarded this as 'important', with the residual 12 per cent saying it was 'relatively unimportant'. However, more than half the respondents analysed their activities only 'irregularly' or 'never'.

Most respondents delegated their analysis and investigations partly or wholly to external institutions. Baerns found that 63 per cent of respondents believed that 'scientific findings' play only a minor part in public relations practice. This corresponds with the 'seat of the pants' attitudes identified in the United States and the UK by Dozier and Watson, respectively. Her conclusion was that when evaluation or monitoring took place, '(it was) mostly as press analyses'.

In her third question, Baerns asked managers if they would rank the majority of their professional colleagues, ie other members of DPRG, as 'communications managers' or 'communications technicians', with the result that 88 per cent regarded their colleagues, to quote Baerns, 'as mere doers, as "communications technicians"', an epithet they did not apply to themselves. In the 1992 study, the German research focused on why practitioners did not evaluate their work (Table 3.4).

Table 3.4 *Ranking of evaluation barriers*

Barrier	Rank
Lack of time	1
Lack of personnel to undertake the task	2
Lack of funds/budget	3
Doubts on usefulness of results	4
Lack of knowledge of methods	5
Aversion to scientific methodology	6

Baerns does not specify percentage data to all the rankings other than for the lowest three, which were doubts on usefulness (20 per cent), lack of knowledge of methods (14 per cent) and aversion to scientific methodology (6 per cent). The German data shows similarities with many other Western public relations cultures, namely that research is not being used as a formative tool and evaluation (or control methods) is based on 'seat of the pants' methods such as media analysis. These shared characteristics indicate that the conclusions for the development of common evaluation techniques could have credence outside a strictly English-speaking culture upon which so much of public relations practice worldwide draws. The German public relations attitudes are shown to be very close to those identified in the United States, UK and Australia.

In 2005, Dr Baerns published a report on the analysis of the German Goldene Brücke (Golden Bridge) PR prize from 1970 to 2001, which found that although 79 per cent of entries claimed that there was an evaluation or assessment of success, only between 33 and 37 per cent could be considered sound in terms of the use of robust social science methods. Some 53 per cent of entrants used 'unscientific methods of evaluation' such as collections of cuttings, sales or usage data, or praise and recognition (Baerns, 2005: 7).

ICCO/GPRA survey

A survey of 107 European public relations consultancies in 1996 (ICCO/GPRA) found similar results to Watson's UK studies. Although more expenditure was available for evaluation, 71.9 per cent spent 0–5 per cent or had no separate budget. Also, the consultancy was most likely to be analysing its output and report to the client. Analysis of media coverage was the most common evaluation tool offered by consultancies and requested by their clients.

The Benchpoint report

Prepared for the 2004 round of the annual Measurement Summit held in the United States, the Benchpoint study was undertaken online in September 2004 by Gaunt and Wright and gained responses from 1,040 practitioners in 25 countries. The key points from that study (Gaunt and Wright, 2004) revealed that:

- Demand for measurement is driven by CEOs: 'measurement is an integral part of PR' (Gaunt and Wright, 2004: 1).
- In external communication, more practitioners measure outputs than outcomes with media evaluation, internal reviews and benchmarking being most used for measuring outcomes (44 per cent of respondents see these as only 'somewhat effective'). Opinion surveying is regarded as the most effective tool. Dashboards, league tables and Advertising Value Equivalents (AVEs) were seen as least effective.
- In internal communication, there is greater use of feedback tools, but 23 per cent use instinct alone. Employee surveys and focus groups are considered most effective; benchmarking and dashboards least effective. Only 18 per cent regard meeting the budget as a success criterion.
- The main barriers to measurement are, cost: 77 per cent, time: 59 per cent, lack of expertise and questionable value of results: 58 per cent each.
- On Return on Investment (ROI), 65 per cent of respondents think it possible to apply this to public relations, although only 13 per cent think this strongly. A large majority (88 per cent) are interested in an ROI tool.
- Some 70 per cent of respondents will be doing more on measurement in future.

Respondents to this study, drawn from public relations professional bodies, mainly from North America and the European Union, were predominantly public relations or communications practitioners and came from most practice areas. Professional and industry bodies are commonly used for data collection in public relations research (Watson and Simmons, 2004). While they give access to self-identified practitioners, the data are more likely to represent those with defined attitudes to the topics rather than the broad spectrum of practice. For quantitative data collection purposes the professional and industry bodies, however, offer the most reliable databases and industry access.

The conclusions from the Benchpoint report are similar to those gathered over more than a decade by Baerns (1993; 2005), Watson

(1992; 1996) and Watson and Simmons (2004, 2005). A report in 2006 by the British media evaluation firm Metrica found related messages: a fall in the number of organizations that do not align business objectives with the objectives of PR programmes, from 30 per cent in 2004 to 6 per cent in 2006, but the predominance of media evaluation over market research and enquiry tracking to measure the results of PR activity. Metrica found that 61 per cent spend 1–10 per cent of the budget on evaluation, followed by 23 per cent spending 11–20 per cent. The use of AVEs was still widespread at 42 per cent of respondents and had risen from 34 per cent in the previous survey in 2004.

Australia and the UK

Research in Australia by Jim Macnamara also detected a gap between saying and doing, but more significantly a reliance on measurement of media indicators and the absence of objective research methods (Macnamara, 1999). He found that only 3 of 50 senior public relations consultancies surveyed could nominate an objective methodology used to evaluate media coverage, despite 70 per cent of respondents claiming that they undertook qualitative judgement of media coverage.

Macnamara found that when asked what methods of evaluation were used, the consultancies nominated discussions with journalists, number of enquiries received, client sales results, share price movements and community participation in events. The research methodology was subjective and variously described as professional judgement, client feelings, word of mouth and general feedback. 'A number of these were hardly objective or reliable forms of evaluation research. Even those that are legitimate forms of measurement were not administered in any remotely scientific way in the majority of cases.'

The public relations profession aspires to shift from a technical (writing, events and information dissemination) to a strategic (managerial decision-making) role in organizations. Practitioners are well known to express frustration at the sidelining of public relations in many organizations, and management failure to recognize adequately the value of communication. Jim Macnamara has highlighted two failings that help explain why public relations lacks credibility in the eyes of management. First is the failure of public relations to evaluate and report the outcomes or effects of communication. A second and related reason is failure to use the language of accountability preferred by organizations (such as MBO, TQM, QA and benchmarking). These factors, he says, are major obstacles to the inclusion of public relations in strategic decision making.

Another survey of senior Australian managers by Steiner and Black (2000) suggests that public relations' transition to managerial status is far from complete. Managers were found to have very low expectations of public relations' role in strategic planning, and rely on public relations officers for information dissemination rather than advice.

United Kingdom

In the UK, a small study of practitioner attitudes was undertaken by Jon White who reviewed practice among a cross-section of consultancies in membership of the Public Relations Consultants Association (PRCA) (White, 2002). The aim of his paper was to offer a qualitative discussion of evaluation issues to the PRCA and so no statistical sample was developed on the actual use.

In 2001, a study of UK marketing directors by Test Research found that only 28 per cent were satisfied with their public relations evaluation, compared with 67 per cent for advertising and 68 per cent for sales promotion. Managerial status will require research and evaluation that give firm evidence of contribution to the organization. Indeed, the IPR/CDF (2004) study recommends explicitly that: 'The cost of PR measurement should be considered against the business case of what PR programmes can achieve rather than against the budget of the programmes themselves. Viewed in this context – helping make a strong business case – the cost of evaluation can be better justified. ... measurement plays a key role in obtaining higher PR budgets by demonstrating the business case of the results achieved.'

CEO'S ATTITUDES

Research by Murray and White (2004) into chief executives' attitudes towards public relations was highly illuminating. They interviewed 14 CEOs and chairmen from major UK and international organizations and discovered that they 'intuitively' valued public relations. CEOs saw it as an essential cost of business, and essential to business and organizational performance. The business leaders also felt that public relations is 'not amenable to precise measurement, being long-term and iterative in effect, or being an aid to avoiding surprises or mistakes. They do not feel a great need to demonstrate a return on investment in their PR' (Murray and White, 2004: 4).

While thinking that practitioners needed to use available measures more confidently and to be able to make the case for the value of their contribution more effectively, CEOs are used to handling information that is not exhaustive. They need enough information to make sensible decisions ('satisficing'), but the quest for definitive information on the performance of public relations appears to be a practitioner's obsession. CEOs feel there is under-investment in public relations and a better case more effectively made would help release resources, but they also identify a lack of talent and expertise among practitioners, 'which – if addressed – would also answer questions about the value of public relations practice' (Murray and White, 2004: 4). Training and education was seen by the interviewed CEOs as critical to improving the calibre of practitioners.

MULTIPLE METRICS

Research by Gregory and Edwards (2004) into the practice of public relations by companies in the UK *Management Today* magazine's 'Most Admired' company list, and by Gregory *et al* (2005) on 'Most Admired' companies and public sector organizations, found that a range of evaluation metrics were used (usually between four and eight), and the most frequently used were informal and/or qualitative, such as journalist feedback and discussions with stakeholders. It is as if the respondents were 'just checking' that everything was on track. This supports the proposition in Murray and White's (2004) research, which indicated an intuitive sense of what is working. As such it reflects life in business generally, where intuition and a general sense of purpose and direction are regarded as vital to success, besides solid research. The one consistent quantitative measure for private sector companies was the share price.

It was discovered that the status of the senior public relations practitioner was high in these admired organizations, with 43 per cent on the board or executive committee, and many others reporting directly to the CEO. Asked why public relations was regarded so highly, it appeared that the handling of crises was critical. Either these organizations had recognized that good public relations had been essential to preserving their reputation in a crisis, or that a lack of such a function had left them dangerously exposed.

THE BARRIERS TO EVALUATION

The barriers to the more widespread evaluation of public relations activity are many. Dozier points to several reasons: previous working experience of practitioners, lack of knowledge of research techniques, the manager/technician dichotomy, the practitioners' participation in decision making. Lindenmann believed that practitioners were 'not thoroughly aware' of research techniques. He also found that respondents to his survey complained of a lack of money, with 54 per cent spending 3 per cent or less (often much less) on evaluation.

Baerns found similar barriers in Germany, with time, lack of personnel, inadequate budgets and doubts about the process all being important. Macnamara's research found that practitioners lacked knowledge of methodology, but did not explore other explanations. In the UK, one strong reason advanced by practitioner commentator Quentin Bell was money and client reluctance to spend it:

> And the problem I fear lies with money – too many clients are still not prepared to allocate realistic budgets to pay for the process. But I concede that it's a Catch 22; until clients have become accustomed to what's possible on evaluation, they won't begin to demand it. That's the basic problem that our industry as a whole must aim to solve. (Bell, 1992)

These barriers follow a circular argument: most practitioners' education does not include social science research techniques; therefore they don't use them but concentrate on technician skills, which means they don't rise into the manager roles and participate in decision making. This would give access to budgets for planning and evaluation, thus creating programmes and campaigns that can enhance their personal standing and meet the objectives of their client or employer.

Unless evaluation becomes less of a mystery and a more accessible process, it would appear that a generation of better-educated practitioners is needed to break the technician mould. Technicians will always be needed to carry out the operational aspects and tactical implementation of programmes and campaigns, especially those that are based on media relations and publications. If the evaluation models are simpler to operate, then technicians can participate in them. As they are producing many of the materials for the strategy, it makes sense for them to aid the evaluation process. Money and time will always be in short supply, but simpler models to enable evaluation to take place more frequently would prove a more convincing case when budgets are set.

PRESSURES TO EVALUATE

Without evidence of the effects of public relations communication, the decision to invest is based on belief. Decision makers generally prefer measures and precedent to guesswork and assurance. Thus investment in public relations communication is threatened by decision-maker perceptions of lack of accountability.

According to Michael Fairchild, author of the *PR Evaluation Toolkit*, the need to strengthen PR's research and evaluation practices in the UK has become even more urgent in recent years (Fairchild, 2002). Recessionary pressures on organizational budgets are causing cutbacks to public relations in the UK, 'indicating yet again that PR is regarded as an optional and dispensable service'. He also discussed a trend leading to increased competition for public relations core business. The convergence of management consulting, legal and accountancy services is resulting in the encroachment of multidisciplinary consultancies on fields such as issues and risk management, communication and reputation. Fairchild notes that, without the esteem of management, public relations is likely to take a publicity rather than strategic role as organizations respond to the increasing (regulatory and non-regulatory) demands to report non-financial performance.

Other pressures upon practitioners include the introduction of payment-by-results (PBR) contracts and the use of purchasing professionals in the negotiation of consultancy arrangements. PBR, which is widely used in advertising, demands evidence of the achievement of mutually agreed objectives or Key Performance Indicators (KPIs). These objectives, or KPIs, are measured by some form of evaluation methodology in order to decide whether the supplier of PR services (in-house and consultancy) can be paid the full contract amount or penalized for missing the targets. It is a similar position where purchasing professionals are involved in negotiating the performance elements of a contract or a campaign. This practice has become widespread in consumer and technology public relations in the UK and North America and is being introduced into the governmental sector in many countries. In the UK, for example, there has been a strong effort by bodies representing purchasers of services and the suppliers to develop a common industry-wide approach which includes evaluation methodologies. Like it or not, PR practitioners are having to face up to the use of evaluation.

CIPR POLICY STATEMENT

Recognizing that the evaluation debate was still developing, and alert to the fact that some practitioners are still seeking the 'silver bullet' of a single all-purpose evaluation metric or methodology, in 2005 the

Chartered Institute of Public Relations (CIPR) set up a small task force of executive board members to produce a definitive policy statement on evaluation. It commissioned Henley Management College, under the guidance of Dr Jon White, to draw together the practitioner and academic literature on evaluation and to examine best practice cases. The resultant policy statement (see www.cipr.co.uk/research) is supplemented by a web-based resource of literature and cases. The policy statement proposes that:

- Public relations is part of the management task and is subject to the same disciplines, such as the need to set direction, allocate and manage resources and monitor progress.
- Measurement and evaluation are problematic in all areas of management. Complexity is a key feature and in the dynamic interrelated business world it is difficult to separate out the effect of one area of management such as public relations.
- Despite this difficulty, the situation can be ameliorated by better planning and objective-setting, particularly better project management where precise, measurable objectives allow for better judgements of progress.
- Public relations can be measured and evaluated in terms of:
    - contribution to social and economic development (for example in Northern Ireland where reconciliation work has led to economic development and community building);
    - contribution to management, leadership and organizational performance by aiding better decision making and avoiding mistakes (for example work by Diageo's public affairs department has led to a more favourable tax regime for alcohol than might have been the case);
    - as a process and as part of programme development and implementation (for instance, the Volvo case study in Chapter 7);
    - contribution and competence of individual practitioners (for example, 'evolve', the UK government's development framework for government communicators).
- Available methods, research-based, provide information that is good enough for decision making for planning public relations programmes. Time and paid resources are practical obstacles.
- Available research methods and approaches are adequate for measuring the contribution of public relations in the areas outlined above. The evidence from the case studies shows clearly that public relations is creating value. ROI may play a part in demonstrating that public relations can build market share; social research can demonstrate value in other areas. Each method has

its limitations, therefore a raft of measures, appropriate to the particular situation, needs to be employed.

CONCLUSIONS

What can be seen as a major change in one researcher's view may not be seen in the same light by another. The claims that there has been progress in the adoption of higher standards of evaluation by both Lindenmann and Blissland are examples of this ambiguity.

Both have used samples chosen to represent the leading edge of public relations practice. Both have found extensive use of the words 'evaluation' and 'research'. Lindenmann, especially, found pious hopes for an expansion of evaluation in the 1990s.

Yet all of the three main studies referred to – Dozier, Lindenmann and Watson as well as small sample research from Baerns, Macnamara and ICO/GPRA – have found that most practitioners rely on 'seat of the pants' research. This is mainly consideration of coverage (cuttings, airtime, etc) in the media. Lindenmann and Blissland's studies could be questioned on the basis of their samples, which may be skewed towards higher achievers and the more research-literate. They certainly do not cover the breadth of public relations practice.

Yet both (as well as Watson) have produced data in line with Dozier, who has looked at public relations practice at all levels from his home area of San Diego to the IABC's membership in three anglo-phone countries.

The culture that he has uncovered, which is confirmed by Baerns in Germany, Macnamara and Watson in Australia and among the IPRA membership, shows that most practitioners, because of their educational background and experience, do not have a working knowledge of research techniques which would aid the evaluation of public relations. Only in the UK research from Watson are there indications of greater imperatives by practitioners for evaluation to be discussed, albeit the most basic output stage.

Finally, it is interesting (and challenging) to reflect on the CIPR's statement about PR evaluation, that the methodology to measure the outcomes and effectiveness of campaigns and programmes is already in existence and that it is time and budgets that are blocking their widespread acceptance and use. The movement from 'seat of the pants' measurement to a more professional approach is, according to the CIPR, in the hands of practitioners now and henceforth. Practitioner culture may now have the impetus to change to a more confident, managerial approach.

Interview

Fiona Wilkinson, Senior Vice President, Corporate Communications, Visa EU, appreciates a dual role of evaluation. Clippings play a prominent role for planning within her communications group and for feeding back results to internal customers: 'a great thump of a large book of clippings is what a lot of people want to hear still'.

However, when justifying the worth of communications to the organization on a higher level, the approach is different. On the surface, it's what she describes as 'gut feel', but it seems that her membership of the management team (and therefore the strategic role of communications) is crucial. 'I walk the floor, talk to people as much as possible, try and understand what the current issues are. I'm involved in board meetings, so I keep in touch with what's going on and can make sure that what I am doing is aligned with the way management thinking is moving.'

When talking about press relations, Wilkinson does not claim a sophisticated approach to evaluation. 'We don't spend a lot of money on evaluation and most of what we do is subjective and quite simple.' Volume of clippings, the proportion that are positive, and how many have Visa in the headline are the type of analysis Visa undertakes. She feels that this reflects the type of advice that she gets from major PR consultancies: 'If we ask for a recommendation on evaluation for a specific campaign, we will get it, but it is primarily of the clippings variety.'

Wilkinson is a wider user of research than at first appears: 'We do measure the attitude of our member banks: how they feel about Visa, how the system works, what they think about the communications they receive, what they feel about the portrayal of Visa in the media.' This is alongside surveying staff and opinion formers, among other research efforts.

Returning to a discussion of media evaluation reinforces her twin-track approach. 'I think it's useful as a communications planning tool. As for convincing the rest of the business about the value of the communications function, I don't think it makes the slightest difference.'

When Wilkinson returned to communications about three years ago, having spent time in other parts of the business, she was very concerned to catch up with the latest thinking on evaluation. Her enthusiasm was short-lived: 'Frankly, I don't think it had moved forwards at all.' In her opinion, one reason for the lack of progress is that there is no single, simple solution. She is wary of AVEs, for example, but does feel they have a role as one element of the evaluation mix: 'It puts some objectivity behind it.'

This thinking is an extension of her view that the management of expectations is important to all aspects of public relations. 'This follows through to evaluation: you won't get a perfect measure; you'll get a number of indicators.'

Fiona Wilkinson is Senior Vice President, Corporate Communications, Visa EU.

QUESTIONNAIRE RESPONSES

Q: How do you encourage clients/employers to include evaluation in public relations programmes?

They only need to see that there will be a return on investment – evaluation/research decisions are not different from other business decisions. **Dejan Verčič**

We are committed to industry best practice as outlined in the IPR (UK) Evaluation Toolkit and include this message in all presentations. **Alison Clarke**

A team of five undertakes evaluation. As there are only 60 staff in the organization, evaluation is a priority and valued. The other positive aspect is that communication is integrated across all programmes. **Fran Hagon**

We build it in from the word go by using our proprietary planning, management and evaluation system. **Crispin Manners**

In presentations we argue that PR is not, contrary to belief, an intangible and demonstrate various measurement and evaluation techniques. **Ray Mawerera**

We make an element of measurement mandatory and build it into the management of any account. Setting the targets upfront also means that measurement of the beginning and end point becomes an automatic activity. Measurement isn't seen as additional or a postscript. It is clear and routine within the programme activity. **Annabelle Warren**

I encourage clients to support evaluation by reinforcing the fact it justifies PR expenditure. **Laurna O'Donnell**

By telling them that this is the only way in which we can justify to them how we spend their money, or what value they have actually received from us. **Clara Zawawi**

By establishing that research is an investment, not an expense; baselines can be set for future research and knowledge acquisition to guide communications activities; programmes can be guided by reliable, detached information instead of best guess and/or instinct. **Tom O'Donoghue**

We now have it as part of any pitch. We offer a basic software-managed measurement service as part of our service so the client does not have to pay extra for it. Anything above the basic analysis does carry a charge. **Mike Copland**

It seems like those that want it, have it, and the ones that don't, don't really care, don't want to spend the time and budget on it. We try to encourage them to build it in, not just as a measurement tool, but also as a diagnostic tool – to determine if the programme needs adjustment or should continue as-is. **Matt Kucharski**

The UK government has always encouraged building in a means of evaluating results. It is regarded as best practice by government. **Richard Offer**

All staff are encouraged to evaluate their campaigns so they are in control of the campaign, maintain records and understand the purpose and target market of the campaign. Records provide a good source of information that can be referred to when required. Information obtained and experiences learned from evaluation are a vital tool for organizing and the success of future campaigns. **Adam Connolly**

We prefer pre-campaign and post-campaign awareness studies. **John Bliss**

4

Gathering and interpreting information

The intimate link between research and evaluation is established and a review undertaken of the current application of research in practice and how different practitioner roles use research. Research methods with relevance to public relations evaluation are outlined together with advice on their application.

Evaluation is a research-based activity, so any progress in evaluation practice has to be underpinned by an understanding of research methods. This is not to say that public relations practitioners have to become experts in research methodology. It does, however, mean that a basic understanding of research methods is part of the professional practitioner's toolkit and that there is a role for research specialists in public relations consultancies and departments. Anyone managing public relations campaigns and activities therefore needs to be an effective commissioner and user of research.

Cutlip, Center and Broom expand on this point: 'Even though it cannot answer all the questions or sway all decisions, methodical, systematic research is the foundation of effective public relations' (2006: 284). They argue that, without research, public relations practitioners are restricted to asserting that they understand the situation and can provide a solution, while, with research (followed by analysis of the data gathered), they can put forward proposals clearly backed up with evidence to support them. Research is the 'scientific alternative to tenacity, authority and intuition'. Cutlip, Center and Broom suggest that training in research sits at the top of the pantheon when it comes to professional development. And while lack of resources and time are often the reasons proffered for not doing more research, a better explanation might be a combination of practitioners lacking an understanding of research methods and clients/employers regarding research as unnecessary.

The importance of market research in supporting evaluation is confirmed by the IPR/CDF (2004: 6) study which makes the following points when summarizing relevant aspects of current communications practice. An important theme of this discussion is the care needed to ensure any effects achieved can be attributed to PR, as opposed to other communications activities, so that any PR effects are clearly isolated:

- Market research can be conducted on a repeatable basis (at least annually to track PR message uptake and spontaneous recall of PR campaigns but care needs to be taken to avoid advertising and other communication message effects).
- Measure customers' and prospective customers' perceptions on a recurring basis (at least annually) against competitor benchmarks (again, care needs to be taken to account for advertising and other communication effects, where appropriate). Similarly, measure employees' perceptions and knowledge, again on a regular basis.
- Measure reach and frequency achieved against target audiences by PR programmes, using media evaluation (such information can be compared directly with similar advertising data as well as cost per thousand reached).
- Use market research to determine changes in spontaneous and prompted awareness before and after specific PR activity (care must be taken to ensure that the results can be attributed to PR and not some other communication activity, such as advertising or direct marketing).
- Measure response to specific PR activity by, for instance, using telephone helpline numbers or micro-website addresses that are only available through PR material. Such response can then be measured against benchmarked sales and other data to assess the impact of PR.
- Use market mix modelling to assess and compare the incremental product sales attributable to PR.

Importantly, research does not have to mean wide-ranging, expensive and highly technical exercises. The US writer Mark McElreath (1997: 203) makes the point that research may range from the informal to the formal. While formal research will have advantages such as the ability to be replicated, all types of research have the potential to yield useful results. 'One insightful revelation from one focus group can be as telling as the key result from a massive opinion poll.' Similarly, Smith (2005: 9) suggests: 'Research begins with informal and often simple methods of gathering relevant information.'

In parallel with this, many practitioners will have access to 'free' research that has already been undertaken for other, parallel, purposes within the organization or client. *IPR Toolkit* author Michael Fairchild (2002: 306) confirms this point when discussing the reasons why the use of research is not yet widespread, one of which he suggests is: 'failure to tap into existing, and often free, sources of research, or to appreciate the value of developing a working relationship with the client's professional market research providers'.

The UK's CIPR has long advocated research as an integral part of public relations planning and implementation. It has promoted the concept of PRE (planning, research and evaluation) through its series of evaluation toolkits, now in its third edition (*IPR Toolkit*, 2003). The five steps of the PRE Process are described as:

1. **Audit:** gather information and conduct research ('inputs') to build a foundation for the PR campaign or programme.
2. **Setting objectives:** align the publicity objectives with the goals and objectives of the client organization.
3. **Strategy and plan:** decide what type and level of research to use.
4. **Ongoing measurement:** how are we doing – what have we learnt from measurement?
5. **Results and evaluation:** quantify the outcome. (2003: 9)

So, evaluation is both a research-based discipline and intimately involved with (if not actually a prerequisite for) professional public relations practice. Its purpose is to inform and clarify and it operates to high standards of rigour and logic. As the orbit of public relations extends from publicity-seeking media relations to issues management and corporate reputation, research will play an increasingly important role in the planning, execution and measurement of public relations programmes.

Similarly, Smith (2005: 9) confirms the integration of research and planning with his 'Nine Steps of Strategic Public Relations', as shown opposite.

Phase One: Formative Research
    Step 1: Analysing the Situation
    Step 2: Analysing the Organization
    Step 3: Analysing the Publics

Phase Two: Strategy
    Step 4: Establishing Goals and Objectives
    Step 5: Formulating Action and Response Strategies
    Step 6: Using Effective Communications

Phase Three: Tactics
    Step 7: Choosing Communication Tactics
    Step 8: Implementing the Strategic Plan

Phase Four: Evaluative Research
    Step 9: Evaluating the Strategic Plan

Research and a strategic perspective on public relations are intimately connected. Most texts which claim to address strategic public relations planning and practice will – quite appropriately – have significant sections on research methods. Why is this? The thinking that lies behind a public relations strategy has echoes of Smith's (2005) nine steps and could be listed as the following:

- analysing the problem;
- establishing objectives;
- building the creative theme;
- segmenting target publics;
- positioning the organization;
- evaluating the results.

A cursory glance at any of these elements confirms the linkage between research and developing a public relations strategy. Analysis (of a problem) requires the gathering of extensive data, for example. Similarly, if 'the big idea' proves elusive you need more information: on the organization, market, environment, competitors, product/ service, whatever.

Here, we have a broader view of public relations evaluation than just research undertaken at the end of the programme to establish effectiveness (important as this is). We extend evaluation to encompass formative research and use the term 'summative' to describe the final research phase. This is aligned with McElreath's (1997: 203) terminology: formative evaluation research and summative evaluative research: 'Research conducted to help a manager better formulate plans for implementing a program is called formative evaluative research. Research designed to help summarize the overall impact of a program is called summative evaluative research.'

Elsewhere (see Chapter 5), we discuss the concepts of *outputs*, *out-takes* and *outcomes* to classify the different categories of results that flow from public relations activities. The point is made (www.instituteforpr.org) that the measurement of PR outputs is relatively simple: 'usually counting, tracking and observing'. In contrast, for *PR out-takes* and *PR outcomes*, 'it is a matter of asking and carrying out extensive review and analysis of what was said and what was done'. The latter often requires the use of research techniques, so the nature of evaluation activity will determine how extensive the research activity to support it needs to be.

THE SCOPE OF RESEARCH

When we defined evaluation in Chapter 2, we confirmed the role of evaluation as a proactive, forward-looking activity. Naturally the collection of historical data is a prerequisite, but evaluation is not restricted to making conclusions on past activity. The emphasis on improving programme effectiveness strongly indicates that the information collected on previous activity is used as feedback to adapt the nature of future activities, and therefore argues for a formative (as well as summative) perspective on public relations evaluation. UK researchers McCoy and Hargie (2003: 305) confirm this orientation and also link formative evaluation into a strategic role for public relations practitioners: 'if practitioners engage in formative evaluation and environmental monitoring it is suggested that this will help them to manage relationships, link PR to organizational goals and make PR more strategic than tactical'.

Professional practitioners base their activities on a body of knowledge as well as techniques. They see public relations operating at a strategic level within organizations: managing relationships with the publics that are key to the success of the organization. This implies an out-take/outcome orientation to public relations research and evaluation.

The current momentum for evaluation in public relations is predicated on the assumption that social scientific methods can be applied to public relations. Broom and Dozier (1990: 14) established the foundations on which much modern thinking associated with research and public relations is based. They identified five major approaches to the management of public relations programmes, based on the role of research in that management. These range from the no-research approach in which 'public relations technicians operate on the basis of their intuition and artistic judgement' through the informal approach, media-event approach, evaluation-only approach to the scientific management approach.

The informal approach uses research but only so-called informal, 'pre-scientific', research that is then misappropriated as the basis for strategic planning. The media-event approach is the province of the visibility study where research (which is usually internally rigorous) is used not in a scientific, knowledge-seeking manner, but rather to create newsworthy, attention-attracting information.

The evaluation-only approach consigns research to an impact-measuring role only, as opposed to a planning tool. This is a common theme, with, for example, McCoy and Hargie (2003: 305) arguing that the focus of public relations evaluation remains on output measures and that, anyway, these tend to be subjective, ad hoc and informal: 'evaluation should include formative evaluation and environmental monitoring rather than just the summative output evaluation that is common in PR'. It is symptomatic of the problems of terminology surrounding public relations in general and evaluation in particular that, while media coverage is often described as the 'output' of public relations activity, many others would argue that media evaluation is at best formative as it focuses on the process of public relations rather than being summative by examining any impact that the PR campaign in question has.

The scientific management approach sees research threaded through every stage of the management of public relations pro-grammes: research is undertaken to analyse the starting point, monitor the programme as it unfolds and ascertain whether objectives have been met.

Earlier research by Dozier (1984) to test whether public relations had adopted 'scientifically derived knowledge' revealed three major approaches to evaluation. Seat-of-the-pants evaluation is a subjective and intuitive method of evaluation which uses casual observation by the practitioner to judge the output of the campaign. It is the tradi-tional approach used by public relations practitioners, particularly those concerned with the process of public relations rather than outcomes, thereby displaying the no-research intuitive approach to the management of public relations programmes.

Scientific dissemination evaluation is another process-oriented approach but with particular emphasis on distribution. It rests on the assumption that wider dissemination means higher impact. It is usually based on numerical analysis of press clippings or broadcast transcripts, the circulation/readership of media used, or analysis of the content achieved. It almost goes without saying that media evaluation falls into this category.

In contrast to scientific dissemination, scientific impact evaluation primarily uses quantitative, social scientific methods of data collection to determine the public relations campaign impact directly. Frequently, practitioners rely upon experimental or quasi-experimental research designs in which measures are taken both before and after a new programme is implemented. This design allows one to determine whether the programme 'caused' the observed change.

Broom and Dozier (1990: 26) mirror the frequent three-step/stage analysis of public relations evaluation (see Chapter 5) when they discuss using research to plan programmes, to monitor programmes and to evaluate programmes. The first stage in programme planning is indeed to analyse the situation, which is effectively an analysis of the public relations 'problem'. This problem concerns the mismatch between the situation as it is and the situation as the organization would ideally like it to be. The public relations programme is designed to align this dichotomy. The key here is to use a cycle of formal and informal, quantitative and qualitative approaches first to confirm and delineate the 'problem', and then to understand and explain it. This approach can be exemplified in this way:

> Somebody tells you that there is a rumour going around that redundancies are in the offing and that staff are worried. Senior management confirm that the rumour is completely unfounded. Informal discussions with opinion formers in the staff canteen confirm that there is indeed such a rumour doing the rounds and 'a lot of people are worried'. You poll a systematic sample of employees to check how widespread the concern is and then talk to a random sample of nine employees to see why they think layoffs are imminent and get a feel as to how the rumour started in the first place.

Once the programme has been launched, research is used to monitor its effectiveness (or otherwise). This can be frightening, but it is essential to avoid wasting resources on pointless activity. The key point is that it is the process that is being examined, but not the ultimate impact (yet). It is worth monitoring process activity because effective processes are *more likely* to lead to successful results. But however good the process, this is no *guarantee* of successful results (see the substitution game, Chapter 5).

When moving on to assessment of the impact of the public relations programme, the outcomes stated in the programme's objectives must be examined. Broom and Dozier (1990: 77) divide these programme outcomes in to three categories: *change or maintenance of a public's knowledge* (including awareness and understanding), *predispositions* (opinions and attitudes), and *behaviour*. This is where direct measurement is required, frequently using formal research techniques, but sometimes using more easily available quantitative data such as sales enquiries (or even sales).

The operational management of public relations is centred on the planning of public relations programmes or campaigns. A common theme of public relations planning models is that they start with a research phase designed to analyse the current situation; the starting point needs to be defined if the correct strategy to reach the end point (objectives/goals) is to be identified.

RESEARCH METHODS

Blaxter, Hughes and Tight (1996: 59) bring a refreshing simplicity – and therefore clarity – to a discussion of research with their discussion of methods at three successive levels: research families, approaches and techniques (see Table 4.1).

Table 4.1   *Families, approaches and techniques*

Research families	● Quantitative or qualitative
	● Deskwork or fieldwork
Research approaches	● Action research
	● Case studies
	● Experiments
	● Surveys
Research techniques	● Documents
	● Interviews
	● Observation
	● Questionnaires

Quantitative research is to do with numbers and qualitative is to do with words. Quantitative answers the question 'what is happening?' and qualitative the question 'why is it happening?' These two terms do not refer to research methods, but how the data acquired by different research methods is treated.

Questionnaires are generally the research method used to gather quantitative data. Qualitative data is usually obtained using an interview technique. This divide is not a ravine, however, and, as is so often the case, terminology frequently confuses. Is the stereotypical market researcher with a clipboard in the high street doing a fully structured interview or administering a questionnaire (probably both!)?

UK researcher Denscombe comprehensively and elegantly defines and distinguishes the quantitative and qualitative (2003: 232–35); see Table 4.2.

Table 4.2 *Families, approaches and techniques*

Quantitative research tends to be associated with:	numbers as the unit of analysis analysis large-scale studies a specific focus researcher detachment a predetermined research design
Qualitative research tends to be associated with:	words as the unit of analysis description small-scale studies holistic perspective researcher involvement an emergent research design

Lindenmann (2006: 5) interprets Denscombe's researcher involvement (or detachment) as subjectivity (or objectivity):

> Primary research is usually either qualitative or *quantitative* in form. *Qualitative* research usually refers to studies that are somewhat subjective, but nevertheless in-depth, using a probing, open-end, free response format. Quantitative research usually refers to studies that are highly objective and projectable, using closed-end, forced-choice questionnaires. These studies tend to rely heavily on statistics and numerical measures.

DESK RESEARCH

Desk research unearths information that already exists: in the form of internal records (can reveal much about the characteristics of customers, what they buy and how) or published information. It is also sometimes referred to as secondary data to distinguish it from primary data, which is raw data obtained by fieldwork (interviews, questionnaires, etc). The main attributes of desk research are that it can be carried out quickly and at a low cost. Unfortunately, it is not always possible to know in advance whether you are going to unearth the information you seek. Sometimes desk research will be fruitless, although usually something of interest will be found. The quality of desk research varies according to the availability of information, how up to date it is, and the time that is available to put it together.

Selecting a sample

Published sources list people or companies to interview. Examples are the electoral register, telephone directory, lists of customers and trade directories.

Obtaining details on products

Approaches include observation (looking at products in action or on the shelf in shops); buying products and stripping them down (yoghurt pots!); getting sales literature on products; and so on.

Providing an economic backcloth

Frequently, it is useful to provide background information as a perspective against which primary information can be set. A survey on the use of plastics in food containers may be made more understandable against a background of the trends in food packaging in general. The broader the scope, the more likely there is to be something available in published form.

Assessment of market size and trends

Government, trade associations and market research companies publish reams of market statistics. Frequently these are only the starting point, particularly if the product of interest is only a niche in that market.

Information on companies

Desk research can provide a considerable amount of information on companies. It can show their turnover and financial performance, the products they sell, their distribution networks, pricing policy, etc. This information can be found in company accounts, press coverage, product literature and directories.

Desk research has one advantage in that the information tends to be collected together in one place, a library for example. A good library will contain under one roof most directories, company information, and journals and magazines covering a bewildering array of subjects. A library may also operate online databases bringing together – usually abstracted – information from newspapers, journals and market research reports.

ACTION RESEARCH

There is much discussion among social scientists about the concept of action research. Its distinguishing feature is that it avoids any two-stage approach: specialist researchers generating some research findings as one stage, and then after consideration and reflection a separate body of practitioners taking some action as a result of those findings as a separate stage. Closer examination indicates that, rather than a research strategy, in a public relations context action research is more a planning and management framework that accepts a rigorous research orientation: 'Practitioner research can only be designated action research if it is carried out by professionals who are engaged in researching, through structured self-reflection, aspects of their own practice as they engage in that practice' (Edwards and Talbot cited in Denscombe, 2003: 75).

The parallels with public relations practice are reinforced (and become almost uncanny) wherever action research is discussed. For example, Blaxter, Hughes and Tight (1996: 64), discussing action research, state:

> It is well suited to the needs of people conducting research in their workplaces, and who have a focus on improving aspects of their own and their colleagues' practices. … It offers a research design which links the research process closely to its context, and is predicated on the idea of research having a practical purpose in view and leading to change. It also fits well with the idea of the research process as a spiral activity, going through repeated cycles and changing each time.

Three parallels immediately appear. First, the focus on improving practice links to the thinking behind formative evaluation. Second, public relations is frequently associated with the management of change. Finally, there is wide agreement that the public relations planning process is necessarily a cyclical one and action research is clearly cyclical as well (see Figure 4.1).

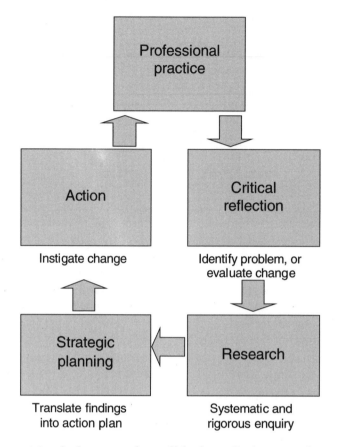

Figure 4.1   *Action research parallels the cyclical nature of PR planning*

CASE STUDIES

The use of case studies (single or multiple) is increasingly popular among social science researchers. By looking in depth at a single instance (or a few instances) it may be possible to derive understandings that are more widely applicable than the single case being studied. For example, a detailed investigation into the organizational behaviour of one complex company may give us an insight into how large companies in general behave. In public relations, case studies are not so much a research technique as a useful means of demonstrating the efficacy of a company's/client's products or services as well as generating third-party endorsement. Case studies sacrifice breadth of study for depth of study: 'Case studies focus on one instance (or a few instances) of a particular phenomenon with a view to providing an in-depth account of events, relationships, experiences or processes occurring in that particular instance' (Denscombe, 2003: 32).

Daymon and Holloway (2002: 105–06) have examined the role of (qualitative) research methods in the context of public relations and marketing communications. They point out that a case study is a distinctive approach because it focuses specifically on the case as an end in itself:

> A case study is an extensive examination, using multiple sources of evidence (which may be qualitative, quantitative or both), of a single entity which is bounded by time and place. Usually it is associated with a location. The 'case' may be an organisation, a set of people such as social or work group, a community, an event, a process, an issue or a campaign.

Many PR and marcomms (marketing communications) people prefer quantitative survey research. The term 'case study' is used to refer to slightly different concepts, indeed not restricted to a research context. 'In public relations consultancies and advertising agencies, "case studies" are compiled of good practice or award-winning campaigns and used for promotional purposes or to generate new business. In education, "case studies" act as a teaching tool to stimulate discussion and debate. Used in this way, they are examples of professional practice within industry contexts' (Daymon and Holloway, 2002).

Stacks (2002: 71–72) is one of the few writers to have examined research issues in a public relations context. He points out that, although case studies are regarded as highly valuable in public relations (frequently to demonstrate examples of good practice), public relations has been slow to adopt them as a research method. 'They provide a richly detailed and complete understanding of the case under study. Case studies are found in most *applied* disciplines, from business to law to advertising to medicine to public relations. They offer insight into good and bad practice. A case study helps us to understand theory, but theory as applied to specific situations.'

EXPERIMENTS

Broom and Dozier (1990: 99) argue that experimental design is always used when a public relations programme is evaluated. This is because a group of subjects (one or more publics) is subjected to a treatment (the PR campaign). The impact of that treatment is then measured by a quantitative comparison before and after the treatment was applied.

Common sense indicates that any application of the concept of an experiment to public relations does not revolve around people in white coats wielding test tubes in a sterile laboratory. Instead, the experimental design predicates field studies, such as the pre-testing of messages among naturally occurring groups of people before the deployment of those messages in a planned campaign. The true scientific experiment seeks to control all the variables associated with the experiment. This becomes increasingly difficult as the experiment moves out of the laboratory and into the field. The latter can only really be described as 'quasi-experimental' in that: 'The quasi (as if) experimental approach is conducted in the spirit of the classic laboratory experiment, but recognizes that the researcher cannot dictate circumstances and needs to take the role of observing events "as they naturally occur"' (Denscombe, 2003: 69).

SURVEYS

A field survey should only be used when secondary sources are exhausted, otherwise you will be wasting time and money finding out what you already know. Unfortunately, however, desk research is not always going to provide all the information that is required. In this case, primary or field research will be required. This is an area fraught with difficulty, theoretically requiring a great deal of technical competence as well as resources in terms of both time and money.

However, in practice a surprising amount of information can be obtained by 'gifted amateurs' and fairly limited surveys, provided no more emphasis is placed on the results than they deserve. All research is subject to error and, in general, the less detailed the research and the smaller the sample size the wider the margin of error. There is no harm in undertaking a brief survey among a small number of people provided that these limitations are taken into account when interpreting the results. Asking six randomly selected people what car they drive cannot be used to calculate Ford's UK market share. It might indicate that Ford is a popular marque (provided that you are not attending a 2CV convention at the time!). This is the province of 'informal research', theoretically a contradiction in terms, but nevertheless, thought-provoking feedback from a few unsystematically polled but influential opinion formers could hardly be ignored.

INTERVIEWS

One of the main techniques when undertaking field research is the interview (administered by telephone or face-to-face). Interviews can vary from being highly structured where a questionnaire has to be strictly followed, while others are completely unstructured and the topic is examined in depth, with the respondent being allowed to lead the discussion in virtually any direction they wish. The less structured the interview, the more skill is required by the researcher in both conducting the interview and interpreting its results.

Because of the cost and time involved, it is normally impractical to carry out a significant number of personal interviews. However, if there are a small number of people with valuable information which requires intricate and detailed questions then this approach might well be appropriate.

The advantages of a personal interview include a low refusal rate by respondents, and the sample is usually less distorted (postal enquiries have an erratic response rate and with the telephone you will not be able to get hold of everybody in the sample). Also, a rapport can be established between respondent and interviewer that breaks down any initial suspicion associated with surveys, and also a wider range of questions can be asked. Dr Kevin Moloney of Bournemouth University has developed a set of rules of thumb for doing research-based interviews which we have adapted (with permission):

Before the interview, ensure that you:

- understand that you are doing qualitative research which may or may not be backed up by survey data;
- can justify how you have chosen your interview sample: randomly, representatively or purposively;
- have a master research question which breaks down into sub-questions.

During the interview, ensure that you:

- ask the questions in a tightly structured way or go with the flow of the responses;
- ensure by the end of the interview that you have asked all the questions on your research agenda;
- tape the interview;
- do not take notes (more than a few key words) – concentrate on what is being said;

- note body language, repetitions and omissions;
- don't ask leading questions;
- don't expect respondents to be overly self-critical;
- realize you may have to get at critical points obliquely.

After the interview, ensure that you:

- write up observation notes on leaving the interview and listen to the tape right through twice;
- are on the look out for topics emerging that you may have missed;
- transcribe everything and do so within two days of the interview;
- remember that a 20-minute interview takes three hours to transcribe (so consider paying somebody else to do it!).

Telephone interviews are cheaper than personal interviews in terms of use of time. They also enable interviews to be completed faster. A wide geographical spread can be covered, the interviewer can take copious notes and is able to study reference or confidential material. Compared with postal questionnaires, the interviewer is able to explain the survey in some detail, even using semi-structured questionnaires that would be totally inappropriate by post. The principal problem is that the length of the interview tends to be restricted compared with a personal interview, and the lack of eye contact makes the relationship between respondent and interviewer less relaxed.

The key benefit of the in-depth interview is the opportunity to probe, to encourage people to expand on their answers. Kane and O'Reilly-de Brun (2001: 206) offer useful advice on probing techniques that are useful for interviews:

- Ask questions that allow people to develop their answers, not questions that can simply be answered by 'yes' or 'no'.
- Pursue information further by asking questions that will tell you 'Who?', 'What?', 'Where?', 'Why?' and 'How?', as appropriate.
- Encourage people to expand on an answer by pausing after the reply, and perhaps giving some sign of encouragement.
- Encourage people to clarify their answers.
- Cross-check the answers by phrasing the question slightly differently.

A focus group can be regarded as a group interview but the interaction between group members gives it particular richness, as well as requiring skill to moderate. Grunig and Hunt (1984: 31) outline three research methods in the context of planning and executing public relations campaigns. In addition to primary research in the form of surveys and secondary desk research they list the focus group:

> *Focus Group interviews* are a marketing research technique that has been successfully adapted to the needs of public relations practitioners. They do not yield the strictly quantitative data that can be gotten [sic] from a survey. But they do have the advantage of being open-ended and permitting members of target groups to speak in their own terms of understanding, provide their own emphasis, and respond to the views expressed by other members of the same group.

Focus groups are undoubtedly a powerful research tool and can provide a useful complement to quantitative approaches to get a deep understanding of the opinions and attitudes of particular publics. However, they do need to be moderated by trained researchers and are not really the province of the 'gifted amateur'. Therefore, the need to outsource their operation has implications in terms of cost.

Daymon and Holloway (2002: 186) suggest that the key features of a focus group are:

● They provide evidence from many voices on the same topic.
● They are interactive.
● They provide a supportive forum for expressing suppressed views.
● They allow you to collect a large amount of data fairly quickly.

The interactive nature of the focus group is important, as one person's comments motivate others to expand upon and develop their own views. They are also useful for involving participants who are suspicious of researching and hesitant to articulate their own views, opinions and perspectives. Typically, focus groups can be used to examine issues that vary from the micro to the macro:

● advertising or concept testing;
● understanding behaviours and attitudes;
● exploring strategic policies and issues;
● developing and understanding brands, products and services;
● exploring organizational and industry issues.

The length of a focus group session varies, but typically is two hours. Similarly, the size of the group varies, with smaller groups preferred for detailed discussions of contentious issues, and larger groups for less intensive discussions of less controversial topics. The facilitator moves from introducing the session, through putting members at ease and outlining the scope of the topic, to the main discussion, with questioning moving from the general to the particular. Note that while contrasting views can be illuminating, an important role for the facilitator is to diffuse any potential hostility:

> The qualities of an effective moderator are the same as those of an in-depth interviewer: flexibility, open-mindedness, skills in eliciting information, and the ability to both listen and interpret. In addition, because you take on a leadership role when moderating, you must have excellent social and refereeing skills. These allow you, first, to guide participants towards effective interaction. Then they enable you to focus and control the discussion without coercing participants or directing the debate. (Daymon and Holloway, 2002: 198)

QUESTIONNAIRES

While it has already been mentioned that a questionnaire can be administered face-to-face, particularly in a market research context, the use of the questionnaire is normally considered when it is administered by post, or increasingly by e-mail where many of the same considerations apply. Denscombe (2003: 145) outlines those situations when this type of questionnaire is at its most effective:

- when used with *large numbers* of respondents in many locations, eg the postal questionnaire;
- when what is required tends to be fairly *straightforward information* – relatively brief and uncontroversial;
- when the *social climate is open enough* to allow full and honest answers;
- when there is a need for *standardized data* from identical questions – without requiring personal, face-to-face interaction;
- when *time allows for delays* caused by production, piloting, posting and procrastination before receipt of a response;
- when *resources allow for the costs* of printing, postage and data preparation;
- when the respondents can be expected to be *able to read and understand* the questions – the implications of age, intellect and eyesight need to be considered.

Questionnaires are generally reckoned to be a relatively cost-effective form of research, and certainly a postal survey can be carried out at reasonable cost. Another advantage is that they can be carried out quite widely, physically and otherwise. Surprisingly, speed is another advantage. Usually, if people are to respond to a postal questionnaire they do so immediately and, although you will find the odd straggler coming in months afterwards, the bulk of response will come back within a few days. The postal questionnaire also eliminates interviewer bias, which is a major problem associated with telephone and face-to-face interviewers. Also, respondents can remain anonymous.

The main problem of postal questionnaires compared with other means of distribution is lack of response. The principal factor governing response is the degree of interest the questionnaire generates among respondents. Providing some sort of incentive to respond (prize draw or free gift) can increase response rate but does add cost. Another problem is getting a representative mailing list in the first place. Another restricting factor is the length of the questionnaire. Once it gets beyond two sides of A4, the length of the questionnaire is going to deter postal respondents. This restriction naturally limits the amount of information that can be obtained.

The chances of a good response rate can be enhanced in a number of ways. First, pay attention to the mailing list; it's worth ringing up a sample to check that names, addresses and job titles are correct. Make sure that the questionnaire is addressed to a named individual rather than a vague job title, and that the questions asked are of real interest. Include a covering letter, which together with the questionnaire itself should be of professional appearance. A reminder sent, say, two weeks after the initial mailing can increase response, but – together with incentives – adds to the cost of the exercise.

Lindenmann (2006: 8) confirms that 'conducting surveys via e-mail or through websites is growing in popularity'. The major advantage of self-administered questionnaires distributed electronically is speed of response, but there can be problems with formatting and incomplete data. Web-based surveys are rather different, 'in that a specialized software program or system is needed to construct a questionnaire and to collect and eventually process the results' (Lindenmann, 2006: 8). One advantage is that survey responses are automatically collected, removing the need for manual entry. However, they are relatively passive as they rely on respondents seeking out the online questionnaire. This has issues for the eligibility of respondents and the representative nature of the sample.

SAMPLING METHODS

Survey research is based on the idea that to obtain representative views from a body of people, it is not normally necessary to talk to them all. The problem is to derive a sample that is large enough and broad enough to be representative of the group as a whole. The sample size is usually a compromise between the resources available to devote to the survey and the accuracy required. There is almost no limit to the statistical knots that some researchers will tie themselves up in trying to perfect sampling techniques. However, much useful information can be gathered using low-cost, small-sample research and, although sample selection should always be approached very carefully, this care should be based on common sense rather than academic statistical theory.

Denscombe (2003: 24) points out that: 'Whatever the theoretical issues, the simple fact is that surveys and sampling are frequently used in small-scale research involving between 30 and 250 cases.' He stresses four points in relation to the use of smaller sample sizes:

- Extra attention needs to be paid to the issue of how representative the sample is.
- The smaller the sample, the simpler the analysis should be.
- Samples should not involve fewer than 30 people or events.
- In the case of qualitative research there is a different logic for the size of the sample and the selection of cases to be included. A small sample size is quite in keeping with the nature of qualitative data.

Briefly, there are two major types of sampling procedures: probability or random sampling, and non-probability or quota sampling. With random sampling, each member of the population to be sampled has an equal chance of being selected. This is not as simple as it sounds, since random does not mean haphazard. For example, picking 20 names in no particular order from a telephone directory does not produce a random sample. There will be some bias in the sample selection (the eye being drawn to familiar or short names, for example). Instead, a preferable approach is to use random number tables.

An alternative approach is quota sampling. Here, those who should be interviewed are specified in terms of specific variables. In consumer terms, this might be a certain proportion of people of a certain sex and age, social class, etc. In industrial terms the aim might be to achieve an equal spread of firms of different size.

QUESTIONNAIRE DESIGN

Crucial to the whole issue of public relations research is questionnaire design. It is the vehicle for collecting the information required. One golden rule with questionnaires is to pilot them by doing a pre-test with two or three potential or typical respondents. Before tackling the questions themselves, two quick points. First, the length of the questionnaire: as a guideline, a postal questionnaire should be limited to 20 questions, a telephone survey to 15 minutes and a face-to-face interview either 30 minutes (in the home or office) or 3 minutes (in the street). The other vital consideration is to ensure that the instructions to both the respondent and interviewer (if applicable) are clear and unambiguous.

Dichotomous questions are the simplest type of questions to ask since, theoretically, there are only two possible answers:

1. Have you heard of EIC (the Extremely Interesting Company)? Yes/No
2. Which of the two products A or B do you think is more attractive?

Questions such as these are easy to ask and analyse but make sure that in the circumstances in which you use them they truly are a two-way choice. 'Don't know' could well be a response to the first question and 'neither' or 'both' to question 2.

With multiple-choice questions, respondents are able to choose from a range of possible answers. Again, these questions are very easy to analyse but it is important to list all possible options and always include an answer 'other (please specify)' in case an option you had not considered emerges.

Where did you buy your trailer from?   Manufacturer
                                         Merchant
                                         Importer
                                         Second-hand centre
                                         Other (please specify)

Scaling questions are an attempt to identify attitudes and strength of feeling. The most common means of attempting to gauge strength of feeling is the so-called 'Likert' scale. A respondent is asked to what extent he or she agrees or disagrees with a particular statement, indicating whether he or she strongly agrees, agrees, is uncertain, disagrees or strongly disagrees.

EIC's products are expensive

5	4	3	2	1
Strongly agree	Agree	Uncertain	Disagree	Strongly disagree

The exact form and phrasing of questions will vary according to the particular research exercise being undertaken. However, there are a number of points to consider:

- Given the subject matter, make it as simple and easy as possible.
- Do not digress: keep to the subject and ask only relevant questions.
- Bear in mind that you will have to analyse the results afterwards.
- Each question should cover one point at a time.
- Questions should be unambiguous.
- Avoid leading and misleading questions.
- Ensure good sequencing and question flow.
- Do not ask unanswerable questions.
- Do not offend or embarrass.
- Introduce some variety; don't be monotonous.
- Use positive questions; try to avoid negatives.

Apparently simple questions can be very difficult to answer. Take the question: Which supplier offers the best price and delivery? There are a number of problems that the respondent may have:

All prices are the same.
The best price does not have the best delivery.
What is 'best' anyway?

Ambiguity is a result of poor use of the English language. For example: Do you use an online database? Is the 'you' the individual, the department or the company? Does the 'use' mean physically and regularly or irregularly? Ambiguity is usually the fault that remains in a questionnaire even when all others have been eliminated. Don't you think that the transfer speed is too slow? is a leading question in that the respondent is not asked to think about an answer but has one suggested. Unless the respondent feels strongly on the subject, he or she will not wish to argue.

Always start with questions that are easy to answer and ensure that they follow a logical progression. In particular, keep any sensitive questions until towards the end of the questionnaire. Also, remember that respondents can only answer questions that are within their own attitudes and experience. Avoid 'How will your competitors react to the situation?' and 'If product X were available, would you buy it?'

ANALYSING INFORMATION

If a simple, well-structured questionnaire has been designed then analysing the information is generally common sense. Remember you have no interest in the responses of individual respondents (on the whole). Rather, the aim is to make generalizations about all – or part – of the sample that was surveyed. If the sample is a representative one then these generalizations can be extended to the population as a whole.

Take this question:

How likely are you to buy a package holiday in the next two years?
(one response only)

Very likely
Fairly likely
Neither likely/unlikely
Fairly unlikely
Very unlikely

A simple analysis of this question might be as follows:

Likelihood of buying a packaged holiday in the next two years (all respondents)

Likelihood of buying	Percentage
Very likely	25
Fairly likely	40
Neither likely/unlikely	14
Fairly unlikely	18
Very unlikely	3
Total	100
[Sample size	200]

This table shows the responses of all respondents but you may be interested in part of the sample or – and this is where analysis of what appears to be 'ordinary' data can start to throw up some interesting results – compare the response of different parts of the sample. This is known as cross-analysis.

Likelihood of buying a package holiday in the next two years (existing buyers)

Likelihood of buying	Percentage
Very likely	40
Fairly likely	0
Neither likely/unlikely	25
Fairly unlikely	30
Very unlikely	5
Total	100
[Sample size	100]

Likelihood of buying a package holiday in the next two years by existing buyers

Likelihood of buying	Total	Existing	Not existing
Very likely	25	40	10
Fairly likely	40	0	80
Neither likely/unlikely	14	25	5
Fairly unlikely	18	30	5
Very unlikely	3	5	0
Total	100	100	100
[Sample size	100	100	100]

This is an example of a relatively simple cross-analysis. This type of analysis can be much more elaborate, with cross-analysis by more than one question and more variables for each question. Another additional analysis for scalar questions, such as this question about the likelihood of purchase, is to assign numeric values to answers and then derive mean scores as shown below:

Likelihood of buying appliance in the next two years by existing ownership of the appliance (all respondents)

Likelihood of buying	Total	Existing	Not existing
Very likely (+2)	25	40	10
Fairly likely (+1)	40	0	80
Neither likely/unlikely (0)	14	25	5
Fairly unlikely (–1)	18	30	5

Very unlikely (–2)	3	5	0
Total	100	100	100
Mean score	+0.66	+0.40	+0.95
[Sample size	200	100	100]

Although mean scores have a tendency to over-simplify the situation, they do show – in this instance – at a glance that non-owners are more likely to buy than owners.

Interview

Anne Gregory emphasizes the confusion that surrounds evaluation in public relations: 'For some people, it's an overall cycle that includes research at the start of the programme, monitoring as the programme unfolds, and then final evaluation at the end. For others, it's purely and simply what the end result is.' Even when evaluation is restricted to looking at the end result, Gregory still thinks the issue is clouded by confusion. 'For some it's ROI. For others it's changes in attitudes and behaviour, while for others it's the "how many column inches did we get?" approach', she adds.

She suggests that the solution is to step back and reflect on what the public relations effort is trying to achieve. Gregory makes a clear distinction between the strategic and the tactical. 'If you take a strategic approach to public relations and your purpose is to change attitudes and behaviour on behalf of, or within, your organization or your client, then that leads to a research-based perspective on evaluation. If your public relations is tactical, focused on a series of defined activities, then you will probably concentrate on measuring specific elements of the process. It really depends on where you are starting from.'

Gregory does not see these two forms of evaluation as incompatible, rather as complementary. She recognizes that changing attitudes (for example) is likely to be a long-term effort so that the evaluation associated with it will involve measurement over time. Also, the evaluation measures required will need to be research-based and probably (possibly) quite expensive, as a benchmark will be required. In contrast, a tactical publicity campaign (short term and restricted to public relations activities) will be relatively easy to monitor and evaluate. 'Probably what is needed is a mixture of the two. Yes, we have reached that particular milestone, but that's within the context of a much wider public relations programme. Also, associated with that are questions such as, am I spending my money effectively, am I managing my resources effectively, do I have the right mix of skills within my team?'

However, when justifying the worth of the public relations effort to the organization as a whole, Gregory's instinct is that, at the most senior levels, public relations practitioners do not have to continually justify the value of their contribution. 'If you get your research right, your planning right, you know where your audiences are, you know where you want to go with them, and you have tested the effectiveness of the channels of communication, then all you need to do at the end is check that you are on track.' Gregory argues that many respected companies focus not on impact evaluation (which is complicated by a range of issues) but on researching the starting point thoroughly and then using a range of qualitative measures to check that the programme is being applied effectively. 'We tend to plunge into a campaign and then say: "Oh, it's achieved something." So, we have to come up with all kinds of elaborate measures to justify having taken money out of the budget. Do it the other way around, and put the effort into planning before you start, then all you have to do is check that you are on track once you move to implementation,' she suggests.

Gregory feels that the public relations industry 'looks inward all the time' and does not ask how other functional areas are judged. 'I doubt very much if an HR director is asked to justify employing John Smith. Instead they will point to soft measures (which may have figures attached to them) such as employer of choice, or a reputation for having enlightened employment policies.' She suggests that similar thinking can be applied to public relations. Gregory argues that public relations will have responsibility for much of the non-financial reporting that will be required under UK and European directives. 'A lot of that will be public relations, because it's about how an organization conducts itself.'

In looking at the future of evaluation, Gregory adds another perspective on public relations justifying its value to the organization. 'At some stage, you have to bridge a credibility gap, but once you have done it, you don't have to justify yourself any more.' She feels that there has to be some sort of trigger that prompts people to accept that public relations has proved its worth. 'Quite often it's an external trigger like a crisis, when all of a sudden there is an understanding of the importance of communication. But it's nothing to do with ROI, it's to do with what might have been had PR not been there, or what actually happened because PR wasn't there.'

Professor Anne Gregory is Professor of Public Relations and Pro Vice-Chancellor at Leeds Metropolitan University and a former President of the Institute of Public Relations.

QUESTIONNAIRE RESPONSES

Evaluation questionnaire for industry leaders

Q: What is the most important role of evaluation – demonstrating effectiveness or planning and monitoring campaigns?

The proof of the pudding is in the eating – for that reason the ultimate value of evaluation/research lies in demonstrating (or disproving) effectiveness and efficiency. Planning and monitoring programmes are means to some ends. **Dejan Verčič**

Both are equally important in my opinion. **Alison Clarke**

Demonstrating effectiveness. **Fran Hagon**

PR as a discipline has sadly failed to demonstrate a cause and effect in delivering demonstrable business value. The right kind of evaluation should focus entirely on proving value. If we do that then we can finally swap the heinous habit of assertion for demonstration or proof. **Crispin Manners**

Demonstrating effectiveness – but it's marginal. Its role in planning is almost as important. **Loretta Tobin**

Demonstrating effectiveness, on the basis that most times that is what the client is interested in: is the cat catching the mice? **Ray Mawerera**

This question is irrelevant. It's like asking which part of the road is more important – the left- or the right-hand side. You can't have a road without both sides. To be effective you must both plan the campaign and continually monitor it. **Annabelle Warren**

I think demonstrating effectiveness, although our clients love the big number at the end of the campaign – it justifies their existence. **Laurna O'Donnell**

Depends – tweaking is extremely important but you need to be sure that you're measuring the right things – ie that your data isn't being skewed by some other element out of your control. If you can't set yourself up to learn from your mistakes though, you're wasting your own time and someone else's money. **Clara Zawawi**

The most significant value is in properly guiding the planning, designing and execution of programmes to ensure effort, time and money are dedicated in the right direction. If the plan is properly designed, executed and funded it should be effective. Supporting research proving success is a bonus. **Tom O'Donoghue**

I suspect that you have to get through the demonstrating effectiveness phase before you can get to the planning element. Clearly the latter looks forward and is the most important, but without a feedback loop even the planning part is meaningless. **Mike Copland**

I believe it's planning and monitoring campaigns. Demonstrating effectiveness is nice, but that's really just self-protection with the client. If you can find a truly effective ROI measurement for PR, then you ought to bottle it up and sell it, because you'll make millions. **Matt Kucharski**

The two are interrelated. Unless you can demonstrate effectiveness, it may be counterproductive planning further campaigns. **Richard Offer**

Demonstrating effectiveness – the Holy Grail of PR. **John Bliss**

5

Evaluation structures and processes

For some time a number of evaluation structures and models have been made available to practitioners to assist them to define and implement evaluation strategies. They have not been universally adopted; the reasons for this are discussed and, together with practitioner research, this discussion is used as the basis of developing more accessible alternatives.

When practitioners undertake evaluation, they tend to take a narrow view of the methods used and concentrate on simplistic methodologies. However, there are a range of structures and models which outline processes for public relations evaluation. This chapter considers those structures and proposes two more based on research among (and feedback from) practitioners.

It is increasingly recognized that the evaluation of public relations programmes/activities requires a mix of techniques: 'In most cases, a skilled practitioner will use a combination of methods to evaluate the effectiveness of a program' (Wilcox *et al*, 2000: 193). This is confirmed by experienced practitioner Walter Lindenmann in his seminal article (1993: 9): 'it is important to recognize that *there is no one simplistic method* for measuring PR effectiveness. Depending on which level of measurement is required, an array of different tools and techniques is needed to properly assess PR impact.'

Frequently a triple-layered or three-stage model is established as a framework for this 'combination of methods'. Typical is Cutlip, Center and Broom's 'Stages and Levels for Evaluating Public Relations Programs' model, which discusses three 'different levels of a complete program evaluation: preparation, implementation, and impact' (2000: 367–68).

PREPARATION, IMPLEMENTATION, IMPACT

Cutlip, Center and Broom's evaluation model (2006: 368), known as PII (Preparation, Implementation, Impact), is a step model that offers levels of evaluation for differing demands. It does not prescribe methodology, but accepts that 'Evaluation means different things to different practitioners.' (See Figure 5.1.)

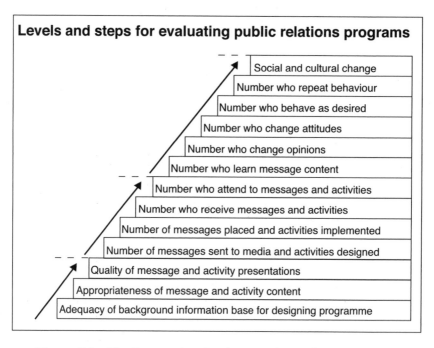

Figure 5.1   *The Preparation, Implementation and Impact model*

Each step in the PII model contributes to increased understanding and adds information for assessing effectiveness. The bottom rung of *preparation evaluation* examines whether adequate background information has been gathered in order to plan the programme effectively.

Next, the content of materials produced is examined to ensure it matches the plan (does the press release carry one or more of the campaign's key messages, for example?). Finally, at this level, the presentation of materials is examined – a professionally produced annual report does not guarantee effective investor relations but it contributes towards it.

At the second level, implementation evaluation considers how tactics and effort have been applied. The starting point is distribution (of materials) and attendance (at events), moving on to opportunities for exposing members of the target audience to organizational messages. This type of evaluation can identify flaws: a professionally written press release will not be effective unless distributed to the right contacts. Although significant numbers can be quoted for Opportunities to See (OTS), these figures are just that – opportunities to see – and give no indication of the extent to which messages were attended to. As an aside, therefore, OTS and similar constructs play a role in media planning, but have limited use in any sort of measurement of campaign effectiveness. Although public relations evaluation is frequently centred around the implementation phase, Cutlip, Center and Broom (2006: 372) sound a warning note: 'The ease with which practitioners can amass large numbers of column inches, broadcast minutes, readers, viewers, attendees, and gross impressions probably accounts for widespread use – and misuse – of evaluations at this level.'

The discussion to date has been concerned with 'process' evaluation. However, at the *impact* level, the emphasis switches to examining the extent to which the outcomes specified in the objectives and overall goals for the programme have been achieved. Impact evaluation is based on measuring the same variables that formed the benchmark for the campaign to establish whether the quantified changes spelled out in the objectives have been achieved – or not. Direct measurement using research techniques from surveys to observation (direct and indirect) is required here and requires both an understanding of research techniques and some ingenuity in establishing indicators of attitude and behavioural changes.

The PII model is valuable for its separation of output and impact and for counselling against the confusion of these different measures. It acts as a checklist and a reminder when planning evaluation. Its most important message (Cutlip, Center and Broom, 2006: 436) bears reiteration as it is a point returned to several times in this text:

The most common error in program evaluation is substituting measures from one level for those at another level. This is most clearly illustrated when practitioners use the number of news releases sent, brochures distributed, or meetings held (implementation efforts) to document program effectiveness (impact). Or if asked to document program impact, they substitute publicity placements, in the form of column inches or airtime, for the changes in the target publics' knowledge, predisposition, and behavior spelt out in program objectives. Evaluation researchers refer to this as the 'substitution game'. Somewhat analogously, to create an illusion, magicians talk of 'misdirecting' audience attention from what is really happening.

MACNAMARA'S PYRAMID MODEL

Since the early 1990s, Australian evaluation specialist Jim Macnamara has developed a model (similar to PII), initially called the 'Macro Model' and now titled the 'Pyramid Model of PR Research'. The Pyramid Model has a 'bottom-up' structure, with the base showing the start-point of the strategy and the peak being the desired outcome of the campaign. Macnamara (2005: 264) says:

> The pyramid metaphor is useful in conveying that, at the base when communication planning begins, practitioners have a large amount of information to assemble and a wide range of options in terms or media and activities. Selection and choices are made to direct certain messages at certain target audiences through certain media, and ultimately, achieve specific defined objectives (the peak of the program or project).

In the Pyramid Model, *inputs* are the components of communication programmes or projects and include the choice of medium, content of communication tools and format. Outputs are the materials and activities produced (such as media publicity, events, and promotional materials) and the processes to produce them, while outcomes are the impacts and effects of communication. A comprehensive menu of evaluation techniques for most public relations situations – from desk research (secondary sources) through media content analysis to observation and quantitative research – is offered.

Macnamara (2005: 266–67) writes that the key steps in the communication process are shown, having been derived from Cutlip, Center and Broom's PII model, but the Pyramid Model offers extra value by listing the measurement methodologies for each of the three stages. Feedback loops are not shown on the model, but 'it is implicit in this model that findings from each stage of research are constantly looped back into planning'. The model includes formative and summative

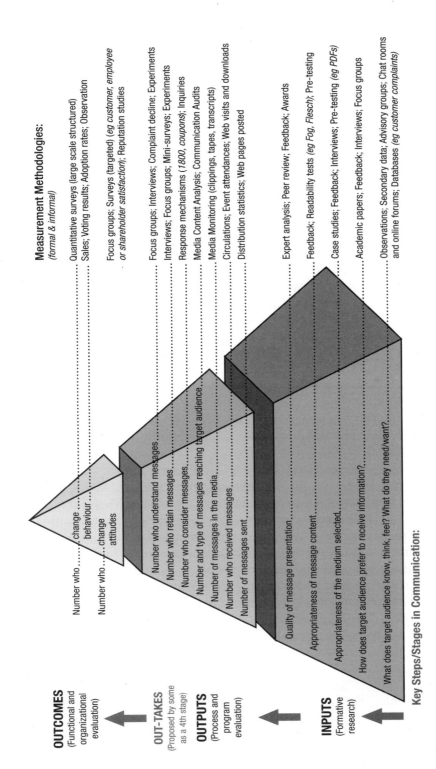

Measurement Methodologies:
(formal & informal)

Quantitative surveys (large scale structured)
Sales; Voting results; Adoption rates; Observation
Focus groups; Surveys (targeted) *(eg customer, employee or shareholder satisfaction)*; Reputation studies

Focus groups; Interviews; Complaint decline; Experiments
Interviews; Focus groups; Mini-surveys; Experiments
Response mechanisms *(1800, coupons)*; Inquiries
Media Content Analysis; Communication Audits
Media Monitoring (clippings, tapes, transcripts)
Circulations; Event attendances; Web visits and downloads
Distribution statistics; Web pages posted

Expert analysis; Peer review; Feedback; Awards

Feedback; Readability tests *(eg Fog, Flesch)*; Pre-testing

Case studies; Feedback; Interviews; Pre-testing *(eg PDFs)*

Academic papers; Feedback; Interviews; Focus groups

Observations; Secondary data; Advisory groups; Chat rooms and online forums; Databases *(eg customer complaints)*

OUTCOMES
(Functional and organizational evaluation)

OUT-TAKES
(Proposed by some as a 4th stage)

OUTPUTS
(Process and program evaluation)

INPUTS
(Formative research)

Number who .... change .... behaviour
Number who .... change .... attitudes

Number who understand messages
Number who retain messages
Number who consider messages
Number and type of messages reaching target audience
Number of messages in the media
Number who received messages
Number of messages sent

Quality of message presentation
Appropriateness of message content
Appropriateness of the medium selected
How does target audience prefer to receive information?
What does target audience know, think, feel? What do they need/want?

Key Steps/Stages in Communication:

Figure 5.2 *'Pyramid model' of PR research*
© Copyright Jim R Macnamara, 1992 and 2001

research methods in order to allow data to be integrated into the continued monitoring and development of communication programmes and so 'work as a continuum of information gathering and feedback on the communication process, not as separate discrete functions'.

PUBLIC RELATIONS EFFECTIVENESS YARDSTICK

The Public Relations Yardstick model, developed by Walter Lindenmann, differs from the other models because its staging does not progress from planning to objectives. It could therefore be criticized for not reinforcing the role of evaluation right at the beginning of the planning process when the situation is analysed and benchmarks established. Instead, it is another three-stage model but the three stages encompass the latter two stages (implementation and preparation) of the PII model and final two stages of the Macro model (outputs and results/outcomes).

Lindenmann (1993: 7) argues that it is possible to measure public relations effectiveness and that there is growing pressure from clients and employers to be more accountable. He adds: 'measuring public relations effectiveness does not have to be either unbelievably expensive or laboriously time-consuming. PR measurement studies can be done at relatively modest cost and in a matter of only a few weeks.' (See Figure 5.3.)

However, the Yardstick is rooted in objective setting and clearly positioned as the second of a two-step process: first, setting public relations objectives and, second, determining at what levels (of expenditure and depth) public relations effectiveness is to be measured. It was also an important development as it was one of the first attempts to sketch out the hierarchy of public relations objective setting, establishing the key role this hierarchy plays in evaluation. At the same time, Lindenmann established the terminology – which is emerging as a de facto standard – of outputs, outgrowths (now out-takes) and outcomes. This important aspect of objective setting in particular and public relations evaluation in general is expanded upon in Chapter 8.

The three levels of the Yardstick gauge the sophistication of the measurement of PR success and failure. Level 1 is the Basic level that measures PR *outputs*: the ways in which the programme or campaign is presented through, typically, media relations. It is measured in terms of media placements and the likelihood of reaching the target groups. The methodology used is media content analysis, measure-

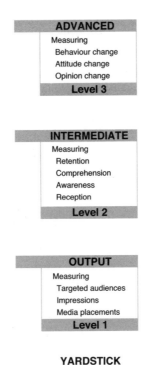

Figure 5.3 *Lindenmann's Effectiveness Yardstick*

ment of placements or opportunities to see, or simple surveys measuring awareness change among target groups. It is essentially the low-cost approach but is more detailed than counting up cuttings or using 'gut reactions', which are informal judgements lacking any rigour in terms of methodology.

Level 2 is termed by Lindenmann as the Intermediate level as it uses *outgrowth* (or *out-take*) measures. These judge whether or not the target audience actually received the messages and so evaluates retention, comprehension and awareness. Practitioners will use a mix of qualitative and quantitative data collection techniques such as focus groups, interviews with opinion leaders and polling of target groups. This stage is more sophisticated than Level 1 and for programmes and campaigns that do not rely solely on media relations for their tactics, this stage will produce data that will be valuable for feedback on strategy and tactics. The data collection methods may not give evidence that attitudes have changed but for practical public relations purposes, it is a lower-cost evaluation strategy.

Outcomes are measured in Level 3. These include opinion, attitudes and behavioural changes. This is where the role of pre- and post-testing comes into its own, with the use of before and after polling, observational methods, psychographic analysis and other social science techniques. It is more complete, takes a longer period to undertake and is more expensive, but for a long-term campaign gives a clear-cut understanding of target audience awareness, comprehension levels and behavioural patterns. It is the comprehensive and valid test of effectiveness and success.

The Yardstick may not be strictly comparable to the other models as it offers a vertical progression of techniques rather than a horizontal movement from Inputs to Results (Macro) or Preparation, Implementation, Impact (PII). It does emphasize the setting of objectives and choosing evaluation methods before starting public relations activity. These are important factors that should be included in any model of evaluation. However, the Yardstick is largely an educational (or promotional) device to encourage practitioners to use evaluation techniques. Its role is to make selection of methodology more accessible to practitioners whose knowledge and understanding of research techniques is poor and to help them bid more accurately for budget in order to undertake evaluation.

THE PRE PROCESS

The three models discussed above have varying provenances. Cutlip, Center and Broom's PII is well known, the Pyramid model much less so. Lindenmann's Yardstick has been publicized in the United States and UK. None of them, however, was mentioned by practitioners in Watson's two surveys among the UK's Institute of Public Relations membership or among public relations practitioners in a multinational firm. They have, however, had considerable exposure in the public relations media of their countries of origin and in other countries. That they have not been adopted by practitioners as appropriate methods can be a result of several factors: practitioners' lack of knowledge, a base of dissemination that is too narrow and academic, or that they lack a practical and universal appeal.

Existing models are too complex; they do not have an integral relationship with effects creation and lack dynamic feedback. They are static, step-by-step processes seen as the final stage in the public relations campaign. Yet public relations is not a 'start/stop' communications process where an organization stops interactions with publics while results of a media relations programme are measured (Watson 1995). All through the programme, it will be informally monitoring and adjusting tactics. At the completion of a particular tactical stage, it may formally measure the effectiveness, but there will be parallel actions continuing and the public relations team will not be in a PR purdah while the evaluation judgements continue. The Pyramid model, with its pinnacle of 'objective achieved or problem solved', is an exemplar of the problem of practical application. In the real world of public relations, nothing stops and activity continues – any valid model must reflect the dynamic, progressive and continuous nature of this process.

IPR *Toolkit* author Michael Fairchild has developed Lindenmann's thinking (particularly with respect to establishing evaluation as a continuous, dynamic process), first on behalf of the International Committee of Public Relations Consultancies Associations (ICO) and more recently through the UK's Institute of Public Relations. The CIPR has published three editions of its Evaluation Toolkit in an attempt to give practitioners practical tools to undertake evaluation.

The Toolkits include a focus on the concept of planning, research and evaluation (PRE). The PRE concept both establishes evaluation as an integral part of public relations planning (not to be tacked on afterwards) and reinforces the close linkage between evaluation and research. Indeed Fairchild's (2002: 36) list of the particular shortcomings related to PRE could be mistaken for the challenges facing public relations in general:

- failure to tap into existing, and often free, sources of research, or to appreciate the value of developing a working relationship with the client's professional market research providers;
- failure to align communications objectives with the business or public sector goals of the client or internal customer;
- the tendency to go into creative mode before constructing a robust planning, research and evaluation framework;
- using terminology for effect rather than for clarity, eg regarding 'objectives', 'strategy' and 'tactics' as interchangeable;
- focusing too heavily on the value of media publicity or failing to assess its value in a broader context.

The PRE process is outlined as a five-step circular process: audit, setting objectives, strategy and plan, ongoing measurement, and results and evaluation (IPR, 2003: 9). Importantly, it is portrayed as a dynamic process (see Figure 5.4).

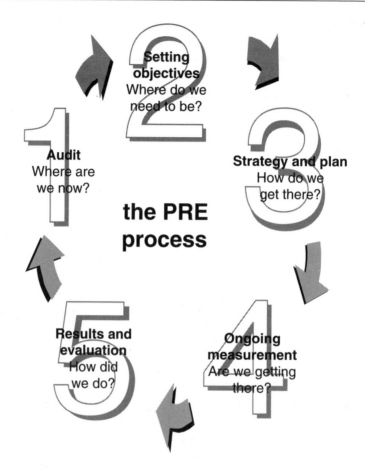

Figure 5.4   *The Planning, Research and Evaluation (PRE) process*

Step 1 (audit) is concerned with conducting research and gathering information to form a foundation on which the programme or campaign is based. Then objectives are set (step 2) and the point is made that as well as being SMART, they should not be set in a vacuum: public relations objectives need to be aligned with organizational goals and objectives. Next, the strategy and its implementation are established (step 3) but even here, research and evaluation are to the forefront, with decisions made about selecting the type of measurement to be used and pre-testing of PR techniques/messages to be employed. Formative evaluation is the province of the fourth step (ongoing measurement), when checks are made as to whether the programme is on track and decisions are made about any adjustments required (or even whether the programme needs to be abandoned). Step 5 (results and evaluation) examines to what degree the objectives set for the campaign or programme have been achieved. While this step is very much summative in nature, there is still a learning perspective, such as what can be fed back into the planning process for the future?

Finally, the dynamic, circular, feedback-oriented PRE process can be mapped onto a four-layered pyramid. This adds 'input' as the base to Lindenmann's three steps, as well as following Macnamara by being pyramidal and linking evaluation methodologies to different levels. PRE steps 1 and 2 (audit and objectives) use research as input, PRE step 3 (strategy and plan) pre-tests and informs the choice of and implementation of tactics, PRE step 4 (ongoing measurement) uses tracking research to monitor progress, and step 5 (results and evaluation) uses direct measurement to examine overall success (see Figure 5.5).

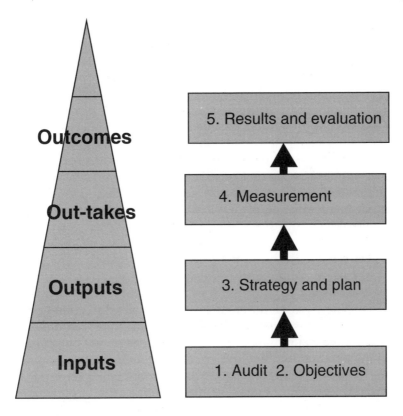

Figure 5.5 *Linking PRE and levels of measurement*

THE UNIFIED MODEL

An analysis of the four existing three-level or three-stage models indicates that, together, they actually describe four steps (as indicated by the Measurement Pyramid) and also that they use a variety of terminology to describe exactly the same – or certainly very similar – stages in the public relations process. Lindenmann does well to separate cognitive and behavioural (also referred to as informational and motivational) effects but maintains three levels by omitting a preparation/input stage. The PII and Macro models feature the latter but fail to make this important distinction at the impact/results stage. The PRE process uses slightly different terms for Lindenmann's three levels but separately recognizes the necessity for an input stage as a benchmark. But PRE does introduce a dynamic perspective to the other – static – models.

However, these approaches remain a useful concept. The first stage to evaluation 'wisdom' in public relations is an understanding that public relations is a multi-step process and that different evaluation methodologies are probably appropriate at these different steps. This is the premise behind all these models and grasping this concept leads to an understanding of the pitfalls of the substitution game.

However, the substitution game continues to be played and therefore the models have not been able to do their job in even this simple respect. The suggestion is that their complexity, allied with confusing terminology, prevents them completing this task. Consequently, the Unified model first takes a relatively simple approach. Second, it is expanded to five levels so that it can accept both an input stage and split out the evaluation of public relations programmes or activities with objectives at the three different levels of the hierarchy.

The integral part of situational analysis in a research and evaluation framework has already been argued. With objective setting such an integral part of a professional evaluation culture, it is a final criticism of the established models that they do not recognize this hierarchy, nor that objectives at different levels will almost certainly require different evaluation methodologies. For both these reasons, a truly representative evaluation structure needs to separate out these three different levels of objective-setting. Consequently, the term 'outcome' is abandoned in favour of a family of outcomes labelled impact, effect and result according to whether the objective(s) set are knowledge/awareness, predisposition or behaviour, respectively. Naturally, as the objectives are hierarchical, impact and effect have to be achieved before result (and, indeed, impact before effect). (See Figure 5.6 and Table 5.1.)

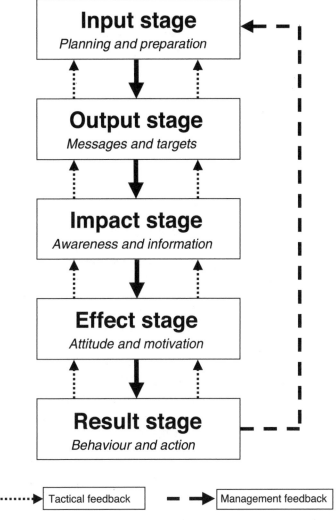

Figure 5.6   *The Unified model*

No methodologies are spelt out in the Unified model. Although it is natural that different methodologies will be required at different levels, the research methodology required should be governed by the particular research problem in the particular circumstances that apply. Consequently, any listing would simply be a collection of likely approaches rather than something of universal applicability. Also, given that an evaluation culture is a research culture, as an evaluation culture develops then so should an appreciation of research methods. As well as accepting the hierarchy of objectives, the Unified model

Table 5.1   *Mapping terminology*

	Unified PII model model		Pyramid model	Lindenmann	PRE
Level/Stage	(S)	(L/S)	(S)	(L)	(L)
A	Input	Preparation	Inputs	–	Inputs
B	Output	Implementation	Outputs	Outputs	Outputs
C (awareness)	Impact	Impact	Results	Outgrowths	Out-takes
D (predisposition)	Effect	Impact	Results	Outcomes	Outcomes
E (behavioural)	Results	Impact	Results/ Outcomes	Outcomes	Outcomes

takes account of the lack of dynamic feedback for which its predecessors have been criticized. This is done in the formative spirit of public relations evaluation but operates at two levels. At one level, there is likely to be formative feedback from one stage to the preceding stage as a means of fine-tuning the current campaign. At another level, there is likely to be lessons learned from one campaign that will feed back into the planning of future campaigns.

PRACTITIONER-DERIVED MODELS

Watson (1995) used four case studies to investigate the real-life constraints and practical difficulties of systematic evaluation. In two case studies, a major industrial redevelopment and a proposal for a new town, it was found that the environmental and development issues embodied in the two projects were so sensitive that it was not practical for pre-testing of attitudes to be undertaken. In the industrial redevelopment programme, research has been used to validate the community relations programme and modify it for the future. An iterative loop was used to sustain the public relations process.

In a third case study – an intensive three-month-long lobbying campaign – there was only one opportunity to make an impact. The proof of performance (ie indication of success) came when the UK government found new money for a project and the threat to the organization receded. Unlike the longer-term campaigns, this intensive campaign had an outcome that was quickly visible and could be expressed as a Yes or No result. The methodology to evaluate the results did not need an iterative loop.

The fourth case study was a community public relations campaign against a new coal-fired power station in an environmentally sensitive area. The results were measured by failure of the public utility's proposals. The campaign's effectiveness demonstrated the value of effects-based planning and the manner in which it creates a feedback to review tactics.

The case studies demonstrated different structures of public relations actions, ranging from the short, sharp lobbying activities to the long-running industrial development and new community programmes. Thus different implications for evaluation theory have emerged. The lobbying campaign pointed to the need for simple models to overcome the barriers to evaluation of lack of time and money (budget/cost factors). It also indicated that a simple Yes/No or Win/Lose outcome from the evaluation process was needed in a short time span.

Evaluation models designed for short-term public relations action must answer the Win/Lose dichotomy. The nature of these types of public relations campaigns is a call to action. Effects are not being created because the objectives are usually concerned with awareness. As a result of these short time spans, practitioners are unlikely to be creating attitudinal or behavioural effects.

The longer-term programmes have different characteristics. They segment audiences and aim to create different effects among target groups by a variety of strategies and tactics. The effects can be judged through continuing, consistent research. They also operate at differing speeds, compared with a short, intense awareness campaign. Indeed, their pace can vary quite considerably over the years. Awareness campaigns largely feature media relations strategies and evaluate the communication of messages through the media filter. Long-term programmes may have minimal use of media relations, preferring lobbying and direct communication with target groups.

Evaluation based on media analysis is thus less relevant for these programmes and so a model suitable for continuing, long-term actions needs to take account of the desired effects and whether these and the objectives are being achieved. It should also offer answers to the Win/Lose dichotomy and to the 'staying alive' factor in mid-campaign. Another factor is that a long-term programme will use a greater variety of strategy and tactics and these will need to be monitored, formally or informally, as the programme progresses.

In summary, the case studies indicated that two different evaluation models are needed to judge two very different scenarios: the common short-term awareness campaign based heavily on media relations and the longer-term programme which has a variety of strategies and tactics.

The evidence of practitioner surveys and the case studies supports the assertion that simpler approaches to evaluation are called for to bring down the barriers hindering the widespread study of impact of public relations activity. Existing models – such as Cutlip, Center and Broom's PII, Macnamara's Macro and Lindenmann's three-level Yardstick models – are too complex, do not have an integral relationship with the creation of effects and lack the dynamic element of feedback. That they have not been adopted widely by practitioners as appropriate methods for evaluation is the result of several factors: practitioners' lack of knowledge, narrow dissemination or they lack a practical or universal appeal.

Essentially, these were static step-by-step models that relied on the public relations activity stopping while evaluation was undertaken. No in-house or consultancy public relations operation can stop and take stock in such a leisurely way. Public relations evaluation models must reflect the dynamic nature of communications in a pressurized world.

The IPRA's Gold Paper No 11 proposed a circular model which links planning with evaluation in much the same way that the PRE process attempts to do. While descriptive of a process of planning and subsequent evaluation for long-term activity, it does not appear to have been developed empirically and practitioner acceptance and understanding are limited, as illustrated by Fairchild's comments. Thus it does not address the barriers and practitioner perceptions that have been identified by so many studies.

SHORT TERM AND CONTINUING PROGRAMMES

Taking into account the need for accessible, dynamic models of evaluation, two models are proposed: the Short Term model for short time span, largely media-relations-based campaigns and activities which seek a rapid result, and the Continuing model for long-term activities where the consistent promotion of messages is a central strategy and the outcome may occur after a long period (a year or more) of continuous activity (Watson, 2001: 267–68).

These models link with Grunig's four summations of public relations activity. The Short Term model is similar to the Press Agentry and Public Information one-way summations as it does not seek a dialogue or feedback. The Continuing model fits with the Two-Way Asymmetric and Two-Way Symmetric models that cover a broader band of communication methods and rely on feedback for campaign monitoring and modification of messages. These models can be expressed graphically (see Figures 5.7 and 5.8).

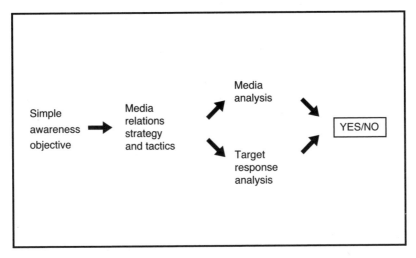

Figure 5.7   *Watson's Short Term model*

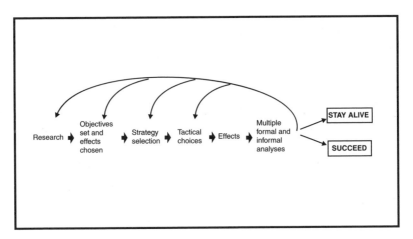

Figure 5.8   *Watson's Continuing model*

The Short Term model has a single track, linear process with an outcome. It does not set out to measure effects and because it does not have a continuing existence, there is no feedback mechanism. Typically, a public relations campaign has a simple awareness objective with one or two strategies. A common example of public relations practice in the Public Information summation is the distribution of news releases about products or services to the media. This is a technician skill of assembling information and photographs or drawings in the manner most acceptable to the media. Measuring achievement of the objectives can be by media analysis, sales response or phone research among the target market.

Using the Short Term model, the objectives could be set on the basis of obtaining coverage in specific media (chosen for its relevance to target audiences), the number of sales responses (realistically set according to the appropriateness of the media and the attractions of the product or service) or quantitative techniques such as phone research or mail surveys. The judgement of success or failure is thus made on whether or not the targets are reached.

This simple model can be applied in different cultures because the accent is on setting realistic awareness objectives and choosing relevant strategies. The terminology can be translated and the model structure is straightforward. If the client or employer sets unrealistic objectives, the model will be as irrelevant as a step-by-step model or informal 'seat of the pants' judgement. The quality of the model's results depends on the professionalism of the practitioner in designing the campaign.

This model has been designed for use in long-term public relations activity. In reviewing the case studies, the need for a dynamic model to cope with ever-changing circumstances was identified. A programme such as that for the new settlement, with multiple long-term corporate and planning objectives, or for the industrial redevelopment, with a medium-term objective of planning permission and a long-term objective of improved relations with the local community, needed a flexible evaluation model.

The Continuing model offers elements that have not been included in step-by-step models. It has an iterative loop and takes into account the effects that are being created by the programme. An additional element is that it offers an opportunity to make a judgement on 'staying alive' – the important stage in a long-term, issues-centred programme when keeping the issue in the decision frame is important. The Continuing model epitomizes VanLeuven's effects-based planning approach. By adopting these principles within the Continuing model, a dynamic and continuing evaluation process is created because the search for consistency means that monitoring is continuous.

The evidence from the long-term case studies reviewed in the research shows that the search for consistency is one of the most difficult practical issues facing public relations practitioners. The Continuing model, using effects-based planning, offers a more disciplined approach that allows the parameters of the programme to be more closely defined and enables continuous monitoring to replace after-the-event evaluation. The consistency of effects-based planning also aids validity and reliability of data.

The elements of the Continuing model are: an initial stage of Research; the setting of Objectives and choice of Programme Effects; from these follow the Strategy Selection and Tactical Choices. As the programme continues, there are multiple levels of Formal and Informal Analysis from which judgements can be made on progress in terms of success or 'staying alive'. The judgements are fed back through iterative loops to each of the programme elements. The loops assist the practitioners in validating the initial research and adding new data, adjusting the objectives and strategy, monitoring the progress to create the desired attitudinal or behavioural effects and helping with the adjustment or variation of tactics. This model is a continuing process that can be applied to a specific programme or to the overall public relations activities of an organization.

UNIVERSALITY OF APPLICATION

The research into practitioner attitudes found many similarities: barriers, reliance on output measures, technician activities and lack of knowledge. The recognition of these similarities has been important in the design of the two models of evaluation and will encourage their use by practitioners in many countries. Their simplicity and accessibility go beyond anglophone public relations. There is no rigidity in the evaluation methodology. Whereas a British practitioner may use a market research approach to analysing response to a campaign among target audiences, a European practitioner may, typically, adopt sociological methodology.

The Continuing model, with its iterative loop, provides the response element that both of Grunig's two-way models require. It is suited to the Two-Way Asymmetrical model as it accepts that the proponent determines the objectives and strategy but this can be equally acceptable for the Two-Way Symmetrical model because the research and objectives setting can be part of a negotiation process in a bilateral or multilateral situation.

The models discussed in this chapter have not been as widely adopted by practitioners as would have been expected, especially in the case of PII, which has been taught to many thousands of public relations students. With the exception of Lindenmann's Yardstick, which is not strictly comparable with the other models, they have 'summative' methods of seeking to answer questions of effectiveness at the end of a programme or campaign. They lack a dynamic element that could offer the formative research to feed back and improve the effectiveness of the continuing campaign or future programmes.

Leaving aside practitioner issues such as setting objectives properly and agreeing evaluation methodology before the start of the activity, evaluation models should provide both formative and summative information. Their role should not be the last stage in a public relations programme, but the springboard to the next stage or, in a campaign, to help adjust strategy and tactics.

The two models – Short Term and Continuing – do not provide answers as to which single method of evaluation gives the universal solution. There is, of course, no single answer to this because each public relations programme or campaign has different objectives and client/employer imperatives. Different methods of data collection and analysis are called for. By using the two models, practitioners can apply an integrated planning and evaluation framework to all public relations activity, and thus test whether objectives have been reached and the desired effects have been created.

VanLeuven's effects-based approach to public relations (see Chapter 2) is a valuable addition to applied theory and should be more widely known among practitioners. The inclusion of Effects elements in the Continuing model was a direct result of testing this approach against real-life practice. These elements strengthen the integrated planning and evaluation style of the Continuing model with its characteristic iterative loop design.

The two new evaluation models proposed give clearly expressed dynamic frameworks for evaluation to practitioners in all cultures. They are based on empirical research and reside in the mainstream of public relations theory and practice. Used by fellow practitioners, the 'black art' reputation of public relations could be minimized and replaced by one of a measurable, effective communications activity.

By highlighting the relative simplicity of short-term, awareness-based, public relations activity, and the complexity of continuing programmes probably associated with attitude and/or behaviour change, Watson's models make an important contribution to clarifying thinking on evaluation. However, they complement, rather than replace, the various three-stage linear models. For example, Watson's Short Term model sits comfortably with Lindenmann's Level 2 and the more complex tasks associated with the Continuing model are appropriate to Level 3.

Modelling evaluation as a continuing activity formalizes and reinforces evaluation as a formative – as well as summative – process. The evaluation of a short-term campaign necessarily means that it cannot provide direct feedback as the particular campaign in question has been implemented by the time the evaluation process has been completed. However, by adding to the body of knowledge and experience of running campaigns it does act in a formative role: providing feedback to the communications management process in general, and thereby increasing the effectiveness of similar campaigns in the future.

Indeed, the Unified and Short Term/Continuing models are complementary rather than competitive, providing different perspectives on the same reality. For example, the Short Term model is exclusively concerned with cognitive awareness objectives (represented by the impact stage in the Unified model) and the Continuing model is likely to be concerned with higher-level motivational and behavioural objectives, represented by the effect and result stages of the Unified model. These models are not detailed prescriptions for undertaking evaluation of public relations programmes. This is a complex problem that does not lend itself to simple, straightforward solutions; nor is a long list of potential evaluation techniques useful for similar reasons. The role of the structures and approaches outlined and discussed in this chapter is to provide a framework that enables the practitioner to apply the sophisticated level of analysis that will lead to some sort of answer to the challenges promoted by this complex issue.

DASHBOARDS AND SCORECARDS

The dashboard is an increasingly used tool for the measurement and evaluation of public relations activity, especially in relation to corporate communications strategy. The term arises from the dashboard of a car in which there are several gauges of performance, such as speed, rpm, fuel, engine temperature and battery charge. Taking the analogy further, these instruments tell you how fast you are going, how the engine (campaign) is performing and whether there are any threats (low fuel, high engine temperature or battery discharge).

This tool has arisen from corporate information systems that brought together various performance data into a single, easily read document for senior management. They were endowed with metrics on sales, revenue and overhead costs. They pushed managers into setting performance targets and continually managing them. Having begun in finance departments, they have been introduced into sales, marketing and more recently communications departments.

Paine says that their usefulness depends on professionals articulating their definitions of excellence. She says they need to be persuaded to look beyond the easy measures of clips and hits and 'to design metrics tied to business performance and organisational mission' (Paine, 2006: 1).

There are six steps to design and implement dashboards (Paine, 2006: 1–5):

1. Ensure that all those who will be operating the communications programmes measured by the dashboard develop it together. Don't have it imposed by others.
2. Identify the measurement priorities by ranking audiences in order of importance.
3. Choose the measures of effectiveness for each of the audiences.
4. Set benchmarks by comparing current year performance with previous years and against similar organizations. (Paine writes of a county in New York state, comparing itself against a similar county by measuring media coverage for both.)
5. Choose the tools for measurement and seek integration between the tools.
6. Make the dashboard report simple and short, no more than a page or two.

Communication scorecards have similarities to dashboards but are more integrated with the organizational operations and strategy. In public relations, they have evolved along two related streams. In 1997, the Canadians Craig Fleisher and Darren Mahaffy proposed a scorecard for the measurement of public relations activity. Others have come from Dutch writers Vos and Schoemaker (2004), who proposed criteria for the communication management elements of a business scorecard; and German consultants Hering, Schuppener and Sommerhalder (2004), who introduced a Communications Scorecard in their market. They have also been used in the form of a Communication Matrix in South Africa for communications in the mining sector, and reported by Putt and van der Waldt (2005).

The main push for them has come from the Balanced Scorecard management tool that was first introduced in 1992 by Robert Kaplan and David Norton. The initial premise was that businesses and other organizations should not be managed solely on a basis where profit and loss and Return on Investment were the criteria for success. The Balanced Scorecard (BSC) was a more extensive control system that tied strategy more closely to performance, but also took account of the human and reputational issues that make businesses excellent. Since then they have developed the BSC further.

Ansgar Zerfass, who has written extensively on the concept and delivery of a BSC-linked Corporate Communication Scorecard, says that the BSC is developed by a process in which managers and staff can identify their own performance's effect on business success, 'including interdependencies to other units and goals' (Zerfass, 2005: 4). When units' goals and KPIs are brought together into the Scorecard, performance can be measured 'across different units as well as continuously adjusting the scorecard for the company and its (other) business units'. In this way communication activity is integrated into the business strategy and operations, rather than remaining separate.

The value of dashboards and scorecards are questioned by some. Macnamara (2005: 311–12) says, 'they are simply ways of collecting measurement data and presenting it in an organization-wide format' and that the research methodologies are those already used widely in measuring public relations. The Benchpoint Report in 2004 (see Chapter 3) found that dashboards were one of the least effective methods of measuring internal communications. But as a tool that aligns communication strategy with business objectives and presents data in a concise and readable manner, they have a lot to offer in creating and monitoring highly effective communication programmes.

Interview

The reaction of Mike Granatt when the subject of evaluation is raised is one of mild despair, 'because, while people talk about it, a lot less is done than is said'. Granatt suggests two reasons for this lack of action. The first is the short-term perspective of many practitioners. 'In many ways, evaluation is not about the immediate, so for many people it is counter-intuitive.' He extends this stricture to both clients of consultancies and to principals of those working in-house, 'who really want to see immediate results rather than some sort of "deep" evaluation'.

Granatt suggests that the second problem for evaluation is the range of techniques that are used. He dismisses evaluation based on the column inches achieved for a particular cause as 'practically useless'. He argues that it says nothing about the quality of interaction with the audience, whether a strategy has been successfully implemented or whether any useful purpose has been achieved.

The word 'strategy' prompts Granatt to warm to his theme. 'You cannot get into evaluation unless you know what your strategy is and in a tactical business, strategy can be seen as a somewhat remote, worthy concept. Getting the strategy right is absolutely key because unless you've got the strategy sorted, what are you evaluating?'

He makes the point that evaluation doesn't start at the end of the programme. The first consideration is the purpose of the campaign. It is at this (very early) point in the 'train of thought' that evaluation's value should be considered. Segmenting target audiences and thinking through their desired reactions helps identify the indicators that will usefully evaluate the campaign.

Granatt feels that understanding the audience is what really counts when assessing the impact of a campaign. After dismissing the outmoded 'all publicity is good publicity' school of thought, he commends the more sophisticated applications of media evaluation, 'where there is a very clear understanding at the outset as to what the strategic purpose is, an examination of changes in reporting, and careful analysis of coverage to identify what is positive, negative and neutral – and why'. Granatt argues that 'this is where it really counts' because you can make judgements as to the knowledge audiences are likely to have gained and what their reactions are likely to be.

But he goes one step further and identifies that many practitioners have not yet moved from outputs to outcomes. They have not moved from using media coverage as their benchmark to measuring whether there have been changes in the behaviour or opinions of the audience.

When asked what distinguishes the more sophisticated users of evaluation, he is unequivocal: 'A research-based approach and a willingness to devote resources to it.' A key problem is that evaluation is regarded as an unreasonable expense. He points out that advertising campaigns are carefully researched, if only because of the expense associated with them. Ironically, practitioners claim that public relations is much more cost-effective, but investment is needed to support this claim.

Granatt sees no distinction between evaluating the process and evaluating the impact of the campaign. 'If you are simply evaluating at the end of the campaign, even if you are running the world's shortest campaign, you are closing your eyes to what is actually happening as it progresses. You cannot take any action without it modifying the environment on which you based your original planning. Not to evaluate as things go along leaves you blind as to whether you are achieving anything or not, or missing opportunities – or even making things worse.'

In summary, he comes back to his strategy theme. 'You can easily evaluate without strategy, but it's meaningless. You can easily have a strategy with no evaluation, but the outcome would be unproven. Strategy and evaluation are in the same bag.

Mike Granatt is a partner at Luther Pendragon, a visiting professor at the University of Westminster, and formerly Director General of the UK Government Information and Communication Service.

QUESTIONNAIRE RESPONSES

Evaluation questionnaire for industry leaders

Q: How much budget is normally allocated to evaluation in annual budgets or major campaigns?

We always do activity-based budgeting and for that reason we have no general rules to apply. Evaluation/research investments are made as appropriate. **Dejan Verčič**

Five per cent. **Alison Clarke**

It doesn't quite work that way. The evaluation team has a budget from each programme area. As we are a corporate service and not regarded as a programme, like evaluation, we too have a budget from each programme. **Fran Hagon**

This varies so much as to be unhelpful to give an average. The key point is to identify the cornerstones of success in any PR programme and establish key milestones to ensuring they are achieved. **Crispin Manners**

We aim for 10 per cent, but by the time the budget is finalized the client often reduces it. **Loretta Tobin**

Unfortunately it remains a non-issue for many clients, but we do internal assessments anyway. **Ray Mawerera**

In many programmes outcome measurement is actually conducted under the auspices of another department – customer satisfaction, market analysis, etc. Some programmes require huge employee opinion surveys, others require small media monitoring programmes. Often the measurement itself is an integral part of the communication campaign that can't be separated from the activity of counsel and advice. There is no set percentage, especially when measurement is integrated into the programme to ensure the team is effective and accountable. **Annabelle Warren**

Normally included in the retainer fee as part of the deal! **Laurna O'Donnell**

It isn't allocated 'normally'. For some clients, it is included in overall budgets from the outset. With one client it's linked to their KPIs, which is very nice (but very unusual). It really depends on what a client is seeking to achieve – a consumer client looks for exposure, a finance client looks for quality media or response to stockbroking presentations, while property clients are seeking sales ahead of a schedule! **Clara Zawawi**

Few clients think of it like this. In reality, I would say that the amount allocated is well under 5 per cent. **Mike Copland**

It varies, but I'd guess between 10 and 15 per cent of budget. **Matt Kucharski**

It is costly in terms of hours spent but generally we spend very little actual cash. **Richard Offer**

6

Developing a media evaluation system

This chapter focuses on practical steps towards establishing media evaluation systems: the first part proposes a simple media monitoring system while the second proposes a more detailed analysis. Both are achievable by consultancies and in-house practitioners and offer usable feedback and data for short-term and continuing public relations activity. The simple system has methodological limitations and may lack social science purity, but it can be set up quickly and at low cost. This could be a major advantage for practitioners who have identified cost as an important barrier to evaluation. The more complex system can threaten to be too time-consuming for manual implementation. However, it can form the basis of a customized in-house system (implemented by an IT department – or database expert) or a specification for an external media evaluation bureau.

SETTING UP A SIMPLE MEDIA MONITORING SYSTEM

The traditional method of measuring public relations success was amassing a collection of media clippings and transcriptions. Mounted on sturdy paper to give added bulk, the clippings were seen as the 'deliverable' of the process and programme. To borrow an analogy from flying, this was like flying on one instrument and ignoring all the others. Kaplan and Norton (1996: 1–2) describe a pilot who uses only an airspeed indicator and ignores fuel gauges, altimeters and other instruments. They conclude that 'we suspect that you would not board the plane after this discussion'. The point for practitioners is that they would not pilot a programme without checking the progress against objectives, yet many rely on a collection of clippings as the sole indicator of so-called success. Sadly, clients and employers often use the same judgement, too.

PR people are communicators, analysts, strategists and tacticians who are always making judgements in fluid environments. So how can they deduce whether the programme is flying fast or heading straight for a mountain of problems? 'Gut feel' and informal feedback are sometimes useful, but often misleading. To make accurate judgements, solid planning and valid, reliable information are needed.

This helps us decide whether we are 'Doing Well', but first we must set measurable public relations objectives. These are the four most important words for the development of both simple and complex evaluation. They tell us where we are starting from and where the programme is heading. 'Measurable' gives the basis of planning and aids validity of feedback data.

> As described in Chapter 3, UK research shows that evaluation supports a professional image of public relations and thus strengthens the position of the practitioner. In the mid-1990s, Tom Watson found that 63.9 per cent of senior British practitioners believed that evaluation increased respect between them and their employer or clients. Only 2.1 per cent said that it worsened the level of respect. This demonstrates that, by demonstrating effectiveness, public relations can be brought into the corporate planning process and can improve its share of budget. (Watson, 1996)

The definition of public relations in Chapter 1 describes PR as a 'management function' and so this is a planned, structured and reviewed process which means more than scoring press mentions. Objectives are the reasons behind the programme in terms of audiences to be reached, messages communicated, channels of communication used and the reactions and responses sought. As a persuasive process, public relations needs measurable objectives or it becomes a random information dissemination activity (see Chapter 8).

Lindenmann's Public Relations Yardstick (as outlined in Chapter 5) has proposed three increasingly complex stages of evaluation entitled Output, Outgrowth or Out-take and Outcomes. For a simple media monitoring system the appropriate Yardstick is Output, which measures production of the PR effort, as opposed to audience response and attitudinal change, which are covered by the others. Output analysis judges where the message was received in the media, the manner and tone of its interpretation and quantitative measurements of its appearance. At this point, it is important to note the limitations of media analysis because it cannot judge the message(s) impact upon non-media targets groups. This needs an additional level of research among those groups, although in practice response to articles via letters, phone calls, sales, literature uptake or visits do give an informal (but partial) measure. Measuring media coverage should be systematic, continuous, part of an overall evaluation process and related to objectives.

The process of creating a simple media monitoring system is essentially a clerical process that has more time spent on the initial set-up stage than on the continuing regular analysis. The raw material is media clippings and transcripts, which can be generated through monitoring of the media by the practitioner or through agencies and broadcast monitoring bureaux. These can be supplemented by word and topic searches by online information organizations and scanning of the internet through search engines.

There are **six** steps to set up the system and fully utilize the information drawn from it:

1. Define objectives.
2. Determine criteria.
3. Choose a benchmark.
4. Select a measurement tool.
5. Compare results with objectives.
6. Modify campaign.

The objectives can include exposure of message, dissemination, education of target publics, sales lead generation, share of voice (vis-à-vis competitors or issues) or others that have been set out in the programme.

When selecting criteria for judgement, there is a mnemonic proposed by the US-based Delahaye media analysis consultancy. Called IMPACT, it sets out these criteria:

Influence or tone
Message communicated
Prominence
Audience reached
Consultant/spokesman quoted
Type of article.

In order of importance, the letters could be reorganized as M (Message communicated), A (Audience reached), T (Type of article), C (Consultant/spokesman quoted), I (Influence or Tone) and P (Prominence). Sadly, MATCIP is not as catchy as IMPACT. The most questionable of factors is Prominence. As McGuire's Output Analysis of the Communications/Persuasion showed in Chapter 2, the way that we awkward humans scan and retain information is not linear. So it follows that we do not necessarily retain the information offered by the largest article on a prominent page or the first report in a broadcast news programme. Indeed, some of the best-read sections of print media are 'fillers' and diary pages that have terse, compressed information.

Having chosen criteria, the next stage is to benchmark media coverage and then choose the repetition by which the analysis will be undertaken. Practically, establishing an effective benchmark is best achieved by reviewing the previous 12 months' media coverage and then repeating the process monthly or quarterly. Once the hard work in setting up the benchmark has been done the period-on-period comparisons take much less time and use frequent repetitions.

Analysing media coverage: the key questions

1. Where has it appeared and how often?
2. Which journalists have by-lines?
3. What is the tone of coverage? 0 to 10 ranking for each item. 0 is completely negative. 5 is neutral. 10 is completely positive.
4. Which products/services/issues have had coverage? (where and frequency?)
5. Coverage of major competitors; where and how often?
6. Classify the coverage as filler, medium or large. Indicate when photos have been used.
7. What are the key messages carried in the press coverage?

In order to get valid information, the project or programme manager should avoid personally judging the 'tone' or favourability of coverage and interpreting the messages carried by the media. If the manager or a close colleague undertakes the analysis role, there is a strong likelihood of 'observer bias', ie they will scan for the positive messages that support their advice and hoped-for results and bypass the negative feedback. The most effective route to take is to establish a panel of independent readers who scan the clippings and transcripts and give their objective opinion. This panel of readers should not be colleagues in the same organization or consultancy but come from outside the business. The media material is circulated among them (at least three people) for analysis using a pro forma. In this way, the level of subjective interpretation is reduced, the analysis is under-

Table 6.1 *A typical form used in a simple media analysis system*

Factors to judge	Data and answers
Which publications have articles appeared in and how often? Use initials for frequently quoted publications.	
List names of by-lined journalists and the publications.	
On a scale of 1 to 10, make a judgement on the tone of the article. 0 = completely negative; 10 = completely positive; 5 = neutral.	
Write a one-sentence summary of what you see as the key message contained in the article.	Use a separate sheet
Identify if it was a small (filler), medium (average of 5 paragraphs) or large (sizeable) article.	F M L
Name any client company spokespeople referred to within the story.	
If competitors or opponents are mentioned in the same story, list them and how often they appear.	

taken on a common basis and the practitioner benefits through valid feedback.

There are varying ways of organizing the reader panel. It can manage itself with one of its members preparing reports, the material can be returned to the practitioner for collation or it can be sent to an independent expert for interpretation. Usually, the panel members are part-time and operate from home, but this is a matter of convenience rather than of methodological importance.

When it comes to interpreting and implementing the information from simple media analysis, a final pitfall to be avoided is the 'substitution game'. These analyses describe the dissemination of messages and their reception and interpretation in the media (the Output phase), but they don't tell of the Impact upon the audiences. To ascribe Impact to the Output analyses will lead to inaccurate modifications of programmes and preparation for new ones. As indicated above and in earlier chapters, impact must be judged by research among the target audiences, not in the channels of communication to them.

In summary, simple media analysis should be continuous and objective. It need not be expensive to undertake and can be operated with in-house resources, with the exception of the reader panel. The information is limited to the programme's output, but it can be linked with other measures on impact to give an overall picture of 'Doing Well?' or not.

A media analysis report based on a real financial services organization. Names have been changed to protect client confidentiality.

CLIENT MEDIA ANALYSIS

'THE SOCIETY'

(12 MONTHS TO THE END OF PERIOD)

1. Publications in which articles referring to The Society have appeared

National newspapers

Financial Times	1	
The Guardian	1	
The Independent	1	
Sunday Express	1	
Sunday Telegraph	1	(Total of 5)

Regional daily and weekly newspapers; business magazines

Southern Daily Echo	9	
Bournemouth Daily Echo	4	
Derby Evening Telegraph	3	
Gateway	2	
Hampshire Chronicle	2	
Isle of Thanet Gazette	2	
Lynn News and Advertiser	2	
Newmarket Journal	2	
Basingstoke Gazette	1	
Birmingham Post	1	
Business South West	1	
Coastal Express	1	
Colchester Evening Gazette	1	
Dorset Evening Echo	1	
Dunmow Broadcast	1	
East Anglian Daily Times	1	
Evening Herald	1	
Grimsby Evening Telegraph	1	
Harlow & Epping Herald	1	
Kentish Express	1	
Leek Post & Times	1	
Manchester Evening News	1	
Mid-Anglia Business Wkly	1	
Northampton Journal	1	
Reading Chronicle	1	
Romford & Havering Adv.	1	
Romford & Havering Post	1	
Tamworth Herald	1	
Western Gazette	1	
Winchester Extra	1	(Total of 48)

Financial publications

Financial Adviser	1	
Investors Chronicle	1	
Money Marketing	1	
Post Magazine	1	(Total of 4)

TOTAL   57

2. By-lined journalists

Jenny Andrews (*Colchester Evening Gazette*)
Anne Caborn (*Chic*)
Michael Freeman (*Southern Daily Echo*)
Martin Ford (*Evening Herald*)
Sean Macdonagh (*The Guardian*)
Vincent Langan (*Grimsby Evening Telegraph*)
Helen Pridham (*Investors Chronicle*)
James Seddon (*Manchester Evening News*)

3. Tone of coverage (0 = completely negative, 10 = completely positive. 5 = neutral)

6.6/10, which is more positive than neutral and well ahead of average scores, which are usually around 5/10. There were three exceptionally high scores of 10/10 given to coverage in the *Reading Chronicle* and *Romford & Havering Post* (twice). The lowest scores of 4/10 went to coverage in *The Independent* and *Post Magazines*.

The strongest tone of coverage came in regional media at 6.8/10, which is a very positive score when set against the sample of 48 stories upon which it was drawn. Tone scores ranged from 5/10 to 10/10, with no scores lower than neutral.

Coverage in the nationals averaged 5.8/10, with four out of five articles ranking between 5/10 and 8/10. In the small number of financial press articles, the tone ranking was marginally above neutral at 5.25/10. The four articles were scored tightly between 4/10 and 6/10.

4. Volume of coverage

Fillers	39%
Medium	39%
Large	22%

5. Client spokespeople

Bob Anderson
John Pollard
Richard Moorecroft
Rod Page
Reg Darlington
Bill Hysom

6. Competitors mentioned in the same story as The Society

Travellers Friendly Society	7
Everton & Sheffield	5
Colchester United Friendly Society	4
Reading Equitable Friendly Society	1

7. Messages carried in the media about The Society

Products and industry comment

The Society has a lot to offer in the world of friendly societies.

Funeral plan launched by The Society.

Society discusses its pre-paid funeral plan.

Family Income Plan outlined by The Society.

Family Income Benefit described (three separate articles).

Chief Executive says products will fit into New Labour's plans.

Chairman talks of the major role of friendly societies in welfare provision.

Low-cost sickness plan offered.

Investors can contribute up to £600 a year for ISAs.

A parent can be valued at £30,000 a year, so insurance cover is needed.

Community

£500 donated to school for wheelchair access.

The Society investing in revival of South's property market.

Society replaces doctor's equipment destroyed in an arson attack.

£500 donated to Salvation Army.

Medical Trust has received £100.

Scout group saved from closure.

Conference to be held at Buxton Cathedral.

Surgery has new equipment, thanks to The Society.

Football team gets new strip from The Society.

Cheque presented to emergency doctors group.

While a manual clerical media evaluation system is simple, very low cost and can be operated in situations of low-volume coverage, it is clumsy to manage for medium to high-volume coverage where frequent reports are needed. There are commercial software packages, such as COMAudit from Media-Monitors-CARMA Asia Pacific in Australia, which offer turnkey solutions. Windows-based COMAudit is available for most world markets and is used to benchmark media coverage and produce reports.

Alternatives can be developed using spreadsheet software, notably Microsoft Excel, which is easy to tailor for different employer/client needs and campaign situations. The main skill is creating and manipulating the macros (mathematical formulae) to relevant data. One example is the apPRaise system developed by the Hallmark Public Relations consultancy at Winchester in England. It has been in use for several years and has been used for clients such as leading professional services firms, government agencies and commercial property agents.

The essence of this system is that the consultancy and the client jointly choose up to six messages that they want to disseminate through the media. (Any number of messages can be chosen, but it is considered difficult for audiences to comprehend or retain more that three to six messages during a campaign.) These messages can be linked to corporate objectives, product promotion, key contact information (such as websites or phone numbers), etc.

The media targets are set and then monitored by regular scanning of publications, broadcast and internet media. While the data entry is essentially a clerical task, it is the analysis of the data that provides value.

The apPRaise system allows for the collection of alternative messages, such as negative comment and competitor response. It also collects data on the media relations activity that generated the media coverage, journalists who are writing about the client organization, corporate spokespeople quoted by the media and the placement of the articles in the media by position in print or broadcast.

A typical apPRaise analysis form (see Figure 6.1, pp. 118–21) will cover Date, Headline, Media title, Media type, Section, OTS (Opportunities to see), Messages 1 to 6, Alternative messages, Media activity, Spokespeople, Reporter/author, Target audience, Placement of article, and Visual impact, and have a space for Comments by the analyst.

From this data, charts and text can be developed to provide information on:

- number of articles per target media;
- OTS received per message;
- OTS per media activity;
- number of times that key messages are featured;
- tone of coverage for each message on a +5 to − 5 scale;

- section in which articles appeared;
- number of articles per media title;
- position of articles;
- visual impact of articles.

Former PR director Steve Osborne-Brown says that for most continuing media analysis purposes, the apPRaise system gives a width of information that helps the consultancy and its clients monitor the progress of a campaign or short-term project.

> With regular production of reports, we know whether the messages that our clients want to express are reaching their media targets. If they aren't, we can decide whether to modify them or put in additional effort. Conversely, if messages are being accepted in the media, we can move on to new challenges.

The apPRaise system monitors the placement of articles but does not allocate a value to them. Hallmark PR says that this requires the development of sophisticated algorithms and that there is still debate as to whether a story on page 1 or page 10 has a differing value. Steve Osborne-Brown argues that the psychology of communication shows that every reader comprehends and retains information in a different manner. 'A short filler story of one or two sentences can have just as big an impact as the page one lead report. It all depends on what the reader's information need is at the time. A media analysis system cannot demonstrate that.'

Another approach has been developed by the Canadian Public Relations Society (www.cprs.ca) and is known as 'Media Relations Rating Points' (MRP). It is a system that 'provides communication and marketing professionals with an easy-to-use tool that measures the effectiveness of any public relations campaign'. In fact, it is restricted to evaluating media coverage – as its name implies. It claims to provide standardized reporting that can be easily used to measure media coverage, and to provide metrics that give an ROI (return on investment) figure in terms of cost per contact.

Each piece of media coverage generated proactively can score up to 10 points. Up to five are awarded for tone (five for positive, three for neutral and none for negative). Predetermined criteria make up the other five possible points to give a rating score. Five criteria are chosen to include in the system. While this is an effort to ensure that the evaluation is undertaken in the context of goals for the campaign, the fact that different campaigns are evaluated according to different criteria weakens the claim for standardization. Criteria suggested by the designers are given below.

Client name/period

Date	Headline	Media title	Media type	Section	OTS

Figure 6.1 *Sample of apPRaise evaluation report*

Client name/period

Headline	Message 1	Message 2	Message 3	Message 4	Message 5	Message 6

Figure 6.1 *Sample of apPRaise evaluation report (continued)*

Client name/period

Headline	Alternative messages	Media activity	Spokespeople	Reporter/author

Figure 6.1 *Sample of apPRaise evaluation report (continued)*

Client name/period

Headline	Target audience	Placement of article	Visual impact	Comments

Figure 6.1 *Sample of apPRaise evaluation report (continued)*

Table 6.2 *apPRaise – key to analysis*

Media type	Refers to whether broadcast, press, national, regional, trade, consumer, etc
Section	Where was the story found? – news, features, health, business, letters, classifieds, etc
OTS	The circulation of a publication or number of viewers/listeners of a programme multiplied by 2.5 (to indicate average readership or audience)
Messages	Indicate the tone of a message in each piece of coverage on a scale from –5 to +5: those messages not featured within a piece of coverage leave blank
Alternative messages	Indicate messages that appear that are not one of your key messages
Media activity	Indicate which activity generated the coverage – press release, launch event, phone call, etc
Spokespeople	Who was quoted?
Reporter/author	Any by-line?
Target audience	Who did it reach?
Placement of article	Its position, using the code below: 10: Front page, DPS (double-page spread), centre pages 9: Pages 2 and 3, feature (article) 8: Pages 4–9 7: Pages 10–centre 6: Back page, columnist's comments 5: Editor's comments, centre–mid-back 4: Letters 3: Neighbourhood/community news 2: Mid–late back 1: Filler
Visual impact	Use the key below A – full page/DPS B – 3/4 page C – 1/2 page D – 1/3 page E – 1/4 page F – 1 column G – 1/2 column H – 1/3 column I – 1/4 column J – couple of lines

> **Suggested MRP Criteria**
>
> | | |
> |---|---|
> | Company/brand mention | Key message(s) |
> | Photo/image | Exclusivity |
> | Colour (photo) | Headline/newscast positioning |
> | Spokesperson quote | Tier 1 vs Tier 2 media outlets |
> | Prominence/position | Competitive/peer inclusion |
> | Target audience | Inclusion of website |
> | Credibility of spokesperson | Call to action |
> | or expert | |

An optional bonus/demerit point can be awarded (outside of the 10-point rating system) for coverage that is either exceptionally positive or negative. With the inclusion of media data, cost per contact can also be calculated by dividing campaign cost by total reach.

Hill and Knowlton corporate blogger Brendan Hodgson (2006), reports a case study of a 'very successful product launch' for one of the consultancy's larger clients. A total of 624 articles were rated using the following five criteria (as well as up to five points for tone):

> 1. Company/brand mention.
> 2. Spokesperson quote.
> 3. Call to action.
> 4. Key messages/product mention.
> 5. Fifty+ words on broadcast segment/print/online.
>
> The results were:
>
> Total articles/stories: 624
> Total impressions (OTS): 123,461,315
> Budget: $149,050.00
> Average Tone: 4.9 out of 5
> Average Rating: 3.5 out of 5
> Total Score: 84% (tone plus rating expressed as a percentage)
> Cost per contact: $0.00121 (budget divided by impressions).

The principal drawback from Hill and Knowlton's perspectives was the time and effort to load 624 articles into the system, described as 'considerable', and – by implication – costly. However, the client was 'thrilled' as the numbers 'satisfied the requirements and expectations of the executives to which that person [client contact] reported' (Hodgson, 2006).

A more complex system than MRP is based on the same principles but adds more flexibility in the choice of criteria/variables to be analysed. The additional complexity – such that it is – comes from the need to go through a 'pre-definition' stage to arrive at the outputs required. These outputs are quantitative in nature in the form of bar charts, line graphs, pie charts and the like.

The 'dimensional' methodology outlined below can be implemented manually, but is ideally suited to automation using database software. There is always a trade-off between the time taken to process the analyses and their usefulness. The key issue here would be to find a balance between capturing all the information that might possibly be useful, and making the process so time-consuming and tedious that it becomes self-defeating.

The health warnings that apply to media evaluation outlined below and elsewhere in this book to do with the 'substitution game' – output not impact – and the like apply equally to the dimensional methodology. Even though the dimensional methodology claims to be relatively sophisticated, it remains concerned with media monitoring and therefore still addresses output only and has nothing directly to do with the impact of the programme, campaign or activity.

The case study shows the type of data captured and outputs produced for a customized in-house media evaluation system developed using the dimensional methodology. In this anonymous (owing to client confidentiality) example, the emphasis is very much on formative – rather than summative – evaluation, a role in which media evaluation is very comfortable.

The ability to design a truly customized approach was key to enabling the organization to derive maximum benefit from media evaluation. It was not seeking to use media evaluation to justify the worth of its activities to the organization as a whole. Instead, it was seeking feedback from the public relations process in order to improve and fine-tune the day-to-day management of its media relations efforts.

So, for example, a key output (see below) is the relative volume of coverage generated by different activities (eg press release). Linking this with the known resources (time and additional costs) required to support this activity would then enable the department to establish which types of activity were most cost-effective. Similarly, feedback on the relative favourability of comment from different media could influence where the emphasis of media relations effort would be placed.

A DIMENSIONAL MODEL OF MEDIA EVALUATION

Media evaluation is concerned with evaluating outputs, specifically the number of messages placed in the media, the number of messages supporting objectives, and the number of people who receive (or have the opportunity to receive) the message. In spite of our repeated concerns expressed here about the limitations of media evaluation, particularly with respect to the substitution game, we enthusiastically accept that media evaluation has an important role to play.

It is equally important to understand the limitations that media evaluation has in fulfilling this role. Media evaluation is concerned with the outputs – not the results – of a public relations programme so it can be used as feedback to improve the quality of those results and – if we accept a link between outputs and results – can be used to make cautious, limited inferences about results where direct measurement is impossible or impractical.

There is a key point here to be made about the use of reader panels. They are important if media evaluation is being used in a summative, judgemental – 'how did we do?' – manner for the reasons already outlined. However, it is acceptable for the practitioners running the programme to undertake the media analysis themselves if the purpose is formative, that is, feedback is being sought in order to fine-tune continuing implementation.

The types of questions that media evaluation seeks to answer are:

- Is the coverage beneficial, neutral or adverse?
- Are the media reporting our key corporate messages?
- Which journalists/publications are reporting us favourably?
- What is the source of the press coverage we are achieving?
- How are we doing compared to our competitors?
- Is our media coverage getting better or worse?
- What are the emerging issues affecting our organization?

The type of analyses that are useful to a particular public relations department will vary according to the organization/client concerned. The dimensional model sets out a media evaluation methodology that first specifies a customized set of reports and then defines how they are produced.

So, in contrast to the media monitoring system outlined above, the dimensional methodology is an approach within which practitioners can develop their own system or systems. It is a structure within which a customized system can be developed rather than being itself a customized step-by-step procedure. The case study gives an example of a system developed using the dimensional methodology.

Indeed, both the simple and more complex systems outlined in this chapter are eminently compatible with some of the specific tools (eg pro formas) developed as part of the generalized monitoring system able to be used for an individual system developed under the dimensional methodology. The latter is essentially a framework for practitioners to develop their own system, customized according to the specific needs of different clients or organizations. It complements Watson's findings, which indicate that the way forward for media evaluation may well be the development of externally designed, but internally operated systems.

Quantitative axes

The dimensional media evaluation model has four sets of four axes: quantitative axes, qualitative axes, focus axes, and time axes. The quantitative axes relate to the output 'layers' of Macnamara's Pyramid model (similarly they can be converted into equivalent levels as outlined by other authors, see Chapter 5):

Table 6.3

Dimensional model – quantitative axes	Pyramid model layer
Number of clippings	Number who receive messages
Volume of coverage	Number who receive messages
Name checks	Number of messages placed
Number of key messages	Number of messages supporting objectives

Number of clippings is self-explanatory, but note that the term clippings is taken to incorporate broadcast media transcripts. It is highly desirable to handle press and broadcast coverage in an integrated manner. This is done by monitoring broadcast coverage through transcripts which then allow the volume of broadcast coverage to be converted into equivalent column centimetres through a conversion based on word counts. Similarly, readership and viewing figures would be considered comparable. Volume of coverage refers to the number of words or can be expressed as column centimetres. Name checks simply refers to the number of mentions of the company or brand name, and number of key messages refers to the number of occasions that specified key messages appear.

Qualitative axes

The qualitative axes start to put some flesh on the bare bones of the quantitative axes.

Different media will have different raw circulation and readership figures, and it may be appropriate to adjust for these variances. It may be appropriate to account for the proportion of readership or audience that fall into the target market. Attribution concerns the extent to which volume can be attributed to one name check; for example, can the whole clipping be attributed to a company or brand name when there is one name check in a two-page article? Normal practice might be to leave the decision to the practitioner but to have a default value of, say, 50 column centimetres. BNA (beneficial, neutral, and adverse) refers to the extent that editorial coverage is positive, negative or neutral.

The impact of an article and the strength with which any messages within it are transmitted are determined by a wide range of factors, many of which are peculiar to particular media or sectors of media. Factors which can affect impact include headlines, photographs, position on the page, position of the page, solus, length and many others.

Table 6.4

Dimensional model – quantitative axes

Circulation/readership
Attribution
Beneficial/neutral/adverse (BNA)
Impact or message strength

Focus axes

The focus axes determine how focused the media evaluation exercise needs to be:

Table 6.5

Dimensional model – focus axes

Source
Medium
Media sector
Total media

The source can either be a particular journalist or third-party commentator. The medium is a particular publication or broadcast programme, while media sector is a classification such as national press, local media, trade press, etc.

The fourth dimension

Science regards time as the fourth dimension and this gives the dimensional model its name:

Table 6.6

Dimensional model – time axes
Historical comparison
Competitive comparison
Objectives comparison
Benchmarking

Specifying a working model

With four sets of four variables, the dimensional model theoretically gives us 256 separate analyses that can be performed. In practice, not all possible combinations are meaningful but, nonetheless, there is a requirement to select a small number of meaningful analyses, from the vast number available, for each evaluation exercise. The process is as follows. First, decide which combinations of time and focus dimensions are required:

Table 6.7

	Source	Media	Sector	Total
Historical				
Competitive				
Objectives				
Benchmarking				

Then for each of these combinations, select a further combination of quantitative and qualitative analyses (see Table 6.8).

Table 6.8

	Circulation	Attribution	BNA	Impact
Clippings				
Volume				
Name checks				
Key messages				

One example might be a competitive analysis in the trade press, using volume adjusted for impact, BNA and attribution. In this way, it is possible to arrive at an evaluation approach, customized for the brand, company or client in question.

CASE STUDY: IN-HOUSE MEDIA EVALUATION SYSTEM

Background

XYZ's Public Affairs department has used a media evaluation bureau in the past but the reports provided were of limited use and the service was discontinued. More recently, one staff member has begun to undertake a manual analysis of media coverage. Time constraints mean that any manual approach to media evaluation is going to be limited in scope.

It is anticipated that the software issues associated with a simple computerized media evaluation system are relatively trivial. The aim, therefore, was to design an in-house, computerized media evaluation system customized to the planning and management requirements of the department. A limited range of specific reports would be produced but more detailed and broader in scope than those able to be produced manually at present.

Input

Key to the whole process would be the electronic coding sheet that would be completed for each press cutting or transcript. Note that the scanning in of press cuttings and broadcast transcripts (the latter may well be available electronically anyway) is an attractive proposition. It would allow some sort of simple automatic content analysis such as the identification of key words and/or messages, as well as being an efficient means of storing press coverage. Finally, internal electronic distribution of key items of media coverage internally via intranet is likely to happen soon anyway. However, the feeling is that the project should be implemented one step at a time so that, initially anyway, cuttings and transcripts will remain paper based.

The design of the coding sheet (actually a screen rather than a physical piece of paper) would be a key element of the next phase of the project. Naturally, its precise content would be dependent on the specific outputs required from the system. However, capture of the following data should enable all likely outputs required to be generated:

- Publication/programme and date plus time of transmission (if appropriate).
- Publisher/broadcaster plus circulation, readership and viewership/listenership (this might be imported from a media directory or entered manually but once only in each case; there would have to be the facility for periodic update of media data).
- Journalist (if known) and position within publication/ programme.
- Presence or absence of a photograph (print media only) and whether the photograph is branded.
- Presence or absence of name in headline.
- Campaign coding (to enable specific campaigns to be tracked).
- Genre (eg documentary, travel section, etc).
- Media sector (automatically prompted from a look-up list).
- Importance of publication/programme (1 = key, 2 = important, 3 = the rest).
- Raw volume in column centimetres (for broadcast coverage either number of lines [transcript] or transmission time [tape] would be entered and a constant used to produce an 'equivalent column centimetre').
- Number of company/product mentions.
- Attributed volume if appropriate, ie only 10 column centimetres would be attributed to each mention up to a maximum equivalent to the length of the item.
- Whether the coverage is beneficial, neutral or adverse (BNA). In the case of beneficial or adverse, a score might be added to indicate slightly, fairly or very.
- The presence of a small range of specified key corporate messages and an indication of the strength (1–5) of those messages. If those messages were directly contradicted, a negative score would be entered. Occasionally, key messages might change so the user would need the facility to update key messages.
- Mention of a small specified selection of key issues. From time to time particular issues would go away and new issues arise.

- A yes/no indication of whether the coverage was generated proactively. If yes, an indication of which type of action from a range (eg press release, facility trip, launch event, VNR, product placement, etc, and which particular release, event, etc).
- Name of any spokesperson quoted.

The key issue here would be to find a balance between capturing all the information that might possibly be useful, and making the process so time-consuming and tedious that it becomes self-defeating.

Outputs

A large number of outputs would be available from the system: the precise range and their nature would be identified as part of the next phase of the project (if appropriate). It is, however, possible to give a broad indication of the type of outputs sought and some specific examples. The output will be quantitative and therefore tabular or graphical (frequently multi-coloured to assist interpretation) in the form of bar charts, line graphs and pie charts. Written commentaries will be added by public affairs staff as a post-report activity.

Normally there will be some sort of measure of volume of coverage. This may be expressed as column centimetres, circulation/readership, or opportunities to see. Column centimetres can be converted into an equivalent advertising cost subject to the availability of suitable data on advertising rates. Circulation figures are available for all media from a computerized media directory already used by the department. Readership figures are available for national media (not always for local or trade publications) and could probably be sourced through the advertising or media agency. These figures (particularly when aggregated, and duplication/overlap cannot be taken into account) are frequently meaningless in absolute terms, but can be useful to indicate trends and make comparisons. They may also provide information on target groups' relationship/audience within the total circulation or audience.

There are a number of ways in which figures for raw volume of coverage can be adjusted. Media coverage can be classified as beneficial, neutral or adverse and also adjusted for impact. Subject to confirmation, the sort of factors that might be taken into account when assessing the impact of media coverage are: whether the article is accompanied by a photograph, whether that photograph is branded, the position of that article within the publication, and whether the brand name is in the headline. Attribution is a further factor to be considered: is it appropriate to attribute the full volume (say, 100 column centimetres) of a long article when there is only a single, passing mention? Equivalent adjustments could be made for broadcast coverage once it is converted into equivalent column centimetres.

Two types of report are of particular interest: first, the presence (or absence) in the media and strength of a limited number of key messages directed at the media; second, whether or not the coverage had been directly prompted by the public affairs department and, if so, what type of activity had acted as the prompt (press release, launch event, facility trip, telephone contact, product placement, etc).

These reports would also be subject to varying degrees of focus. It may be desirable to analyse the coverage prompted by one particular journalist or emanating from one particular publication or programme. More likely, coverage might well be broken down into media sectors: national, consumer, trade, local, etc. Coverage could also be analysed according to target media, important media, and the rest.

It would be highly desirable to handle press and broadcast coverage in an integrated manner. This would be done by monitoring broadcast coverage through transcripts, which would then allow the volume of broadcast coverage to be converted into equivalent column centimetres through a conversion based on word counts. Similarly, readership and viewing figures would be considered comparable.

Sample outputs

This is a list of possible outputs to give an indication of the type of outputs that are envisaged. Their precise nature and scope would need to be discussed/examined in more detail. *The absence of a particular output does not necessarily mean it could not be generated.* Also given is some indication of the perceived management benefits:

1. Raw (unadjusted) volume of coverage in column centimetres or number of mentions by month (*bar chart*). **A crude indication of presence in the media and how it compares with previous periods.**
2. Weighted volume (adjusted for readership/viewership, attribution, BNA and impact [position of page, name in headline, photograph, branded photograph]) of coverage in column centimetres per month for a) target/important/other and b) media sectors (*two bar charts with multiple bars per month*). **Media presence taking into account nature of coverage and where it appears; again allowing historical comparison.**

3. Relative volume of coverage (percentage) for a specified period (eg 3 months, 6 months, 12 months) according to activity that prompted the coverage. This volume could be weighted and the analysis carried out for different media sectors (*pie charts*). **An indication of the effectiveness of different activities which could then be compared with the time/resources devoted to those activities.**

4. Number of mentions of specified key issues in national media over time (*number of mentions against month/week with a line for each issue*). **Inevitably historical, but past trends might give early indication of those issues which will dominate media interest in the future.**

5. Volume of coverage attributed to key messages (adjusted for strength) per month in target media (*bar chart with multiple bars per month, each bar representing a specified key issue*). **Success or otherwise of persuading the media to report the organization's key messages.**

6. Separate rankings of journalists and publications/programmes according to the beneficial, neutral and adverse comment (*table*). **A clear indication of those journalists or media who report the organization's particularly positively or negatively.**

7. A campaign analysis listing the volume of coverage (column centimetres for press, time for broadcast, and a combined figure using equivalent column centimetres), both raw and adjusted, including opportunities to see, for a particular campaign. This could be split by media category and/or genre if required (*probably a table according to complexity*). **Quantitative data to support reporting on and analysis of a specific campaign.**

8. An activity analysis listing the volume of coverage (column centimetres for press, time for broadcast, and a combined figure using equivalent column centimetres), both raw and adjusted, opportunities to see, and advertising value equivalent for a particular activity such as a press trip (*table*). **Quantitative data to support reporting on and analysis of a specific activity.**

The first point that Dermot McKeone makes when the subject of media evaluation is raised is to clarify what exactly is meant by media evaluation: 'What people are looking for when they use the sort of services and products that media evaluators supply is media analysis – media content analysis, in particular.' He then goes on to accept that the argument that media evaluation is only part of the evaluation issue in public relations is absolutely true. However, he stresses the important role that media evaluation plays: 'If you are going to evaluate a PR programme properly, analysing the media coverage you have generated is one of the things you have to do. There are all sorts of things that PR people get up to these days, but the content of media coverage is one thing that needs to be looked at carefully.'

However, McKeone argues that media analysis has benefits beyond a narrow view of PR programme evaluation: the media profile of the organization you are looking at can tell you a lot more than how effective its media relations office is. 'Particularly in a large and complex organization, much of the media coverage will be nothing to do with the PR department, but nevertheless it deserves measurement. Even though the corporate communicator hasn't caused an article or news item to appear, nevertheless, as guardian of the organization's reputation, the PR people have a good deal of responsibility for how that organization looks to the outside world.' So, media profile is what media analysis is all about, not just the simple evaluation of the public relations programmes or campaigns, he argues.

McKeone then moves on to extend the scope of media evaluation to competitive monitoring. 'You can analyse other people's PR efforts, other people's campaigns, in much the same way that you can analyse your own. If you've got a rational, sensible way of dividing your coverage up; looking at different elements; analysing it by message, subject area, favourability, media type; you can find out an awful lot about the sort of direction a company is happening to move – it's a sort of media intelligence.' He suggests that by analysing your own profile alongside those of your competitors, as well as analysing things like messages and favourability, you can see how well you are doing against the competition.

At its best, media analysis can give an organization a three-dimensional view of its media profile. By measuring parameters like overall tone and delivery of messages separately from each other, analysts can obtain two mutually helpful but different views on the way issues and broad subject areas are being reported in the media. 'It's like reconciling your bank statement with your profit and loss accounts. You're looking at the same thing in two different ways to get a full picture, a complete understanding,' he says.

Especially in the big company environment, there are increasing demands for numbers that reflect performance, and the PR function is no different from any other. 'Just as the manufacturing division has to meet productivity targets, so the public relations function has to meet its own targets.' McKeone points out that the advantage PR people have – for the moment at least – is that they are invited to choose their own targets and benchmarks. 'Nevertheless, once they have set those targets, it is up to them to reach them, and it is not unreasonable to regard the company's media profile as being within their remit, so they can analyse facts and figures about that.' He suggests that there are several broad questions the PR practitioners should be asking of themselves: 'How well did we perform as a department/consultancy? How well did we communicate the things we were asked to communicate on behalf of our employer/client? How well have we been performing as guardians of the reputation of our company/client, and to what extent have we been successful in keeping it good and shiny?'

When he turns to the changes taking place in the media evaluation world, McKeone naturally stresses the impact of the internet, 'both as a channel for spreading news around, but also as a medium in its own right'. He stresses the role of technology in getting televisual and audio material in front of audiences. 'You can now reach virtually any programme you want from virtually anywhere in the world over the internet. This may well become the main way that people – in the future – receive news and information, and therefore form attitudes and opinions, rather than via terrestrial, satellite and cable broadcasters.'

Nonetheless, McKeone suggests that the traditional media evaluation activity of using people to analyse media output by making judgements about message content and favourability (and the like) will continue for the foreseeable future, as will analysing the type and numbers of people that traditional, offline media are reaching. 'It's the weighting and applying of those numbers that are going to see big developments, and also there will be other numbers coming into play. For example, how well are we able to measure the different terms people are searching for on an internet site?' He mentions search engine profiling, which looks at what happens when a company name is put into major search engines: which pages come up, how many people have been looking for that information, and so on. However, there are plenty of problems to be addressed: 'A lot of key sites don't readily publish their readership statistics. Similarly, finding data for some important blogs as well as the online media associated with national press is difficult. Getting to grips with the "readership" data associated with the spill-over from offline to online media is going to be a big challenge', McKeone concludes.

Dermot McKeone is Chairman of Impact Evaluation.

QUESTIONNAIRE RESPONSES

Evaluation questionnaire for industry leaders

Q: Getting started on evaluation of public relations activity is often a challenge to practitioners. What advice would you give them?

Either you learn how to do it well or you need to have a qualified and reliable supplier. Margins of error are smaller than in any other public relations activity. **Dejan Verčič**

Use the CIPR Evaluation Toolkit as it gives a helpful step-by-step guide. Start modestly and see the results. **Alison Clarke**

1. Develop your own evaluation processes and demonstrate to the rest of the organization the value you deliver.

2. Evaluate your work from the beginning (research methodologies, processes, activities, budget, and outcomes).

3. Make sure it is evidence based (not just media either).

4. Make sure senior management/board receive report.

Fran Hagon

Identify the desired outcome at the planning stage – shape what this outcome will look like to the client and then set about delivering it – with milestones identified so everyone involved knows that they are still heading to the correct destination. **Crispin Manners**

Think outside the box – don't take a formulaic approach – think about all the stakeholders in the PR programme and what they would like to see. **Loretta Tobin**

It is important for clients to understand and appreciate the contribution of PR programmes to the bottom line. Practitioners need to take time to devise and implement evaluation mechanisms that are easy to follow to show if they are achieving objectives. **Ray Mawerera**

Don't think of it as evaluation. Think of it as celebration points. Every time you can say to a client 'We've done it, we hit the target!' get out a bottle of champagne. Learn to enjoy evaluation as part of the good side of our industry. **Annabelle Warren**

I encourage them to use evaluation by reinforcing the fact it justifies PR expenditure. Invest in a good software package, train your staff properly and educate them about the importance of evaluation – it's increasingly becoming a 'must have' for all clients. **Laurna O'Donnell**

The hardest thing can be picking exactly what it is that could be measured. For example, would it be readership, in which case you can use data issued by the media – or is it in outcomes, in which you could measure sales? You don't always have to set up and perform the evaluation yourself – think about how you can identify and piggyback on what other people are doing. **Clara Zawawi**

Identify proven evaluation methods that apply to the programme in question; closely check references and track record of performance when engaging a research firm; seek out observations, suggestions and opinions of fellow practitioners. **Tom O'Donoghue**

Start from what you are trying to achieve rather than thinking of measurement as an optional extra (which can be cut when the budget is cut). Think in particular about how you justify your role and worth and also realize that senior management does want to see the return on any investment: failure to measure, even at a basic level, puts your job in jeopardy. **Mike Copland**

Make sure that the objectives are well defined and measurable. Without that, any evaluation attempts will be pure conjecture. **Matt Kucharski**

Build it in at the start. Plan the evaluation when you plan the campaign. If you have the budget, measure beforehand and measure afterwards. **Richard Offer**

Allocating time is considered one of the most challenging aspects for evaluating campaigns. Encroaching deadlines and

additional work heavily influence practitioners' management methods of the campaign. Before commencement of a public relations campaign, a practitioner should be aware of the repercussions if extensive evaluation is not undertaken. Ultimately, the success of the campaign will be apparent from the results and if they are not favourable, some form of evaluation is required to recognize problems and areas of improvement.
Adam Connolly

7

Evaluation in practice – case studies

PRICEWATERHOUSECOOPERS

Benchmarking tunes PR performance

Hard-core data convinced senior management at PricewaterhouseCoopers to spend more on public relations. 'Our public relations programme moved from the anecdotal and subjective to the realm of fact', said Peter Horowitz, senior managing director for global public relations.

The proof prompted management to increase the PR budget after analysis revealed that PwC was the most written-about firm in the accounting/consulting industry and enjoyed the most favourable reputation among journalists.

'Our research on the effectiveness of the public relations programme swept away management's subjective negativism such as "Why aren't we getting press?" when of course we had been', Horowitz said. 'I had been fighting that battle for 20 years, but now I have definitive proof of public relations' effectiveness, and it has changed the way our management views what we do.'

PwC's analytical approach to media research and evaluation began in July 1998, when Price Waterhouse and Coopers Lybrand merged. With help from Echo Research, PwC's PR programme was fine-tuned by quarterly reports that monitored the percentage of negative and positive stories, tracked journalists who regularly write about PwC, and helped identify the strategies that drive favourable press. 'Without regular benchmarking to measure the impact of PR, we'd be walking around blind', Horowitz reported.

Measuring awareness

Measurement helped PwC determine how well it communicated its new brand name and brand attributes following the merger. 'We wanted to make sure the new PwC name was reported correctly and our messages about the merger weren't overlooked', Horowitz said.

Initially, media tracking of domestic and international publications revealed many negative articles that quoted business analysts who scrutinized the merger. Reporters also positioned the merger as a takeover of a larger firm, Coopers Lybrand, by the smaller Price Waterhouse rather than a merger of equals.

Research helped PwC focus on journalists from *The Financial Times* and *The Wall Street Journal*, as these were found to be the key media influencers. In follow-up interviews, PwC emphasized the merger was equal in name and that an equal number of senior managers from Price Waterhouse and Coopers made up the merged firm's board of directors. 'It was important to communicate those actions and not spin some nice words', Horowitz said. 'Our CEO and senior team played a significant role by making themselves available for interviews to answer any questions reporters raised during that time.' Subsequently, journalists portrayed the merger as one of equals and the number of negative articles decreased.

Measurement also proved PR's impact on reputation during the US Security and Exchange Commission's investigation into potential conflicts of interest between PwC's auditing and consulting division. Although the investigation shifted PwC's reputation rating into a negative area for the first time, research showed that within four months, media coverage shifted back to positive, thus easing management concerns. 'During that time, we communicated the positives about PwC and we were able to show the impact our communication had on reputation', Horowitz said. 'Measurement showed how, over time, we completely recovered from that crisis.'

Improving your campaign

Research also demonstrated key methods of improving PR programmes:

- Favourable press coverage increased when a chart or graph accompanied a press release. 'If you offer a graphic, the chances are very good that the story will run', Horowitz said.
- Evaluation showed that articles written by senior managers are 'the most powerful way of generating positive press and influencing readers'. Getting the CEO to participate in press interviews results in articles that are more favourable than an article on the same topic without him or her.
- Media evaluation identifies the reporters, publications and wire services that wrote most often about industries and topics. Without benchmarking, effort can be misdirected.

AIRBUS

'GPS' for the communications roadmap

Airbus, the major aircraft manufacturer, has been tracking media coverage since 2004, initially to inform its position in European and US markets and in comparison with its main competitor Boeing.

At first the coverage was analysed for products and interpretation of corporate values, but as political opposition in the US rose against the subsidy that Airbus receives from the European Union, it looked in more depth at politics and political commentary.

Because of the worldwide nature of this debate and its impact on aircraft purchase decisions by many airlines that were choosing between the Airbus A350 and the Boeing 787 Dreamliner, Airbus and its media analyst Echo Research widened the media evaluation brief.

- Deliver a wider global picture of Airbus's media profile.
- Detect emerging issues and potential problems.
- Provide guidance on raising Airbus's profile and favourability in the United States.
- Identify ways to reduce and manage the on-going political commentary, especially from the United States.

- Measure the visibility of the CEO and country representatives, and their impact on overall media profile.
- Gauge Airbus's reputation, globally.

Asia was added to Europe and the United States as continental regions being analysed. Analysts were employed in the 15 countries or had worked in them. In addition to coding the media coverage using Echo's methodology, they were asked to comment from a personal perspective on the issues they were researching, which gave a national perspective to the identification of opportunities and risks.

The monthly evaluation report included a regional table of media volume and favourability, comparison of Airbus and Boeing media coverage, tracking of press releases and key messages by region, and emerging issues. Echo also advised Airbus on targets for overall coverage and in main areas of business. One aim was to reduce the political coverage by putting more effort into human resources and technology/environment media activities.

The results included:

- A wider global perspective on Airbus's media coverage.
- Emerging issues were identified. Each month Echo highlighted opportunities and risks and offered recommendations. This has included the problems over the delays on production of the A380 super-jumbo, which has led Airbus to a weekly report as it has become a major reputation issue.
- Profile and favourability of media coverage in the United States has risen, without too much *schadenfreude* towards Airbus over the A380 problems.
- Evaluation has also identified the increased visibility of Airbus's CEO position, although with several changes in Airbus senior management this would have been inevitable.

Although Airbus ultimately makes its own reputation through its products, customer service and policies, it recognizes the role that media evaluation plays in monitoring delivery of messages to the media and in fine-tuning communication strategies and actions.

Hubert Faure, Airbus's Head of Communication, says that the media evaluation work undertaken by Echo 'does a job for us similar to a GPS (Global Positioning System). It shows our precise position on the communications roadmap, so that we understand our strengths and the challenges that face us on the journey.'

This case study won the Association for the Measurement and Evaluation of Communication Gold award for Best Use of Media Evaluation – International Multi-Market Activity in 2006.

COMALCO

Using measurement to plan and manage stakeholder engagement

Comalco, a subsidiary of Rio Tinto, is a supplier of bauxite, alumina and primary aluminium to Australia, New Zealand and export markets. In 2000, opinion research indicated that perceptions of Comalco in Australia were in need of improvement. The results were problematic – the reputation of the company and the credibility of its messages were lowest in the town of Gladstone in the state of Queensland, where it was considering investing $2 billion in a new smelter. The company had few well-developed relationships with opinion leaders, except those formed on an ad hoc basis.

To measure the company's reputation, Burson-Marsteller, New York, had initiated a stakeholder dialogue. More than 700 local government and opinion leaders were identified and surveyed. They were chosen on the criteria of being opinion leaders from government, community, NGOs, education, business and others who could impact the company in some way or influence those who do so.

The survey investigated stakeholders' awareness and their view of the ideal mining and minerals company. It helped benchmark their awareness of the company's external initiatives and activities and indicated whether they were receiving information on Comalco. In addition, interviews were conducted between Comalco managers and Gladstone community leaders. This gave the managers the opportunity to listen, learn and develop a dialogue with opinion leaders.

The objectives of the plan to improve Comalco's reputation were:

- Understand the expectations and views of stakeholders critical to Comalco's success.

- Improve stakeholders' perceptions and credibility of the company.
- Maintain Comalco's 'operating licence'.
- Provide a road map for the company's external communications programme.

Comalco decided that it must improve a wide range of relationships within its plant communities to support the expansion plans, and so set a target for its External Affairs team to 'provide external communications for the purpose of improving Comalco's business through managing the company's reputation'.

The survey data helped focus communication strategy and create meaningful community programmes. Community Needs Assessment research, also undertaken by Burson-Marsteller, found that there were issues of communal concern – drug and alcohol abuse, healthcare, employment, youth activities and educational opportunities. These provided the opportunity for Comalco to engage as a prominent 'good corporate citizen'.

The company published the results of the research and developed community outreach programmes. Managers became more involved in community and charitable giving through existing programmes and, in 2002, the company started a Community Fund in Queensland and at Weipa on Cape York Peninsula in north Queensland, a major mining site on ground traditionally owned by indigenous Australians.

Through the Community Fund, Comalco committed over A$520,000 to community development in 2003 and has given over A$1 million to the Gladstone community since 2002. It also leveraged A$3.2 million in funding from other sources.

In early 2004, Burson-Marsteller conducted a follow-up survey with the same stakeholders. The results, it says, were impressive.

- A 50 per cent increase in perceptions of Comalco.
- A 60 per cent rise in Comalco's overall credibility.
- An increase in the frequency of mentions of all company sources, whose credibility had also risen.
- Overall, perception gaps were significantly lowered between 2000 and 2004.

> ● A 100 per cent increase in awareness of some Comalco-led initiatives in health and safety and in schools, and large increases in awareness of community and indigenous initiatives.

Business results

The investment in reputation research, using accepted social science methodology, has led to stakeholder engagement programmes and communication activity that rebuilt Comalco's reputation and furthered its business interests. The stronger relations with the Gladstone community led it to invest A$2 billion in the smelter; improved community relations in the Weipa area resulted in a new agreement extending Comalco's right to mine on indigenous lands; and other important relationships with government, business and NGOs have moved ahead over a three to four year period.

This case study won the Golden Ruler Award for Excellence in Public Relations Measurement by the Institute for Public Relations (US) in 2004.

INFOCOMM DEVELOPMENT AUTHORITY OF SINGAPORE

Tracking global positioning as an 'IT hub'

In the early 2000s, the Singapore government launched a major policy initiative to promote the island state as the primary location for leading international IT and telecommunications companies wishing to establish head offices, joint ventures and manufacturing facilities in the Asian market. Success in this potentially means billions of dollars to the Singapore economy.

With China widely predicted to become the world's largest market, much attention has turned to Beijing and Shanghai, while Hong Kong continues to vie for international investment, and new emerging economies such as Malaysia and India are also competing for international investment dollars.

Through the Infocomm Development Authority of Singapore (IDA), working in conjunction with the Economic Development Board of Singapore and other government agencies, Singapore launched an international public relations campaign to promote key messages that position Singapore positively as an 'IT investment hub' in Asia, including:

- Government support and incentives for international investment.
- The wide availability of technology infrastructure including broadband in Singapore.
- A skilled workforce.
- Geographic centrality to the emerging economies of China and India.
- Multicultural and multilingual capabilities, with Singapore having large Indian and Chinese speaking populations as well as English.
- A safe, secure environment to invest and establish facilities.

An international firm was engaged to communicate key Singapore messages to target audiences, such as CEOs, CFOs and CIO (Chief Information Officers) of large international IT and telecoms companies in the United States, Canada, the UK, Europe and Australia.

The public relations campaign identified the key media that are influential within these target audiences in each market. These included publications such as *The Wall Street Journal*, *Fortune*, *Forbes* magazine, *Financial Times*, *The Economist*, *Bloomberg*, *The Times* of London, *Australian Financial Review*, *BRW*, and key CEO, CFO and CIO trade journals. Then the IDA and the firm set about distributing Singapore's messages to these key media through news releases, fact sheets, interviews, and other communication activities.

Two stages of research were planned to evaluate the effectiveness of the campaign.

Media analysis tracks message placement and positioning

First, media analysis firm CARMA International was engaged to analyse the content of target media. This identified the extent to which key messages were effectively placed in media read by the target audiences. Furthermore, media analysis tracked Singapore's competitors (other countries in Asia including China, Japan, Korea and Hong Kong) to identify Singapore's 'share of voice' and positioning. From analysis of leading messages and the favourability of coverage, as well as 'share of voice' of various Asian countries, media analysis could show the success of the PR efforts as well as draw inferential and predictive conclusions concerning likely market impact; see Figure 7.1.

Comparison of global coverage for competitors
by volume & favourability

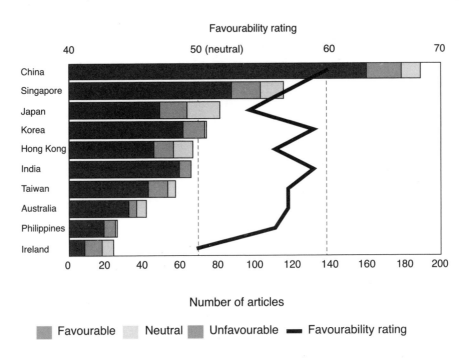

Figure 7.1 *IDA Chart 1: CARMA International media analysis showing media coverage*

Audits identify awareness and perceptions

To 'close the loop' and gain conclusive data on outcomes of the campaign, IDA also commissioned a research firm to conduct interviews with CEOs, CFOs and CIOs in target countries every six months to identify their awareness of Singapore's attributes and their attitude towards investing in Singapore. Early in the campaign, perception audits showed low awareness of Singapore's key messages and the presence of several negative messages concerning

Singapore (eg it was perceived as autocratic, having strict censorship, and more expensive than other Asian countries). However, after more than 12 months of public relations activity, awareness and perceptions among target audiences confirmed that Singapore's messages were getting through, with an increased number of senior executives being able to recall unprompted key positives about Singapore such as its high technology and skilled workforce, as shown in Figure 7.2.

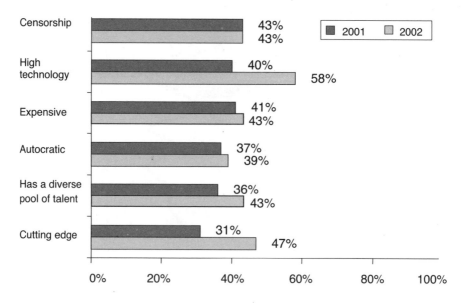

Figure 7.2   *IDA Chart 2: findings of a perception audit among CEOs, CFOs and CIOs in target markets following PR campaigns*

LIFT06 CONFERENCE

Measuring events with blogs, mash-ups and wikis

The methodology for measuring the impact of a conference or event has long used a post-event survey tool, typically inserted in the conference or event pack. The simple questionnaires gave a quick snapshot of participants' views on the quality and relevance of the event and of the speakers or production that had been witnessed.

The limitations of this approach are usually that there is a low level of response, unless there is an incentive or a strong push by conference organizers to extract the survey from departing delegates. There is also little depth in the response, other than approval/disapproval comments.

At a Geneva IT conference in 2006, called LIFT06, an experiment was undertaken using new technology tools such as wikis, blogs and mash-ups to evaluate the event. Glenn O'Neil of Benchpoint sought greater depth of response during the event and not just as an *ex post facto* survey. He also wanted to identify the manner in which LIFT06 influenced the knowledge, attitudes and behaviour of conference delegates.

Blog – a blog (or weblog) is a website in which messages are posted and displayed with the newest on top.

Wiki – a wiki is a type of website that allows anyone visiting the site to add, to remove, or otherwise to edit all content, very quickly and easily.

Mash-up – a website or web application that combines content from more than one source into a single web page.

The aim of LIFT06 was to 'connect people who are passionate about new applications of technology and propel the conversations into the broader world to improve'. The research methodology combined qualitative and quantitative methods.

In collaboration with the conference organizers, Glenn O'Neil developed a three-level evaluation framework to elicit responses from the 285 delegates who came from all over Europe; see Table 7.1.

All delegates were sent an online survey with questions focusing on the key measures, which had a 60 per cent response rate. During the conference, 10 participants, selected randomly, were interviewed for a 15–20 minute period. There was a wiki for the conference programme, in which each speaker had a one-page website set up for them on to which both delegates and speakers could leave comments. It was estimated that 20–30 per cent of conference delegates had laptops in use during conference sessions and were thus able to comment during and after speakers' presentations.

During the conference, more that 20 delegates actively posted their comments on to their own blogs, with 680 postings mostly during and immediately after the event. These postings were fed into a mash-up report from which 50 posts were randomly selected and analysed.

The results of the evaluation using these conventional and new technology research methods were as follows:

Table 7.1   *Evaluation framework for LIFT06*

Evaluation objectives	Key measures	Research methods	Data sources
Immediate reaction of participants to LIFT06 Interviews to wiki Program wiki	Quality Relevance Planned actions through posts	Participant survey Participant	Participants Participants
Change to knowledge and attitudes of participants as a result of LIFT06	Knowledge Attitudes	Participant survey Blog monitoring	Participants Participants' blogs Mash-up feed
Changes to behaviour of participants as a result of LIFT06	Actions undertaken Initiatives launched Contacts made	Participant survey Post-LIFT survey	Participants

- The range of methods gave both immediate feedback on delegates' views and attitudes during the conference (which offered formative data and enabled immediate change) and afterwards (summative data for future planning).
- Based on self-assessment measures, 82 per cent of delegates indicated that their IT knowledge and 70 per cent of their attitudes had changed as a result of the conference.
- The participant survey also showed that 93 per cent would attend the next LIFT conference and 96 per cent would recommend it to others.
- The monitoring of a random sample of 50 blog postings showed 62 per cent positive, 30 per cent neutral and 8 per cent negative, often as reactions to speakers. O'Neil also noted that 26 per cent of blog posts came from non-delegates, indicating that LIFT06 had generated discussions outside its halls and the immediate circle of participants. (This is information not normally gained through end-of-event questionnaires.)

- Overall, 94 per cent of delegates met new contacts, with 57 per cent meeting between one and five new people.

In addition to new methods of collecting quantitative data, O'Neil commented that the use of blogs is akin to the use of 'learning logs' in the education system. He says that this is a rich new area of evaluation research as its gives an immediate 'insight into participants' changes in attitudes, concerns and practices'.

This case study has been drawn from O'Neil, G (2006) Blogs, mash-ups and wikis – new tools for evaluating event objectives: A case study on the LIFT06 conference in Geneva. *It is available from* PRism 4 (2), *the online academic PR journal at http://praxis.massey.ac.nz/file admin/Praxis/Files/Journal_Files/Evaluation_Issue/ONEIL_CASE_STUD Y.pdf*

SOUTHWEST AIRLINES

Measuring the link between PR and sales

Each month, millions of people use online news services and search engines to find the latest information on topics that interest them. When conducting this type of news research, they often find press releases from companies as well as thousands of articles from a wide range of sources. Recognizing this phenomenon and that many travellers gain information on carriers and schedules to inform the purchase of tickets and accommodation and, as well, that press releases distributed by wire services are directly searchable by web crawlers, Southwest Airlines and its PR consultancy, SEO-PR, have adopted a strategy of optimizing press releases for the major news search engines. In this way, they sought to place news about Southwest Airline, the largest carrier in the United States in terms of scheduled domestic departures, before both the media and potential customers.

The strategy also sought to demonstrate a method of definitively linking media relations activity to consequent sales, which has often been implied but seldom demonstrated. As Linda Rutherford, VP (Public Relations) at Southwest Airlines, and Greg Jarboe of SEO-PR comment, 'While increased brand awareness ultimately leads to sales, it was virtually impossible to prove that a particular press release made a sale happen – until the advent of news search engines.'

Here's how they made press releases ready for news search engines and made the outcomes measurable:

At the beginning of 2004, the Southwest Airlines/SEO-PR team adopted a five-step process.

Step 1. Conduct keyword research to identify what people are looking for

Online tools such as Wordtracker and Yahoo Search Marketing's bidding research tool were used to find out the terms that consumers use when making a search. These tools are mainly used by pay-per-click advertising agencies but can be used by PR practitioners, too. They found that in October 2005 'Southwest Airlines' got around 1.3 million searches for the month, but that 'Southwest' got just fewer than 400,000 searches. So, using Southwest Airlines instead of Southwest made it relevant for three times more searches.

Step 2. Edit press releases to include search terms

Although the press release must be newsworthy to maintain credibility online, the team trained themselves to optimize headlines and body copy for online search engines. They would write a standard release and then edit it to include specific search terms in the headline, first paragraph and a few more times in the body copy. This was undertaken because news search engines place more weight on the 'visible' text in the headline and body copy, rather than on keyword meta tags. 'Optimization requires copywriting skills designed primarily for humans, with keyboard research for search engine considerations secondary', say Rutherford and Jarboe.

Step 3. Have special hyperlinks on hand, and use them wisely

Many online news readers won't scroll all the way to the bottom of a press release to find a clickable link or response number. Southwest Airlines made it easier for them by routinely including a hyperlink at the end of the first or second paragraph of the optimized press releases. This wasn't the company's main website address, but a unique hyperlink generated for each press release. They were not only trackable – so that the number of people who clicked on them and their subsequent actions (including ticket purchase) could be monitored – but they were also 'deep'. So a press release about a particular offer would link directly to the web page, where the visitor could purchase it.

Step 4. Distribute via wire service that is crawled by news search engines

Most press release distribution services are 'crawled' by Google News and some are covered by Yahoo News and AOL News. Southwest Airlines uses two wire services to distribute press releases to get the widest coverage on online news.

Step 5. Test a variety of press releases

In 2004, Southwest Airlines conducted three tests on seven press releases and found:

- The decision to optimize a press release about launching a new service to Philadelphia with 'airfare to Philadelphia' and 'low fares' in the headline and body copy led to $80,000 in ticket sales. Also, the press release and story were covered in more than a dozen media outlets including the *New York Times* and *Washington Post*.
- The launch of a new Spanish-language online ticket capability was announced in two press releases – one in Spanish and the other in English. As many Hispanics in the United States use both languages when conducting searches, the English language version used 'en Espanol' in the first paragraph. The launch press releases led to $38,000 in ticket sales.
- On 15 July, described by Rutherford and Jarboe as 'PR Hell Day', Southwest Airlines had to break its rule of one press release per day. In addition to two releases from the investor relations department on quarterly earnings and dividends, the airline's CEO unexpectedly resigned, which led to a third corporate announcement. In the meantime, Southwest Airline's marketers had scheduled a major fare sale with '22 new daily non-stop flights with low fares starting at $29 one-way'. With so much news, the PR department considered that the marketing release 'had no hope of breaking through the buzz from the other news', but they optimized the marketing release with a hyperlink in the first paragraph and 'crossed their fingers'. The outcome was unexpectedly positive, with more than $1 million in ticket sales as there was a spike in online searches of the corporate news, which found the marketing press release at the very top of news search engine results.

From February 2004 to April 2005, Southwest Airlines was able to directly track more than $2.5 million in online ticket sales as a result of optimized press releases. They also found that results start with a sharp spike in sale for the first few days and then dribble in slowly for the next four weeks.

By optimizing press releases, Southwest Airlines has been able to measure and evaluate this strategy continually, as well as demonstrating a real link between media relations and sales.

This case study won the Golden Ruler Award for Excellence in Public Relations Measurement given by the Institute for Public Relations (US) in 2005.

SURREY POLICE

Scorecard summarizes all aspect of media coverage

By using media evaluation, a UK police force has been able to tailor its communications more closely to the attitudes and anxieties of communities and individuals.

Surrey Police, which covers parts of the London conurbation, turned to Echo Research to monitor media coverage in the county. Its brief had seven objectives:

1. To establish measurable performance indicators for ongoing evaluation.
2. To identify coverage of key messages and create targets on key messages.
3. To monitor reputation.
4. To monitor impact of coverage on fear of crime.
5. To monitor effectiveness of proactive communications.
6. To monitor impact of critical stories.
7. To evaluate effectiveness of communicating key messages.

A high proportion of media coverage of Surrey Police is generated from uncontrolled incidents – the stuff of hard news – which have a strong impact on perceptions of the force and its effectiveness. As these are outside the ability of Surrey Police to manage, Echo Research proposed separation of analysis from the force's proactive communications.

Its solution was to create a Critical Incident Chart to illustrate the overall ratings, volume and favourability of media coverage that was drawn from hard news events. This is viewed alongside analysis of proactive work, as well as monitoring of perceived fear of crime, as expressed by local people in the media. Echo Research condenses the data into a two-page monthly scorecard-style report that is widely circulated.

It is tailored to Surrey Police's needs and contains charts reviewing overall favourability of local and national press coverage, coverage by fear of crime impact, media sources, divisional performance, reputation drivers, mentions of key messages, and the impact of critical stories and proactive communications. There is a bullet point commentary on the month's highlights and key findings. This is accompanied by a 'strengths and weaknesses' analysis of the force's PR activities, and recommendations on how to put the data into planning of future activities.

Echo had identified six 'reputation drivers' that shape the Surrey Police's reputation as a public sector organization: accountability, competence, communications, transparency, social engagement and trustworthiness. These drivers are tracked in the media by Echo, which can advise Surrey Police on its progress or not on reputation development and maintenance.

Among the outcomes of this media analysis reporting and Echo's subsequent recommendations is a concerted effort by Surrey Police to include key messages in press releases and spokespeople comment. Echo and Surrey Police continually monitor messages to ensure they are current, relevant and strategic. Additional scorecards have also been developed by Echo for specific campaigns.

Commenting on the value of the media analysis, Tim Morris (Surrey Police's press and publicity manager), said that Echo had given the force 'a much better idea of how the public actually see Surrey Police portrayed through the eyes of the media'.

Echo also helps Surrey Police benchmark its communications performance against other organizations that are clients of the firm. Over time, the force has consistently improved its rating, scoring higher than many other organizations and private sector companies.

This case study won the Association of Media Evaluation Companies' Platinum award for 2005.

TOYOTA AUSTRALIA

Planning for a launch using media analysis

Despite being Australia's top-selling automotive brand, Toyota was trailing third behind Ford and GM (Holden) cars in the family sedan market with its Camry and Camry V6 models. With the imminent launch of new models in 2005–06, Toyota Australia decided to assess the media exposure potential of the new cars. Turning to Millward Brown Precis, this was the first time that it was using media analysis research to inform the model launch's communication strategy.

To assist Toyota in setting key performance indicators for its in-house and agency teams, the consultancy started with research into best practice model launches as conducted by Toyota and its competitors. Millward Brown Precis analysed the previous unveilings of the three competing Toyota, Ford and Holden family sedans in 2002, as well as the more recent roll-outs of the Ford Territory SUV and Mitsubishi's competing 380 sedan range. This was conducted by reviewing coverage of the launches in some 40 leading Australian newspapers and magazines. Analysis included month-on-month comparisons of the media exposure the cars received for three months before the launch and four months afterwards, with tone and quality of reporting about each of the five car ranges taken into account.

Toyota included the analysis in its communication planning for initial product announcements, corporate statements by senior managers, motor show presence, sales figures, award ceremonies and export news. Millward Brown Precis was also able to provide Toyota with an understanding of the factors driving media coverage in the launch period and the level of interest expressed by individual journalists and publications.

The outcomes of the research also set benchmarks for the KPIs by which Toyota's in-house team and consultancies were able to demonstrate performance. 'This metric has increasingly become the PR currency within Toyota Australia and our use of the analysis has raised the appreciation of PR with senior management and marketing,' says the manufacturer's PR manager Mike Breen.

This case study won the Association for the Measurement and Evaluation of Communication (UK) Platinum award for 2006.

WESTMINSTER CITY COUNCIL, LONDON

'Bin There, Done That' recycling campaign

Increasing the level of household recycling to meet national government targets by 2010 was the objective of a campaign started by Westminster City Council (WCC) in central London in 2003. The Council's area covers many of London's most famous landmarks such as Big Ben, Buckingham Palace and Piccadilly Circus. Large increases in taxation on rubbish sent to landfill sites and the costs and pollution caused by the alternative of incineration were also powerful drivers to make a new cleansing contract's recycling service a success.

To tackle the communication of the benefits of recycling and the new service, WCC developed a campaign called 'Bin There, Done That', using the planning, research and evaluation principles set out in the (now) Chartered Institute of Public Relations' PRE toolkit.

The objectives of the campaign were to:

- Change the behaviour of residents so that they increased their use of the recycling service by one quarter (over previous levels) and increase the amount of waste to be recycled from 30 tonnes per week to 50 tonnes per week.
- Position the Council as the leading recycling local government area through raising the City Survey satisfaction from the existing 43 per cent to 60 per cent.
- Increase awareness of the recycling service among the target audience so that the recycling usage rose and the Council met national government targets for tonnage of recycled waste by 2010.

Planning and implementation

Audit and targeting

When planning the campaign, WCC audited local residents and found in a sample of 502 residents that 60 per cent didn't feel informed about the service; 98 per cent agreed that recycling is important; and 72 per cent said they would recycle only if the Council made it easier. It also conducted two focus groups and found that one recycled regularly while the other had never done so.

The focus group findings were that there was a 'shocking lack of knowledge' about WCC's recycling service, confusion over what could be recycled, and an emphatic desire for the process to be made easier. Two campaigns were tested with these groups and both unanimously chose one with the theme of 'We've made it easier, you make it happen.'

Strategy

As a result of the audit and research, the Council's strategy was to improve the information sent to households. It had to be clear, concise and accurate on the types of material that could be recycled. The communications had to:

- Reinforce the message that the service was easier to use (a single bin for all goods).
- Promote two-way communications, via a helpline and website.
- Deliver strong, easy-to-understand messages.

The campaign name chosen after trialling several alternatives was 'Bin There, Done That', as it met these criteria.

Delivery

As the research showed that messages had to be clear, simple and recognized as coming from Westminster City Council, the campaign had five stages:

1. a two-week teaser campaign;
2. roll-out of service information;
3. advertising;
4. field marketing follow-up; and
5. follow-through information campaign.

Measurement and evaluation

Four methods of evaluation were used to measure different objectives and the progress of the strategy. Trained Council staff surveyed over 16,000 homes. As a result some new messages (such as how to order replacements for bins stolen by neighbours) were adopted. There was a survey on communication messages and their reception, analysis of the tonnages sent for recycling and the residents' participation rate, and a comparison of the Council's annual survey of residents with the previous year's data.

The results were:

- Tonnage for doorstep recycling rose from 30 tonnes per week to 177 tonnes per week, compared with the objective of 50 tonnes.
- As a result of the 'Bin There, Done That' campaign, 68 per cent who were aware of it said they were active recyclers, whereas only 45 per cent who were unaware did so.
- 73 per cent of those who were aware of the campaign thought the Council had made it easier for them. This was nearly double the 40 per cent who had not seen the campaign.

> - There was also a rise in the position of the Council as the leading recycling authority, from 43 to 61 per cent, above the target of 60 per cent.
> - The number of households participating in doorstep recycling rose from 4,843 in May 2003 to 12,572 in December that year.

In the next two years, the evaluation of the campaign continued. It found that the 'Bin There, Done That' communication continued to help the Council reach and exceed its targets, with the headline figure of tonnage for recycling rising to 279.5 tonnes per week, with 48 per cent of households participating by December 2005. In terms of residents' attitude, 63 per cent of residents are satisfied or very satisfied with the recycling service and 96 per cent think recycling is a good thing.

This case study won the IPR Excellence Award in 2004 for Planning, Research and Evaluation.

VOLVO XC90

Measuring an integrated consumer launch

The small 4×4 vehicle market has been the fastest-growing automotive sector. In the last decade in the UK, it has grown by 400 per cent. Volvo's presence in this sector had been limited to one model, which had not been very successful. With a new entrant on its way, Volvo placed a substantial budget behind the launch of its new 4×4, the XC90, as it wanted to ensure success in this highly competitive marketplace.

Volvo invested heavily in qualitative research prior to launch, especially against the key segment competitors, the BMW X5 and Mercedes M-Class, in order to give the XC90 the best possible start. Once the launch phase was under way, the Swedish carmaker wanted to assess the success of the promotional campaign and to acquire integrated research that judged all aspects of the launch activity.

Volvo commissioned Millward Brown Precis with the objective of assessing the UK launch of the XC90 in as comprehensive manner as possible by integrating all available data collected between July 2001 and April 2003. The measures used were:

- Evaluation of the quality and quantity of PR coverage, its perceived strengths and weaknesses and overall effect on the brand:
  - comparison against key competitors;
  - tonality of coverage.
- Measurement of consumer perceptions about the XC90 and Volvo brand.
- Monitoring internet traffic tracked on the Volvo website.
- Measuring personal and web-based customer enquiries.
- Assessing target audience segmentation analysis.
- These measures were then integrated to assess the campaign in its entirety.

The XC90 was launched at the Detroit motor show in January 2002. It was immediately reported favourably by the media due to its looks and for its overall package. However, many models launched at motor shows enjoy a short burst of success then fade away, so did the XC90 fall into that trap?

The first task was to compare the XC90 launch against a successful launch of another Volvo vehicle using a more traditional PR campaign. The Volvo S80 was considered to be the most recent example of such a launch. The S80 achieved a huge peak in media attention around its launch, but then interest diminished and dwindled to current levels, where it is a low-volume player within its sector; see Figure 7.3. XC90 was also mapped against the BMW X5, the sector leader, which also followed a similar strategy.

XC90 employed a different tactic whereby it built on its launch coverage to increase its impact quarter on quarter. Since its launch in early 2002, it has become a benchmark vehicle in its sector, thus ensuring a place in major vehicle group tests.

Contribution to the brand

XC90 boosted the brand across a 15-month period, contributing around 45 per cent of the PR impact generated for the whole Volvo brand. It also boosted Volvo's core attributes of design, safety and practicality, pushing these to their highest-ever levels versus other manufacturers. It continues to be the highest-impact model for the brand.

The first element of integration was to investigate how public relations activity had reached Volvo's key target audience. For most of the

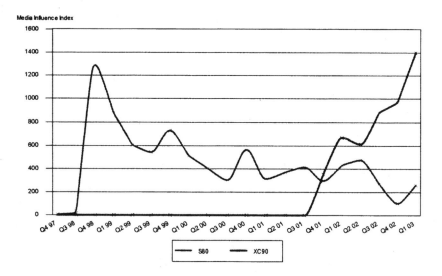

XC90 and X80 launch comparison (by Quarter)
Q4 1997–Q1 2003

Figure 7.3 *Volvo XC90 and S80 launch comparison chart*

analysis, the target audience remained broad, in order to be able to compare the XC90's performance against other competitors. Then the broad audience was segmented into a core group of target consumers. These were men or women aged 25 to 44 with a household income of over £50k, educated to degree level, and who have a keen sense of adventure. This target group totalled 609,000 people.

Among the general public, XC90's presence was very high, with 85 per cent of the total adult population having an opportunity to see XC90 messages at least once. This was well above expectations. In the core target audience, 96 per cent of people had the chance to be exposed to media coverage on the XC90, and over 90 per cent had at least two opportunities to be exposed to coverage.

Consumer response

Almost twice as many people claimed to be very familiar with the XC90 than either of its two key rivals. The largest increase in familiarity during the analysed period was directly attributable to its highest peak in PR in 2003. Not only did consumer awareness and familiarity of the model augment significantly, but some of its key attributes also improved in consumers' opinions. Safety was one of these, with the XC90 matching and exceeding its rivals. The favourable design coverage was also responsible for a sharp uplift in perceptions at a brand level of Volvo being a company that makes stylish vehicles.

As PR efforts translated into media coverage on the XC90, consumer enquiries increased in line. Two sources of information regarding enquiries were used: web traffic and personal enquiries. The initial peak of activity around the Detroit show saw an immediate surge of people accessing the internet to request information, which at that time was the only source. Over time, web enquiries decreased and personal enquiries began to build as models became available to view in showrooms; see Figure 7.4.

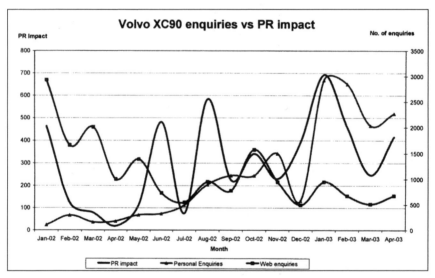

Figure 7.4   *Volvo XC90 PR stimulus chart*

Orders placed for the XC90 showed a strong growth over time, before the vehicle became available, and far exceeded forecasts. This culminated in a peak in orders just after the final PR action that announced the on-sale date for the model. Because demand was higher than anticipated, people ordering the vehicle at this stage were placed on a waiting list.

The small amount of advertising undertaken by Volvo gave a minor uplift in enquiries, but not sales. However, on the basis that the orders already far exceeded forecast when the advertising was due to be aired, Volvo deferred some of its broadcast advertising budget and as a consequence made a saving of over £2.5 million. This was attributed to data showing that PR had helped to sell the required number of vehicles and they would not be able to produce many more than this in the time available; see Figure 7.5. The advertising budget was then diverted to support other models.

This case study won the AMEC Platinum Communication Effectiveness Award in 2003.

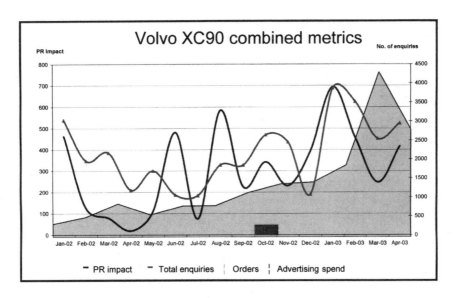

Figure 7.5   *Volvo XC90 combined metrics chart*

8

Objectives and objective setting

This chapter stresses the pivotal role that objectives play in public relations evaluation. Their relationship with goals and their contribution to strategic public relations management are examined. The hierarchy of communications objectives is outlined before the concept of process objectives is introduced as part of the effort to address the complexity of objective setting in public relations.

OBJECTIVES IN CONTEXT

The bedrock of the effective evaluation of public relations programmes and activities is setting appropriate and effective objectives. Formative evaluation is about measuring progress towards objectives and summative evaluation is about establishing whether stated objectives have been met. Indeed, evaluation becomes relatively trivial if clear measurable objectives are established at the outset. Vague, unspecific objectives lead to unsatisfactory evaluation. So objectives are pivotal to the evaluation of public relations programmes. And it is because objective setting is not simple in public relations that public relations evaluation is also not simple.

There is a widespread and almost universally uncritical assertion that effective evaluation starts with the setting of appropriate objectives. Appropriate in this context means that the objectives are clearly defined, measurable and quantifiable. Countless authorities assert that achieving objectives is the simplest (only) way to evaluate any communications programme or campaign. For example, when talking about the credibility of measurement and evaluation in communications, Lindenmann (2006: 13) stresses that the starting point is indeed to set specific, measurable communications objectives. 'This has to come first. No one can really measure the effectiveness of anything, unless they first figure out exactly what it is they are measuring that something against.' Broom and Dozier (1990: 76) develop this point further: 'To learn if your program worked, you must use the criteria established in the objectives and goals.' They then go on to point out that if at the evaluation stage the criteria for evaluation have to be refined – or even defined from scratch – then the only reason is that the criteria spelt out in the objectives were not specific enough. Indeed, a common fault of ineffective evaluation is a mismatch between (so-called) evaluation undertaken at the end of (and during) the programme, and the objectives spelled out at the start of the programme.

However, objectives are a key issue in a much broader context than public relations and communications. For example, when discussing the role of objectives in corporate strategy, marketing communications writer Chris Fill (2005: 361–62) outlines a number of reasons why objectives play an important role in the activities of individuals, social groups and organizations:

1. They provide direction and an action focus for all those participating in the activity.
2. They provide a means by which the variety of decisions relating to an activity can be made in a consistent way.
3. They determine the time period in which the activity is to be completed.
4. They communicate the values and scope of the activity to all participants.
5. They provide a means by which the success of the activity can be evaluated.

All of these general attributes of objectives have key benefits when specifically applied to public relations programming. In particular, the last two points cover the potential value that objectives can play in proving the worth and assessing the value of business activities.

Figure 8.1 shows how objectives (and goals) are the link between the organization's mission and values, and the strategies and tactics required to fulfil that mission. In this way, public relations practitioners do not derive objectives in isolation. They are identified and selected specifically so that their achievement makes some contribution to solving the problems and seizing the opportunities that face the organization. If a number of communications objectives can be established (and then met) that ultimately contribute to an organization achieving its mission, then public relations can truly be described as playing a strategic role within that organization.

Figure 8.1   *Strategic planning pyramid (based on Austin and Pinkleton, 2001)*

While any discussion of objectives tends to be uncritically approving, it is worth adding one note of caution. The desire to be specific and crystal clear when outlining objectives should not go to the extent of creating a straitjacket. As Mullins (2005: 153) states:

> An explicit statement of objectives may assist communications and reduce misunderstandings, and provide more meaningful criteria for evaluating organizational performance. However, objectives should not be stated in such a way that they detract from the recognition of possible new opportunities, potential danger areas, the initiative of staff, or the need for innovation or change.

In other words, objectives have significant benefits in providing focus and direction for a public relations campaign or programme. But this should not be at the expense of stifling creativity or eliminating the flexibility to respond to opportunities that were not anticipated when the plan was formulated. For example, the outbreak of a computer virus is a good opportunity for an anti-virus software vendor to raise its profile, irrespective of whether this type of activity was anticipated at that time.

AIMS, GOALS AND OBJECTIVES

The terms aims, goals and objectives tend to be thrown around as if they are interchangeable. Attempts of varying specificity are made to distinguish between the three. For example, James Grunig and Todd Hunt, while accepting that the dictionary definition of goals and objectives is the same, move on to 'define goals as broader and more general than objectives' (1984: 116):

> Goals are generalized ends – ends that provide a framework for decision making and behaviour but that are too broad to help much in making day-to-day decisions.

> Objectives, on the other hand, are ends in view – expected solutions to day-to-day problems that we can use to deal with that problem and to evaluate whether we have solved it.

An example given to illustrate the difference is that the goal of a PR department might be to ensure public acceptance of the organization. But the practitioners working in the department will need more specific objectives in order to enable them to plan and evaluate day-to-day activities. These might be along the lines of getting a certain percentage of an important public to understand the organization's stance on a particular issue.

Here, we will be no more precise than accepting that goals and aims are frequently slightly broader and less closely defined than objectives and concentrate on understanding and applying the latter. It may be helpful to set overall campaign goals but, by and large, these will not be measurable. Indeed, many statements that are described as objectives in public relations proposals and programmes are no more than vague goals. Typical examples are 'to raise awareness of...' or 'to position as...'. Such a goal may possibly be achievable in some loose way, but is certainly not measurable unless quantifiable elements are added. Purists might even argue that if an objective is not measurable then it is not achievable, as the fact of its achievement cannot be identified. Frequently, public relations – quite appropriately – sets broad outcomes such as raising awareness but it is unhelpful (indeed incorrect) to describe these as objectives, although they are almost universally so described.

This is a key point. Virtually every public relations plan or proposal has stated objectives that are expressed in these vague terms. This reflects not so much lazy thinking on behalf of the practitioners involved, but rather (as we will see) the peculiar challenges of objective setting in large swathes of public relations activity. Simply stated, but more difficult to implement, public relations planning frequently requires the statement of broad aims and goals underpinned with more specific – and necessarily, therefore, limited – objectives.

Note that this interpretation of the relationship between goals/aims and objectives is not universally accepted. American planning commentator Ronald Smith (2005: 69) points out that in public relations and marketing contexts, goals are indeed couched in general terms and objectives are specific. However, some other business disciplines 'either reverse the meanings of the terms or use them interchangeably'. This is not the first time – nor will it be the last – that codifying and developing the practice of public relations is bedevilled by terminology rather than true content.

So, unhelpfully, in actual practice these terms (goals and objectives) are used differently by different people. Public relations practitioners need to decide on their preferred definition and then stick to it. We commend the use of the terms as outlined by Smith (2005: 69–72) as follows and this is the approach used here:

A **goal** is a statement rooted in the organization's mission or vision. Using everyday language, a goal acknowledges the issue and sketches out how the organization hopes to see it settled. A goal is stated in general terms and lacks measure; these will come later in the objectives.

An **objective** is a statement emerging from the organization's goals. It is a clear and measurable statement, written to point the way forward toward particular levels of awareness, acceptance or action. Objectives often are established by communication managers responding to broader organizational goals. Like goals, objectives deal with intended outcomes rather than procedures for reaching them. A single goal may be the basis for several objectives.

This is nothing new. Indeed, Grunig and Hunt (1984) outlined this distinction between goals and objectives while also highlighting the relationship between them. This is demonstrated in Figure 8.2.

In much the same way that the term objective is frequently used without too much care, so there tends to be confusion with the associated (but not overlapping) concepts of strategy and tactics. While the objective is the end-point that the programme, campaign or activity is attempting to reach, the strategy is the overall approach to be used in pursuance of reaching that end-point: not to be confused with tactics, the particular set of actions required in order to implement the strategy.

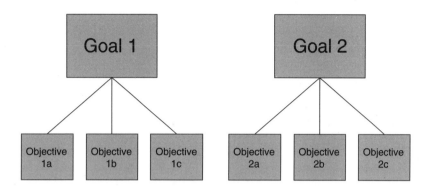

Goals are broad and abstract and cannot be tested directly.

Objectives are derived from goals. They are specific and measurable.
Meeting an objective contributes to attaining a goal.

Figure 8.2   *Goals and objectives*

So, if an individual desires to travel from point A (Newtown) to point B (Smithsville) then the objective is patently to reach Smithsville, probably by a specified time. This may well be in support of a broader goal, perhaps to appreciate a part of the country previously unknown to the traveller. The choices of strategy are to travel by car, train, aeroplane, bus, etc. The tactics would depend on the strategy chosen: in the case of travelling by car, they could be a set of driving directions. Note that tactics are relatively easy to change, but this is not the case with a strategy. So, while the taking of a wrong turning can normally be corrected fairly quickly, abandoning a car journey in favour of going by rail can be done but is likely to be disruptive and take some time to implement.

MANAGEMENT BY OBJECTIVES (MBO)

In a general business context, the term objective is most commonly associated with the concept of management by objectives (MBO).

Indeed, this is nothing more than common sense in public relations where we have already established that objectives play a key role before, during and after the implementation of a communications programme, and we have established that public relations is a management process.

This reinforces the central role that objectives can, and frequently do, play in modern management thinking. As Kotler and Keller (2006: 54–55) explain, while most business units pursue a range of objectives, for an MBO system to work, the business unit's various objectives must meet four criteria:

- First, objectives must be arranged hierarchically, from the least to the most important. By proceeding this way, the business can move from broad objectives to specific objectives for specific departments and individuals.
- Second, objectives must be stated quantitatively whenever possible.
- Third, goals [ie objectives] should be realistic. They should arise from an analysis of a business unit's opportunities and strengths, not from wishful thinking.
- Finally, the company's objectives must be consistent [with each other]. It is not possible to maximize both sales and profits simultaneously.

These exhortations will be echoed in much of the discussion of public relations objectives outlined below. For instance, a hierarchy of objectives implies the linking of public relations objectives, directly or indirectly, with organizational objectives. Taking another example, the encouragement for objectives to be quantified is a mantra oft repeated in a public relations context. In terms of being realistic, public relations objectives need to be communications objectives. Finally, realism also points towards being realistic about the effects sought. Public relations practitioners too often fall into the trap of promising/ assuming over-optimistic results from their efforts. This may breed euphoria in the short term, but certainly disappointment and disillusionment follow in the medium to long term.

A more careful review of classic MBO thinking also throws up clear parallels with public relations evaluation when undertaken in a formative rather than summative guise. This parallel also illustrates the contention that public relations thinking is continually hampered by the need to reinvent the wheel: quicker and more effective progress could easily be made if practitioners had the confidence and good sense to borrow and adapt ideas that have been tried and tested in related fields of endeavour (note that the phrase Management by Objectives has been in use for nearly half a century).

'The underlying basis of a system of MBO' is described by Mullins (2005: 249) as:

- the setting of objectives and targets;
- participation by individual managers in agreeing unit objectives and criteria of performance; and
- the continual review and appraisal of results.

This introduces a number of ideas which are directly applicable to objective setting in a public relations context and will be echoed in the discussion of objective setting below. The use of the term 'targets' alongside 'objectives' is an indication of how objectives can made measurable without a 'near miss' condemning the programme to failure. Performance criteria firmly imply that thinking about how the success of the programme is to be measured needs to take place as soon as planning starts (not when implementation has been completed). Finally, 'continual approval and appraisal' points to a dual formative and summative approach to the evaluation of public relations activities.

Translating this thinking to PR programme management, we have another plea to concentrate on the impact of what is being undertaken rather than being sidetracked into concentrating solely on the process of the programme. As discussed below, process objectives can be useful but need to be treated with caution. They can easily result in the misplaced approach to evaluation represented by the substitution game.

HIERARCHY OF OBJECTIVES

Looking at this issue from a mainstream public relations perspective, Cutlip, Center and Broom (2006: 315) integrate the discussion of management by objectives, goals/objectives and a hierarchy of objectives:

As now applied, MBO operates at two levels of outcomes: goals and objectives. Goals are summative statements that spell out the overall outcomes of a program. ... Goals establish what will be accomplished if the objectives set for each of the publics are achieved.

Objectives represent the specific knowledge, opinion and behavioural outcomes to be achieved for each well-defined target public, what some call 'key results'. The outcome criteria take the form of measurable program effects to be achieved by specified dates.

In fact most authorities would argue that there is no way to evaluate public relations activity *except* by comparing programme outcome with the objectives set for the programme. For example, Wilcox *et al* (2000: 192) state quite baldly: 'Before any public relations program can be properly evaluated, it is important to have a clearly established set of measurable objectives.'

They then make four general points which approach some key principles associated with public relations evaluation, including an appreciation that the nature of the objectives set is a key factor in the planning and evaluation of the campaign required to achieve them:

● Agreement on the criteria that will be used to assess the attainment (or otherwise) of the objectives set is a prerequisite.
● The end of the programme is not the time to start determining how that programme is to be evaluated; it is the beginning.
● If an objective is 'informational', evaluation involves assessing how successfully information was communicated but this says nothing about changes to attitudes and behaviour.
● If an objective is 'motivational' (which is more difficult to achieve) then it is important to demonstrate that public relations activity caused the effect and 'before and after' research might be required in order to quantify the percentage of change achieved.

This starts to indicate what Smith (2005: 74) describes as 'an ordered hierarchy' of communications objectives. They grow out of 'a logical progression through three stages of persuasion: awareness, acceptance and action'. The word hierarchy is used to indicate that higher-level objectives can only be achieved once objectives below them in the hierarchy have been achieved. For example, people will not buy your new product before they have first been made aware of it and secondly are positively disposed towards it.

Don Stacks (2002: 29) is another authority who confirms that there is a 'sequencing' of public relations objectives: from informational (or awareness/knowledge), through motivational to behavioural objectives:

Informational objectives establish what knowledge should be known or is needed by the publics the campaign or program is intended for. ... Motivational objectives test whether or not the information is having an effect and whether tactical strategies are having an impact on future behaviour. Furthermore the relationship between informational and motivational objectives is interactive; that is, if motivational objectives are not being met, informational objectives can be changed to overcome identified blockages. The behavioural objectives are often what 'count', and they in the end define the success or failure of a campaign.

While instinctively we might appreciate that awareness/knowledge objectives are the most common and easiest public relations objectives to achieve, they can be relatively difficult to measure. Survey research is often required but frequently practitioners seek to infer (rather than prove) effectiveness by concentrating on measuring media coverage. However, efficient delivery of the message does not prove anything about changes in awareness and exposure to messages does not necessarily mean increased awareness.

Awareness objectives, and even motivational objectives, can be regarded as – and may on occasion overtly be – process objectives in pursuance of behavioural objectives. If so, the standard health warning associated with the substitution game applies. As Don Stacks points out above, behaviour is frequently the ultimate aim. However, it is not necessarily the province of public relations/communications. Product sales might reasonably be regarded as a marketing/sales objective but supported by public relations/communications objectives which concern themselves with raising awareness of the product and even motivating prospects to buy.

Behavioural objectives tend to be more difficult to achieve but ironically they are frequently easier than awareness and motivational objectives to measure. The former are based on clearly measurable results that can be quantified and observed directly, rather than implied (eg product sales or attendance at an event).

In short, behaviour is easier to observe than cognitive effects. However, it is more difficult to prompt. Below are examples of public relations objectives for three levels of outcomes:

- **Knowledge/awareness outcome:** within six months, to increase by 20 percentage points the number of UK homeowners who are aware that smoke detectors halve the chance of death or serious injury in a house fire.

- **Motivational/predisposition outcome:** to ensure that over the next 12 months at least 75 per cent of local residents (living in the Borough of Eastleigh) have a positive attitude towards the airport.
- **Behavioural outcome:** to increase the percentage of employees who donate to the company's chosen roster of charities through 'pay as you earn' from 13 per cent to 25 per cent by the end of the financial year.

SPECIFYING OBJECTIVES

Perhaps the most common acronym to be applied to objectives is SMART. Even here, authorities differ in their interpretation (with at least one extending it to SMARRTT):

- **Specific** because objectives should be clear, precise and give direction about what is to be achieved.
- **Measurable** because a quantified measurement statement (eg a percentage or absolute amount to be achieved) enables precise evaluation of the campaign.
- **Achievable** because the resources must be available to achieve the objectives set.
- **Realistic** because – even with adequate resources – the objectives should be capable of being met.
- **Relevant** because objectives should be appropriate for the task at hand.
- **Targeted** because all objectives should be related to the target audiences that are being addressed (and with more than one target audience there needs to be separate objectives for each).
- **Timed** because a clear time-frame indicating when objectives are expected to be achieved enables the campaign to be monitored and evaluation to be undertaken.

The public relations department of one major FMCG retailer has 'Are your objectives SMART?' plastered across the walls of its (substantial) public relations department, and no doubt the same could be said of many other high-profile organizations. But, in spite of these exhortations, it is common practice to lapse back into the comfort of high-minded, impressive-sounding but ultimately unedifying objectives. For example, Ridgway (1996: 6–7), when discussing media relations programmes, makes a good if standard start when she states:

If an objective is to be measured effectively it needs to be defined clearly. There is no point in stating that the objective is 'to increase awareness' or 'to change attitude'. This is not enough. You must include the answers to the questions 'of what' and 'by whom?' which will lead you into defining target audiences.

Unfortunately she immediately contradicts her own advice when suggesting the objectives for the example of a media relations programme for a small company producing torches:

i.   To increase awareness of the more recent products
ii. To show that these products are up to date and invaluable to the modern man or woman
iii. To give the company a more go-ahead image, while retaining the dependable aspect.

In contrast, marketing academic/consultant Paul Smith (1998: 43) provides examples of communications objectives which encompass some of the SMART principles, even if they might not all be wholly achievable through the use of public relations alone:

● To increase awareness from 35 per cent to 50 per cent within eight weeks of the campaign launch among 25–45-year-old ABC1 women.
● To position the service as the friendliest on the market within a 12-month period among 70 per cent of heavy chocolate users.
● To reposition Guinness from an old, unfashionable, older man's drink to a fashionable younger person's drink over two years among all 25–45-year-old male drinkers.
● To maintain brand x as the preferred brand (or number one brand) of photocopiers among at least 50 per cent of current UK buyers in companies with 1,000+ employees.
● To include Bulgarian wines in the repertoire of possible wine purchases among 20 per cent of ABC1 wine buyers within 12 months.
● To support the launch of a new shop by generating 50 per cent awareness in the immediate community one week before the launch.
● To announce a sale and create 70 per cent awareness one day before the sale starts.

Broom and Dozier (1990: 44) go into further detail when describing the anatomy of an objective. They discuss the nature of the intended change, the target public, the outcome to be achieved, amount of change desired and a target date for achieving the outcome:

1. *Begin with 'to' followed by a verb describing the direction to the intended outcome.* There are three possibilities: 'to increase', 'to decrease,' and 'to maintain'.
2. *Specify the outcome to be achieved.* Again three possible outcomes: knowledge, predisposition or behaviour. Each objective should spell out a single, specific outcome.
3. *State the magnitude of change or level to be maintained in measurable terms.* The watchwords are quantifiable and realistic. A combination of judgement based on experience, and benchmark data is used to set outcome levels.
4. *Set the target date for when the outcome is to be achieved.* Typically, outcomes must be achieved in order with one necessarily before another.

As with SMART objectives, this guidance is frequently an ideal to be aspired to rather than anything that can be followed to the letter. Frequently, there may be major environmental influences (recession) and/or other communications efforts (failed sales promotion) that will result in a professional public relations campaign failing to (help) achieve the effects sought.

Finally, the Institute for PR (www.instituteforpr.org) echoes Broom and Dozier's recommendations for an objective while focusing on the key aspect (but most frequently ignored) of SMART, measurability:

1. Specify a desired outcome (increase awareness, improve relationships, build preference, adopt an attitude, generate sales leads, etc.
2. Directly specify one or several target audiences.
3. Be measurable, both conceptually and practically.
4. Refer to 'ends', not 'means'. If your objectives outline a means by which to do something (often prefaced by the words 'leverage' or 'use'), you have a strategy, not an objective.
5. Include a time-frame in which the objective is to be achieved, for example by 1 July.

Note that this advice could be criticized for implying that one objective can encompass more than one public. Our advice is that PR planners should indeed set separate objectives for each public, but it may often be the case that different publics happen to be given similar (or the same) objectives.

THE NATURE OF OBJECTIVES

Nonetheless, on some occasions, the achievement of public relations objectives is simple to assess. Frequently, this is when public relations is not operating in a marketing context. A campaign to amend a piece of legislation will either succeed or fail and establishing this success or failure will be a trivial matter. Similarly, a company's share price will either reach a target level or it will not and the evidence will be in the public domain.

Frequently, meeting public relations objectives is not a simple pass/fail issue. The nature of the objectives themselves has a major effect on the type of the public relations campaign required, what needs to be achieved and therefore how the campaign is to be evaluated:

- The nature of public relations objectives varies according to virtually every conceivable criterion.
- The nature of the objective will determine the techniques required to evaluate the programme concerned.
- Behavioural objectives are more difficult to achieve than objectives which seek to achieve simpler effects.

Chris Fill (2005: 364) confirms that there are differing opinions as to what communications seeks to achieve and the resulting complexity means that many managers fail to set promotional objectives at all. When they do, 'they are inappropriate, inadequate or merely restate the marketing objectives'. Setting sales-related promotional objectives, for example, fails to accept the contribution of other elements of the marketing mix: 'Two distinct schools of thought emerge, those that advocate sales-related measures as the main factors and those that advocate communication-related measures as the main orientation.'

There are a number of problems with what Fill describes as the 'sales school', the view that: 'the only meaningful measure of the effectiveness of the promotional spend is in the sales results'. These include:

1. Sales result from a variety of influences which can be marketing related or even the wider social, political or technological environment.
2. Promotional effort may influence the eventual purchasing decision but this can take some time to become apparent.

3. Sales objectives do little to assist in the development of the communications programme, that is, they do not have a formative role.

However, there is an argument that, at least on occasions, sales-oriented objectives are appropriate. This is when direct response is sought from a targeted message through clearly identified channels. Frequently retail organizations operating in mature markets can use sales response to evaluate public relations effort. Such organizations often use loyalty cards and the customer database that they represent can be powerful in trying to model and evaluate customer response to communications efforts.

Sales, of course, are not the only goal and the aim of the communications campaign is to enhance the image or reputation of an organization or product. A number of models have been developed to aid our understanding of the processes involved. The challenge now is to link communications objectives to sales objectives in such a way that they are mutually consistent yet are able to be measured while recognizing that communications by itself frequently only contributes to the sales effect.

Often, the ultimate impact of a communications programme is behavioural, but cognitive effects are sought as part of the process of achieving the organization's ultimate objectives. For instance, UK marketing professor Peter Doyle (2002: 274) argues that public relations can be highly effective and that PR campaigns frequently address changes in awareness and attitudes but 'it is very difficult to disentangle the effects of PR from the variety of other factors affecting business performance'.

For example, adopters on new products are described by Kotler and Keller (2006: 659) as moving through five stages:

1. *Awareness:* The consumer becomes aware of the innovation but lacks information about it.
2. *Interest:* The consumer is stimulated to seek information about the innovation.
3. *Evaluation:* The consumer considers whether to try the innovation.
4. *Trial:* The consumer tries the innovation to improve his or her estimate of its value.
5. *Adoption:* The consumer decides to make full and regular use of the innovation.

Imagine that a distinctive new toothpaste is launched (perhaps it incorporates baking soda to deliver a fresh taste and feel). A consumer is made aware of the innovation through a television advertising campaign, is stimulated to seek more information, and does so through editorial coverage in a consumer magazine (achieved as part of the PR effort). Suitably impressed, the consumer makes a regular visit to the local supermarket and notices a sales promotion for the toothpaste (half-price trial offer) which prompts purchase.

The toothpaste would probably not have been purchased if the PR campaign had not got the right coverage in the right media. But sales objectives could not have been set for the PR effort as it was the sales promotion that 'closed the sale' (and the sales promotion agency would quickly claim the credit). So frequently, public relations is essential to the process but not the only factor in achieving the marketing/corporate objective. So objective setting in public relations is frequently problematical, and consequently so is evaluation of public relations activity. At its simplest, evaluation is no more than establishing whether the objectives set have been achieved.

It is tempting to throw up our hands in horror and take the despairing perspective that could be described as the 'curse of public relations': that any objective which is achievable through public relations alone is not worth measuring, and that any objective worth measuring is not achievable through PR (alone). This is, indeed, most applicable when public relations operates in a marketing support role.

The purpose of a marketing communications campaign may be to move a significant number of prospects from one set to the next. However, public relations tends to be effective at the early stages of the process (raising awareness, for example) while other elements of the communications mix will be more effective at the end of the process. Thus, it is the latter that 'close the sale' and maybe receive the plaudits, but all their efforts would have been in vain if the PR campaign hadn't successfully raised awareness of our new product so that it made it on to the short list. So, public relations does not work in isolation and its effects tend to be cognitive: towards the beginning of the adoption process rather than behavioural towards the end.

If public relations evaluation is intimately connected with objective setting, then the evaluative process must take into account the varying nature of those objectives. Frequently, those objectives whose achievement is completely within the control of public relations – and therefore relatively simple to evaluate – are at best process objectives only (eg obtaining media coverage).

The contribution of public relations to the attainment of true impact objectives may well be crucial, but nonetheless often partial and early in the process. Frequently, public relations makes the ground more fertile for complementary communications activities. Under these circumstances, disentangling the public relations contribution is complex and a pure 'evaluation by objectives' approach becomes inappropriate.

PROCESS OBJECTIVES

As well as a more realistic approach to objective setting, there is a useful concept to which we have alluded but not yet explained that can help guide us through the objective-setting maze. This is the concept of process objectives: on the surface an oxymoron, as an objective is an end-point and process revolves around reaching that end-point.

US writers Crabble and Vibbert (1986: 391–92) articulate a general theme when listing Evaluation by Objectives as the last of six evaluation 'standards'; they describe it as a system based on management by objectives. This links the discussion back to both the pivotal role that objectives play in public relations evaluation, and the concept of MBO.

> When public relations is managed by a system of objectives, the measurement of those efforts is incorporated into the system. There are two key aspects to management by objectives in public relations: objectives are derived mutually, between public relations manager and supervisor; and these objectives set a series of intermediate goals that define what should be done and when. When public relations projects, programs, or problems are managed 'by objectives', those objectives are the result of consultation between public relations manager and supervisor.

This introduces the concept of process objectives (or targets): a very useful concept for public relations where the process is frequently complex and the ultimate impact is a result of range of influences of which public relations is one, but only one. Process objectives are best illustrated by our fictitious traveller from Newtown to Smithsville. Having left Newtown and made substantial progress towards Smithsville, the traveller comes across a milestone indicating that Smithsville is now only 10 miles away. This milestone is like a process objective: it does not guarantee that the traveller will ever reach Smithsville. However, it does indicate that progress is being made in the right direction and that it is likely that by keeping on the chosen road, the desired destination will be reached (objective achieved).

So, it is possible that a combination of broad goals supported by a number of process objectives can approximate to ideal objectives. This is when the complexity of the communications process means that truly SMART public relations objectives cannot be set. Frequently, in public relations, SMART objectives are an ideal to be aimed for rather than anything that can be fully achieved.

However, there is a concomitant danger: too much emphasis on the process can prompt a mindset where communications activity is undertaken for its own sake rather than to achieve identifiable effects.

So, process objectives run the risk of the substitution game. But if this risk is appreciated, they can become useful elements (but no more) of the evaluator's toolbox as they relate to milestones in the communication effort (but not the destination), to the reaching of which public relations has made a major contribution, even if other elements of the programme help us continue on to our final destination.

To reiterate this point, this discussion of objectives finishes with the case for the prosecution with regard to process objectives from the Institute for PR (www.instituteforpr.org):

> In general, process goals, such as 'get publicity', 'launch a product' or 'create a brochure', make poor objectives. They do not relate to broader organizational goals and are not measurable in any specific, concrete, or truly meaningful manner. ('I did it'/'I didn't do it' does not count as measurable.) A useful way to replace these 'process' objectives is to ask yourself, 'what is the purpose of (insert objective).' The answer to this question is likely to move you closer to a clear, actionable objective.

The role of objective setting is put into context with an evaluation questionnaire for a 'sales' seminar/workshop. The objectives associated with the questionnaire (see Table 8.1) are eminently SMART and range from pure process (event administration) through to genuine impact (sales lead generation).

Table 8.1 *Objectives of XYZ sales seminar*

At least 100 attendees, of whom 80% are decision makers/key influencers.

80% of delegates felt their objectives in attending were met.

80% of delegates would attend another XYZ event.

The average overall rating of the event is over 3.5.

The average rating for how well the event is organized is over 3.5.

The average rating for the usefulness of information from interactive voting is over 3.5.

The average rating for speakers will be over 3.5.

80% of delegates who don't already receive them will request Loaded and Currant Bun.

80% of delegates wish to be invited to future XYZ events.

At least five qualified sales meetings arise directly from the event.

80% of journalists who attend use material in some form within six months of the event.

Interview

Andrew Wallis sees the impetus for evaluation coming from the public relations function itself rather than from other parts of the organization. 'Compared to other people who may be asked to justify their activities, we try and set our own benchmarks or to look at how we can improve ourselves as a department.' One explanation is that evaluation is seen as costly and therefore is not a priority within the organization.

Indeed, Wallis sees evaluation (or at least process evaluation in the form of media evaluation) as the 'currency' that his department offers other areas within the organization. This currency is the profile of the organization generated by reactive and proactive media relations activity, complemented by qualitative feedback from influential people within the organization. This feedback is obtained from other influential people within the organization, people Wallis describes as 'marketing mavens' because other people seek their advice. 'I am seeking to understand not only the effect that the media in particular might be having in terms of reputation and therefore staff morale and other soft measures, but also gauging what the workforce thinks of your own performance in either promoting or defending the organization.'

Focusing back on to professional practice, Wallis stresses the integral role that evaluation plays in any form of planning or strategy. He says that the public relations process is not a linear one, but operates to a more advanced cyclical model. 'Consequently, there is some form of control, review and – indeed – learning. In a learning organization, that is one of the key ways you can contribute in a systems way, learning from what you do and improving it individually and on behalf of the organization as a whole.'

Keeping the learning theme, Wallis's advice to the junior practitioner is to take copies of anything they do that succeeds. 'Look at things that have worked and keep in your mind what has brought success because that is what you will want to replicate in the future. Conversely, you will want to learn from what has caused you, or your organization, grief and learn how to deal with that. Then there is learning from others. Not only collecting your own work, but identifying how others do things. And then there is the more systematic, research-based, approach of looking at case studies.'

Wallis devotes effort to monitoring broadcast and media coverage but appreciates it examines output with no real link to outcome. Again this comes down to organizational constraints and cost. 'Any systematic approach is going to cost so it goes on the back burner. Performing best practice: doing an audit, seeing how things are done, and improving on it normally involves cost. And in my experience, the reaction is why don't we spend the money doing some PR rather than learning. Ironically, the organization tends to put pressure on not improving.'

Wallis regards process evaluation as tactical: 'those things that you can change here and now, switching effort between one activity that isn't working and another that is'. While impact evaluation is difficult to disaggregate and expensive, process evaluation related to a specific campaign is a very 'here and now' activity. Cost is not such an issue with the latter, if only because its immediacy tends to categorize it as a campaign expense rather than an evaluation cost.

While Wallis cautions against 'expensive media evaluation dressed up as PR evaluation', he is strongly in favour of employing people with an understanding of research in public relations. 'Not everybody has to be an expert, but there is certainly a place for somebody with an understanding and appreciation of research and scientific principles.'

Andrew Wallis is former head of press and PR for Thomas Cook UK & Ireland.

QUESTIONNAIRE RESPONSES

Evaluation questionnaire for industry leaders

Q: What other tips and advice on evaluation do you have for practitioners?

You have to start doing it, do it and do it again. As you become accustomed to doing it, it becomes a part of your everyday work. Of course, education and training help. **Dejan Verčič**

It is worth doing and as you see the benefits of the results you will be encouraged to do more. **Alison Clarke**

Take the time to do it. Just because it is a process and can be tedious, don't undervalue its effect and how it ensures credibility and understanding of the work we do. It adds to our professionalism and our reputation as an industry. **Fran Hagon**

Don't use a sledgehammer to crack a nut – focus on what is important to the client and only evaluate in this area. Make the output of the evaluation process something that can also fuel the communications, marketing or sales process – rather than be a sterile report that will never be read by anyone in a position of real power. **Crispin Manners**

Package it up for clients as part of the programme – not a bolt-on. It has to be integral. **Loretta Tobin**

Textbook prescriptions, really: common sense in evaluation methods; real measures that are tangible; quantitative evaluation methods (media count: mentions, website hits, publicity, word counts, area in sq m, etc); qualitative (positive and negative opportunities to see [OTS], reading pattern studies, advertising value equivalents, etc); PR events are evaluated on the basis of attendance figures, the calibre of people and their level of participation (if it's interactive), general level of interest and feedback. **Ray Mawerera**

Step up and get at least a little bit mathematical. Use numbers in your conversation. Don't be embarrassed by a lack of information – scavenge whatever is available and use it to really counsel your clients. You can create benchmarks over time, over previous campaigns by others or for other clients, by researching on the internet for guidelines and so on. **Annabelle Warren**

Set targets at the beginning of the campaign in order that the clients' expectations are realistic and agree key messages before the campaign begins to allow you to evaluate quality of coverage as opposed to simply quantity. There's no point in setting goals and messages retrospectively. **Laurna O'Donnell**

Do it! Our industry will never lose its fluff and bubble image if we don't, it needs to be real and it needs to be hard core. But be creative and don't be afraid to take responsibility for your actions – it doesn't have to be expensive or time-consuming. **Clara Zawawi**

Always present it to the client as a valuable investment, but ensure skilled, ethical and seasoned research practitioners are engaged. **Tom O'Donoghue**

Get it into the DNA. You can't separate it from the full analysis/planning/execution/measurement cycle. Make sure that every campaign has measurement built into it: don't let it go ahead without this, even if the degree of measurement is limited. **Mike Copland**

Evaluation of individual campaigns is important but the wider question must always be: Where are we overall? What do the public think about us? And that comes from attitude research. **Richard Offer**

Evaluation does not have to be carried out at the end of a campaign, it can be actively carried out through the planning and organizing stages of a campaign, during the campaign and post the campaign. On completion of a public relations campaign evaluation, the information obtained should be used when implementing other campaigns. It is vital to learn from experiences. **Adam Connolly**

9

Relationship and crisis communication measurement

Although the term 'public relations' has been in place for many decades and definitions of PR such as 'the management of relationships between an organization and its publics (stakeholders)' have been widely used, it has been in the past decade that the theorization of public relations as relationship management has made progress. In defining relationship management as 'the development, maintenance, growth and nurturing of mutually-beneficial relationships between organizations and their significant publics' Thomlinson (2000) has made a direct link with the Grunig and Hunt definition of public relations (see Chapter 1).

MEASURING RELATIONSHIPS

The relationship management paradigm of public relations helps move it out of the media relations and publicity model and shows that:

public relations is captured as the value of relationship quality between organizations and their publics and the supportive behaviours from stakeholders that are more likely to result when organizations and publics have a positive relationship (Jo, Hon and Brunner, 2004).

Bruning and Ledingham (1999: 158), who have been proponents of relationship management as the public relations model, also commented that there has been a shift 'away from the manipulation of public opinion and towards a focus on building, nurturing and maintaining organization-public relationships'. This revised conceptualization of public relations has appeal to practitioners and scholars because it changes the purpose of public relations from a persuasional practice to one that creates mutual benefit. It also gives the public relations industry a new focus, 'which knowing that it deals with wide-ranging objectives and methods has struggled with ways to define itself and its value' (Hibbert and Simmons, 2006: 3).

Lindenmann links this emerging consensus with the standard view of PR activities producing outputs, out-takes and outcomes. But he drops out-takes and adds 'measuring the success or failure of long-term *relationships*' (Lindenmann, in Hon and Grunig, 1999: 5):

> As important as it can be for an organization to measure PR *outputs* and *outcomes*, it is even more important for an organization to measure *relationships*. This is because for most organizations measuring outputs and outcomes can only give information about the effectiveness of a *particular or specific PR program or event that has been undertaken*. In order to answer the much broader question – '*How can PR practitioners begin to pinpoint and document for senior management the overall value of public relations to the organization as a whole?*' – different tools and techniques are required.

Hon and Grunig (1999) reviewed research that shows PR contributes value to an organization when its communications programmes result in quality long-term relationships with strategic publics (stakeholders). They identified two types of relationships, with four characteristics.

The relationships are, first, *exchange*, where one party gives benefit to the other only because the other has provided benefits in the past or is expected to do so in the future. A party that receives benefit incurs an obligation or debt to return the favour. Exchange is the essence of marketing relationships between organizations and customers. But, Hon and Grunig argue, it's not enough for a public, which expects organizations to do things for the community without expecting immediate benefit.

The second type of relationships are *communal*, where parties are willing to provide benefits to the other because they are concerned for the welfare of the other – even when they believe they might not get anything in return. 'The role of public relations is to convince management that it also needs communal relationships with publics such as employees, the community, government, media and stockholders – as well as exchange relationships with customers.' Communal relationships are important if organizations are to be socially responsible and to add value to society as well as client organizations.

The quality of relationships

> John Ledingham has proposed relationship management as a general theory of public relations (Ledingham, 2003). There are three planks to the theory (Bruning, Castle and Schrepfer, 2004: 442–44):
>
> 1. There is a linkage between organizational-public relationships and results such as enhanced satisfaction and improved loyalty.
> 2. Organizations and publics should set common interests and goals.
> 3. Public relations practitioners take the lead in preparing strategies and actions that help organizations and publics to 'enhance mutual understanding and benefit'.

Hon and Grunig (1999) also nominate four outcomes that are indicators of successful interpersonal relationships but can be applied with equal success to relationships between organizations and their publics. Importance declines as we go down the list:

1. *Control mutuality:* the degree to which the parties in a relationship are satisfied with the amount of control they have over a relationship. Some degree of power imbalance is natural, but the most stable, positive relationships exist where the parties have some degree of control. It doesn't have to be exactly 50:50. The ceding of some control is based on trust.
2. *Trust:* the level of confidence that both parties have in each other and their willingness to open themselves to the other party. Three factors are important:
   - integrity: an organization is seen as just and fair;
   - dependability: it will do what it says it will do;
   - competence: has the ability to do what it says it will do.

3. *Commitment:* the extent to which both parties believe and feel the relationship is worth spending energy to maintain and promote.
4. *Satisfaction:* the extent to which both parties feel favourably about each other because positive expectations about the relationship are reinforced. Each party believes the other is engaged in positive steps to maintain the relationship.

The suggestion is that relationships are evaluated through a questionnaire that asks a series of agree/disagree statements (using a 1–9 scale). A complete list of the relevant statements is given at www.instituteforpr.org, but Table 9.1 gives Lindenmann's shortened list of statements used to measure relationships outcomes.

Grunig later wrote a paper on qualitative methods for assessing relationships between organizations and publics (Grunig, 2002) that use non-statistical methods such as interviews and focus groups to evaluate the relationship. It includes a guide to questions about the six dimensions of the relationships and the analysis of the information gathered. There have been two published studies that have used Hon and Grunig's (1999) or Grunig's (2002) qualitative model.

The first measured the relationship between a university and its students (Jo, Hon and Brunner, 2004: 24). Some 687 students took part in two surveys, which used a seven-point measurement scale to investigate the factors in the relationship. The researchers found that the two groups of students 'perceived the six factor measures as a valid and reliable instrument for measuring their relationship with the university'.

Hibbert and Simmons (2006: 7–8) used Grunig's qualitative approach in a quite different situation to measure the relationship between Australian political and defence media and the public affairs staff from the Australian Defence Force in the context of the 2003 Iraq War. They found it 'provided a useful guide to the research and analysis at the points of planning, exploring, labelling and reporting the relationship' but that there were limits to its facility in reporting the width of relationships because of its bilateral focus on what occurs between an organization and a public, when the real influences on the situation are more complex. They also found that some of the language had to be modified for an Australian situation and that, in its standard form, it is awkward in use.

A critic of Grunig's approach is the US consultant Angela Sinickas, who recommends that communicators should avoid using the language of communal relationships. They are best to proffer relationship measurement to their executives in terms of an 'exchange scenario, even if the reciprocation is far down the road. In my experience, neither executives nor members of society regularly make

Table 9.1   *Measuring relationship outcomes*

Control mutuality
1. This organization and people like me are attentive to what each other say.
2. This organization believes the opinions of people like me are legitimate.
3. In dealing with people like me, this organization has a tendency to throw its weight around. (Reversed)
4. This organization really listens to what people like me have to say.
5. The management of this organization gives people like me enough say in the decision-making process.

Trust
1. This organization treats people like me fairly and justly.
2. Whenever this organization makes an important decision, I know it will be concerned about people like me.
3. This organization can be relied on to keep its promises.
4. I believe that this organization takes the opinions of people like me into account when making decisions.
5. I feel very confident about this organization's skills.
6. This organization has the ability to accomplish what it says it will do.

Commitment
1. I feel that this organization is trying to maintain a long-term commitment to people like me.
2. I can see that this organization wants to maintain a relationship with people like me.
3. There is a long-lasting bond between this organization and people like me.
4. Compared to other organizations, I value my relationship with this organization more.
5. I would rather work together with this organization than not.

Satisfaction
1. I am happy with this organization.
2. Both the organization and people like me benefit from the relationship.
3. Most people like me are happy in their interactions with this organization.
4. Generally speaking, I am pleased with the relationship this organization has established with people like me.
5. Most people enjoy dealing with this organization.

Exchange relationships
1. Whenever this organization gives or offers something to people like me, it generally expects something in return.
2. Even though people like me have had a relationship with this organization for a long time, it still expects something in return whenever it offers us a favour.
3. This organization will compromise with people like me when it knows that it will gain something.
4. This organization takes care of people who are likely to reward it.

Communal relationships
1. This organization does not especially enjoy giving others aid. (Reversed)
2. This organization is very concerned about the welfare of people like me.
3. I feel that this organization takes advantage of people who are vulnerable. (Reversed)
4. I think that this organization succeeds by stepping on other people. (Reversed)
5. This organization helps people like me without expecting anything in return.

---

decisions based on societal good at great expense to the self' (Sinickas, 2004: 12). She also opines that using the language of communal relationships puts PR into the category of 'nice to do' rather than 'business critical'.

This discussion of public relations being about managing relationships has been integrated with the emergence of the three levels of PR measurement (output, out-take and outcome) in a slightly more logical manner by British consultant James Thellusson (2003: 1). He retains out-takes (as well as outputs and outcomes) and simply adds a fourth 'O' to address the evaluation of relationship building:

> But while the PR industry as a whole is still exploring the implications of these existing measurement frameworks, an elusive fourth question is beckoning. What really matters is: 'what effects did those actions create – on other stakeholders in the business network, on productivity of relationships, and therefore, ultimately, on total shareholder return?' This is the ROI question for PR, as it is for other marketing disciplines. I will refer to it, in the context of multi-stakeholder communications, as the 'outflow' question.

Thellusson goes on to list the four 'Os' in the context of PR measurement:

1. *Output:* volumes and quality of messages that reach defined audiences.
2. *Out-take:* what the audience understands from PR messages.
3. *Outcome:* the achievement of specific objectives.
4. *Outflow:* the establishment of a measurable relationship with stakeholders.

He also links crisis communication with relationship being 'the outcome', arguing that the value of the 'relationship asset' created by PR is a latent one that may not prove its worth until a crisis occurs which threatens the goodwill established by previous public relations activity. Thellusson also admits that evaluating this sort of PR is 'a significant undertaking':

> It requires an organization or brand to develop a relationship model of its unique web of stakeholders, which diagnoses shifts in stakeholders' level of empathy and trust, and correlates them to behaviour changes within the business web.... Over time, accumulated evidence will prove which links are causal and which are mere serendipity. (Thellusson, 2003: 1)

In conclusion, the measurement of relationships is a relatively new area of public relations evaluation, although it has been widely used in other disciplines, especially psychology and counselling for interpersonal relationships. More papers are coming forward all the time and should give a wider range of methods and case studies.

EVALUATING COMMUNICATIONS EFFECTIVENESS IN A CRISIS

The 11 September attacks on New York and Washington brought the effectiveness of crisis communication into sharp focus. Many organizations whose headquarters were obliterated or severely affected by the attacks in lower Manhattan completely lost their ability to communicate externally. They lost key staff, crisis plan files, internet sites and all telecommunication capacity, as well as the buildings from which they operated.

This terrible example of a terrorist attack has had two outcomes. Corporations are now organizing crisis plans on a dispersed model that is not knocked out by a single act, and they are placing more emphasis on monitoring and measuring their performance in crisis situations.

The likelihood of another 11 September may be considered to be on the outer edge of probability, but there are many other crisis situations that can be considered. These range from an incident at a factory that results in injury or environmental damage, through product recall, to hostile takeover, to a major conflict with government or legal processes. This list can be developed in numerous directions of threat, which should be considered by corporate communications managers.

Grunig comments that: 'communication with publics before decisions are made is most effective in resolving issues and crises because it helps managers to make decisions that are less likely to produce consequences that publics make into issues and crises' (Grunig, 2001, cited in Paine, 2002a). This could be described colloquially as planning and consultation help avoid the 'law of unintended consequences'.

Grunig proposes four principles of crisis communication:

1. *The Relationship Principle:* An organization can withstand crises if it has well-established relationships with key stakeholders.
2. *The Accountability Principle:* An organization should accept responsibility for a crisis even if it was not its fault. (For example, recall a product that has been threatened or tainted by an extortionist.)
3. *The Disclosure Principle:* In a crisis, an organization should disclose all it knows about a crisis or problem. If it does not have immediate answers, it must promise full disclosure once it has additional information.
4. *The Symmetrical Communication Principle:* In a crisis, the public interest should be considered as equal in importance to the organization's interest.

To measure its performance in a potential crisis and against these principles, the organization needs to prepare itself by monitoring current issues in the media being discussed by employees, customers and stakeholders. The media scanning should also include internet chat rooms and news rooms as well as conventional print and broadcast media.

Using a variation of the Lindenmann's Three-Step Yardstick (see Chapter 5), Paine (2002a) proposes three elements to measuring effectiveness:

1. *Measuring outputs and process effectiveness:* Constant monitoring of media to determine if key messages are being communicated and to whom.
2. *Measuring impact:* Determining if messages are having the desired effect, if they are being believed and whether they are swaying public opinion.
3. *Measuring outcomes:* Has the crisis impacted on reputation, sales, employee turnover, shareholder confidence and other factors?

'Which type of measurement you select should be driven by your internal needs for better decision making tools' is the pragmatic advice given by Paine (2002a: 2). In an analysis of situations that includes organizations such as IBM, Nabisco, HCA Healthcare, Levi Strauss and Kodak, Paine comments that 'a well managed crisis gets all the bad news over with up front by aggressively dealing with a problem. A poorly handled one can drag on for months'. By 'aggressively dealing', Paine means that the response is prompt, accurate and clearly communicated.

Using case studies cited by Paine, it is possible to apply three of Grunig's four principles of crisis communication with relative ease; see the box below. It is more difficult, and probably inherently impossible, to apply the Symmetrical Communication principle to a crisis.

---

1. *Relationship* – Levi Strauss, famed for its branded jeans, hit a downturn and chose to close 11 plants and lay off nearly 6,400 workers. Paine says that the jeans-maker took a 'novel approach, simultaneously announcing grants to all the communities affected by the layoffs. As a result, media coverage spiked in the first week and steadily decreased after that'. Putting aside the description of best practice in stakeholder relations – simultaneous communication – as 'a novel approach', Levi Strauss's strategy minimized media comment in less than a month and allowed it to continue its negotiations and repair community relationships with less pressure than if it had taken a 'drip, drip' communication approach.
2. *Accountability* – The Odwalla natural juice organization was found to have sold batches of apple juice that caused illness and, in one tragic outcome, led to the death of a child. Paine argues that by 'owning' the problem and not blaming others, Odwalla was able to contain the crisis to a three-week period and avoid lawsuits. Media analysis showed an early peak in coverage that tapered away to almost nothing over 21 days.

3. *Disclosure* – The reverse case to Levi Strauss came when Kodak was stricken by leaks over future strategy and suffered a prolonged crisis played out in the media, as well as among other stakeholders. Paine (2002a: v5) says Kodak 'suffered a series of leaks about potential layoffs, eventually announced layoffs, and then had to announce even more layoffs because the cuts hadn't been deep enough'. Again, she says, 'the result was many more weeks of bad news. It could be argued that if Kodak had followed Levi Strauss's open and fulsome announcement, it could have built relationships that helped it manage the change'. However, the outcomes of its strategy were tracked by media analysis as three spikes of negative coverage over a three-month period.

4. *Symmetrical Communication* – This is a new usage by Grunig of his most debated descriptor of public relations practice. In essence, it is the sum total of relationships, accountability and disclosure set into a public safety scenario. The most famous of all product recalls, Johnson & Johnson's prompt and complete removal of the Tylenol branded analgesic from sale after an extortioner tainted the product, is the closest example. But this is not the same as Grunig's normal description of symmetrical communication. In the Tylenol case, J&J's action was prompted by an ethical and commercial decision to protect consumers and save the reputation of the company and the product. The fact that Tylenol remains a respected and popular product in North America is a tribute to that decision. It is not, however, an equally balanced, continuous dialogue between an organization and its publics as enunciated by Grunig for two decades or more.

After the crisis is over, evaluation can assist measurement of position and deliver lessons for future strategy and crisis communication. Paine suggests that questions to consider could include: 'Did consumers change their behaviour, did employees leave at a higher than normal rate? Did the stock drop?' To which could be added qualitative and quantitative judgements on the attitudes of regulators, the media, commercial partners, and employees and their families.

Crisis communication is a major subject by itself but media analysis and other measurements of attitude and perception play an important role in monitoring the evolution and maturity of a crisis. They advise strategies to manage and respond. However, the principles espoused by Grunig of relationship, accountability and disclosure are the bedrock on which those strategies should be based.

Interview

Pascoe Sawyers feels that the importance of evaluation is beginning to be recognized in local government. 'I get the impression that communications is much higher up the agenda in local government that it was five years ago. As a consequence, evaluation is being taken much more seriously.'

There are two main reasons. First, tools are now available which were not around a few years ago. Second, there is much more sharing of best practice. 'People are looking at what colleagues are doing. They are not developing communications strategies in isolation: they are looking at what others are doing, seeing evaluation in there, and so they are more inclined to think about it', adds Sawyers. He doesn't claim that the evaluation being undertaken is as robust or as effective as it could be, but argues that the importance of evaluation is receiving increasing recognition.

Sawyers feels that the different environment in which local government operates compared to the private sector can encourage a less serious approach to evaluation. In a commercial environment, short-term financial imperatives prompt evaluation, making it almost an automatic part of the communications process. Local government is concerned with political and democratic issues, 'arguably more important, but their long-term perspective means that some may think there may not be immediate pressures to examine communications effectiveness'.

Nonetheless, Sawyers reflects many of the frustrations experienced in public relations as a whole. 'It amazes me how often I see a strategy that doesn't really get to grips with evaluation, or throws it in at the end as an added extra – something we will do if we can afford it – rather than regarding it as an integral part of the whole process', he adds. Sawyers questions whether there is any point embarking on major communications projects if there is no intention to evaluate them.

Even when evaluation is undertaken, Sawyers calls for a more sophisticated approach. He is concerned that there is a tendency to look at evaluation in terms of outputs as opposed to outcomes. 'So my programme says that I must issue 50 press releases a year, but what happened to those releases? How many got used? How many releases with positive messages ended up as negative stories?' The solution could, at least in part, lie in educating senior people to understand not just the business case for effective communications (relatively easy to do) but also the more difficult task of appreciating what the features of an effective public relations campaign are. 'They get a communications strategy presented to them and probably give it the thumbs up because they respect the professionals who have produced it. As they may not understand what they should be looking for, you can get problems in distinguishing between outcomes and outputs. It's one thing to get councillors to commit; it's another to get them to actually understand what they should be looking for.'

Another aspect of evaluation which Sawyers sees as benefiting from a more sophisticated approach is benchmarking. 'It really irritates me that people don't make the connection between audit and evaluation. People develop communication strategies but don't think that if they are going to evaluate it, that's going to be difficult – if not impossible – to do in a vacuum. They need to undertake an audit in order to understand their starting point. It's really important, in terms of being able to evaluate effectively, that the audit process takes place. That's where it all starts and that's what helps make sense of the evaluation, appreciate the progress that's been made.'

Given the increasing pressure in the private sector for organizations to seek 'permission to operate' from the communities they operate in, one driver of evaluation in local government could have increasing applicability across the board. Sawyers says that consultation is a key aspect of local communications activity, and one where evaluation has a crucial role. He concludes 'Evaluation requires two-way communication, which is what consultation is all about. Robust evaluation in your initial strategy ensures you do not fall into the trap of asking the questions, going through the process, but not responding in any meaningful way.'

Pascoe Sawyers is former principal consultant at the UK government's IDeA (Improvement and Development Agency).

10

The challenge of the online environment

The focus with online public relations in general, and online evaluation in particular, is monitoring: monitoring the online conversation, researching trends, identifying issues and nascent crises, seeing who your promoters or detractors are, and benchmarking. It is also much more push-oriented than offline PR; so, for example, press releases are optimized (for search engines). Almost every online technique has an offline equivalent (and, by definition, the reverse): for example, podcasts relate to VNRs. Consequently, the skills required for offline PR are transferable to the online environment.

PUBLIC RELATIONS ONLINE

A key public relations skill is developing relationships with people (stakeholders and journalists, for example). Online PR is all about persuading people to comment positively about the organization or client that is being represented. The round table is a typical PR tactic offline; now it can be replicated online without the overhead of arranging for a group of people to meet at one geographical location.

However, it is in the nature of the internet that some of the control is lost (so the need for more, and early, intelligence in what is going on), because the audience can bypass the journalist/media and transmit messages direct. So listening (monitoring) becomes even more important. We are used to having influence over the key messages that are being transmitted about us. Now that influence and authority are dissipating, so we need a much more flexible PR strategy with multiple objectives and multiple tactics. Authority online is not popularity, but a function of who links to you in the context of a particular topic. If you are influential, the people who reference you are also influential. They check on who is referencing whom and why on particular issues or brands.

Currently, inspiring action is probably the most important aspect of online PR: driving people to websites. So, at present at least, online PR is being led by people who have some technical knowledge of the internet environment. As online public relations is frequently about influencing behaviour, there is the potential for evaluating online PR to be relatively simple. We have commented before that changing behaviour is relatively difficult to achieve but relatively easy to evaluate (if only because it can be observed directly). There is the potential therefore to demonstrate, for example, that a piece of content placed online has driven traffic to a website and even that the result was a specified number of sales. (See the case study in Chapter 7 on Southwest Airlines.)

It is also the case that online and offline are threaded through each other. The vast majority of journalists search online to support and develop stories. Similarly, news stories leap from one environment to the other. Even to be in the offline conversation, you have to be online.

The key to offline content is to make it accessible in a place your consumers want to look at and which they can find easily. Very few people using a search engine such as Google go beyond the third page of search results. The first batch of organic listings are key and are known as 'above the fold' (not having to scroll down), to use an offline metaphor. If your organization is not there you will not be noticed, and if there are negative messages about you above the fold, then that is what people will understand about you.

Online PR is about engaging people in conversation so they become advocates for your organization. The more independent comment there is about an organization online, the more people will trust you. But this is a double-edged sword as it does not take much for advocates to become detractors very quickly. Unlike offline, online material actually has surprising longevity; a good (or bad) review, can be accessed – and maybe acted upon – years later.

If your target for online PR is to drive traffic to a website, it is possible to track what is going on by using web analytics tools. You can identify where that traffic came from. For example, if a press release (with embedded links) goes on to a wire site, it is possible to prove a direct link between an enquiry generated from that site and the press release issued. You can track the customer journey.

If you are running a blog, you can also look at the frequency of comments back to see how many people are engaging with you. This can be an effective indicator of objectives such as generating awareness or changing attitudes. If lots of people are talking to you, something must be happening. One area where online evaluation is waiting to catch up with offline evaluation is historical data. There is a lack of historical data online, simply because it is relatively new, and it is historical data which is the raw material of econometric analysis (see Chapter 11).

Until recently, the internet has not had as dramatic an impact on pubic relations in general, and PR evaluation in particular, as we might think. The focus has been on the use of the web as a distribution channel; the biggest impact for most people has been e-mail. The technology and devices used to access this communication channel have also changed. The first portable computer, the Osborne, was known (not by the brand owner) as a 'luggable', weighing in at 30 kilograms – and housed in a suitcase because that seemed appropriate. Today it is a museum piece, which would engender a wry smile. But, connectivity aside, it is the progenitor of the modern laptop.

The essential relationship between organizations, their press agents (public relations practitioners), the media, and the deferential public has remained much the same until now, but things really are starting to change. We may have paid lip-service to dialogue and two-way communication while continuing to lobby journalists to report our agenda to benefit from the credibility associated with third-party endorsement; credibility associated with a passive public's acceptance that you 'believe what you read in the papers'. In the PR world, media distribution lists got a bit longer and more complicated, but the humble press release, and pitching stories to key journalists by phone, changed little.

Increasingly, messages will no longer follow the straight, one-way path from the organization to intended audience, frequently mediated by journalists. The one-to-one communication afforded by the net, compounded by the death of deference ameliorating the authority of the conventional media, means that people are turning to their own kind as sources of unbiased, authoritative information. They are responding by pumping out messages and information to quench the thirst for unmediated information. The one-to-all model is being replaced by an all-to-all model. Enabled by digital technology, the 'person in the street' is beginning to be a creator of content (not simply a target for it) and as they surf the web more and more, they are encountering content that is not created by the big media companies, but created by people like them. The blog is perhaps the prime example.

The rise of the blog

Personal web pages enable individuals to publish virtually what they like to an unsuspecting world. But their creation requires skills that are beyond the average web user. In contrast, a blog can be created by anybody who can type (with two fingers or more).

Much of the focus for the public relations evaluator has been on message delivery. One of the key trends over the past 25 years has been an increasing focus not just on the volume of coverage but its quality. The prime indicator of that quality has been the presence or absence, strength or weakness, positive or negative reporting of key corporate messages. That was easy enough when messages took a straight (and signposted) path to their intended audience. Now, the message can be changed, developed, added to, hijacked and contradicted along the way. This provides peculiar challenges to communicators; challenges that can be met by the technology that begat them.

The challenge for the public relations evaluator in the 21st century is this. Formative monitoring of who is saying what about you will become essential to enable the rapid intervention and rebuttal necessary to influence the online conversation before it is set in stone. The digital environment has a ghostly permanence, only rivalled in the traditional world by the seminal events of the past such as the famous gaffe committed by Gerald Ratner back in 1991, when he admitted selling 'crap' in his High Street shops; pale examples reported offline are referred to as 'doing a Ratner', but quickly forgotten.

The Kryptonite example reported later in this chapter shows how control online is lost forever without rapid and early intervention. It also underlines the point that online and offline impinge on each other and need integrated, not separate handling. The web is a giant, searchable archive.

When dealing with the traditional media, there was a feeling that you were dealing with a finite quantity. With the pervasive nature of online coverage and in particular blogging, anyone can now publish electronically a newspaper, or run their own radio or TV station. A new skill will be understanding which of these are significant to stakeholders.

The credibility of offline media is well documented; many would argue that (in its media relations guise) the supposed 'killer benefit' of PR is the credibility afforded by the media's third-party endorsement.

As a more recent phenomenon, the credibility of online media is less well established, although common sense indicates that it is likely to be high as an extension of powerful face-to-face, word-of-mouth communications.

Johnson and Kaye (2004: 624) suggest that, initially, the credibility of the internet (compared with traditional media) should have been questioned. The ability of anybody to publish their views, lack of editorial oversight, circulation of rumours and misinformation are all given as reasons: 'However, the public, particularly internet users, did not share those fears.' Similar arguments are advanced to question the credibility of blogs: created by anyone, no professional standards, lack of objectivity, no editing and the use of pseudonyms. In response, there are claims that other bloggers peer review blogs, the independence of blogs lends credibility, and blogs frequently cover stories ignored by traditional media.

Johnson and Kaye (2004: 625) point out that while the blogging community is critical of traditional media, they do not ignore them: 'Because most bloggers are not independent news gathers, they must rely heavily on the web for their content, and much of that content comes from traditional media.' They also note that many bloggers give their sites credibility by providing links to traditional media. In parallel, many journalists, although dismissive of bloggers, rely on blogs for input to their own stories as well as being bloggers themselves.

Dearstyne (2005) summarizes why blogs have become so popular. They:

- are relatively easy to set up and maintain;
- enhance information sharing by capturing fresh insights and opinions;
- are unedited and unfiltered, so they appeal to those suspicious of corporate announcements and the mainstream media;
- may include links to other blogs and sites, so acting as a conduit to further information;
- have the capacity to form 'blogswarms' by sharing and spreading information quickly.

Dearstyne (2005: 40–41) then places blogs into five categories:

1. **Individuals' personal news and views.** These are personal journals set up by individuals to share news about their lives, families and personal developments, and for personal expression.

2. **News/commentary/journalism.** These blogs report the news, provide interpretation and commentary, and in some cases confront and upstage mainstream media.
3. **Advertising/promotion/marketing/customer service.** Some blogs promote products and services or communicate with potential customers.
4. **Business/professional issue commentary and insight.** The most influential blogs in the business world fall into this category. They may include commentary by CEOs, views of professionals and other employees, trial balloon ideas, results of research projects, and interpretations of the events and trends in the field.
5. **Internal information sharing/knowledge management applications.** These applications are new, and descriptions are just beginning to make their way into the literature. CEOs are using blogs to share perspectives and policies with employees. Project managers use them to direct and coordinate complex projects, eg giving direction but at the same time inviting updates and commentary. Technical experts use them as convenient records of engineering or design projects.

While traditional offline media will remain influential for the foreseeable future, the rise of online media in the digital environment is obvious for all to see. As with many sectors, those working in public relations will need to get to grips with this 'mixed economy'. We need to be placing our messages and holding our conversations where those we want to communicate with are spending their time. Increasingly, this is online.

Most of people's time on the internet is spent communicating: it was the e-mail that made the web an integral part of the modern experience. Now, e-mail has been joined by blogs, podcasts, RSS feeds and even viral marketing campaigns. Layered on this is the PR-friendly concept of participative dialogue with publics. As people have become more comfortable with new technology, there is a steady move towards consumer-created content.

In November 2006, blog search engine Technorati reported the following highlights in its quarterly review of blog usage statistics and trends, 'State of the Blogosphere':

● More than 57 million blogs are being tracked, of which 55 per cent are active (updated at least once in the past three months).

- As of October 2006, about 100,000 new weblogs were being created each day.
- About 1.3 million postings were made per day.
- Integration of blogs and traditional media sites on the web continues: the top 100 sites are still made up of traditional media sites like the *New York Times* and CNN.
- By the time you reach the top 5,000, blogs have essentially taken over with very few well-funded mainstream sites listed.

Technorati establishes the authority (or influence) of a blog by tracking the number of distinct blogs that link to it. The 'very high authority' group is defined as having 500 or more blogs linking in six months. This blogging elite represents more than 4,000 blogs. They have been in existence for 18 months on average and post nearly twice a day. Some are fully fledged professional enterprises that post many times a day and are increasingly looking like mainstream media.

Cymfony (which describes itself as a market influence analytics company) claims that usernet groups and discussion forums receive over twice as many posts a day as blogs (4–6 million). It argues that the popularity of discussion boards persists because of enthusiasts' desire to find a community that shares their passion. Increasingly, people are moving beyond reading content or buying merchandise on the net. They are creating their own content, engaging with others' content, and remixing content found online and in traditional media.

As the influence wielded by traditional journalism and advertising declines, then so consumers' reliance on other consumers increases. In short, consumers trust each other. Word-of-mouth has always been the most powerful of communications; now the internet enables people to seek advice from an infinitely wider circle than the traditional set of friends and family. The influence of online media, however, spreads beyond the online community. Many journalists use blogs and other online media for researching stories for offline (and online) reporting. In parallel, a significant proportion of search engine results for major brands are from user-generated content.

The Kryptonite blogstorm ('How ten days of internet chatter crippled a company's reputation', *Fortune*, 2005) illustrates the power of the blog and the amplification that can result from offline and online media resonating with each other.

On 12 September 2004, a complaint was posted on bikeforums.net to the effect that a Kryptonite bike lock could be easily picked using a Bic ballpoint pen. Within two days, a video was posted demonstrating the trick, reaching hundreds of thousands of blog readers a day. Soon after the company issued a statement downplaying the issue, the *New York Times* and other traditional media picked up the story, and the amplified awareness reached millions of people. By the time the company announced a free product exchange 10 days after the first posting, the damage had been done. The exchange announcement received little coverage and, years after the event, negative stories dominate searches for 'Kryptonite lock'. Kryptonite has survived to tell the tale, but *Fortune* magazine reports estimates that the direct costs of the episode was $10 million.

Dell Hell – the influence of blogs

A white paper produced by Market Sentinel, 'Onalytica and Immediate Future' (2005) analysed the effect of the 'Dell Hell' episode on Dell's corporate reputation. This paper argues that there are problems with the conventional means of measuring the influence of a blog that are based on the general influence of a website. However, a site's influence is not the same on every subject. So the paper examines online influence according to topic and by using keywords.

In June 2005, blogger Jeff Jarvis complained about the after-sales support (or rather lack of) he was receiving from Dell on his new laptop. Jarvis coined the term 'Dell Hell'; his blog postings (www.buzzmachine.com) prompted numerous responses from other angry Dell customers and he became their spokesman. Dell responded by offering Jarvis a refund but maintained its policy of not reacting to blog commentary. In July 2005, Dell closed down its online customer service forum and that autumn issued a profits warning. The white paper looks at the extent to which Jarvis influenced attitudes to Dell's customer service, and whether a single consumer really had an impact on the Dell brand.

First, two key search terms were examined: 'Dell Hell' and 'customer service' referenced to Dell. All sites mentioned in the context of Dell Hell were listed and referred to as 'stakeholders'. They were then ranked according to three measures:

1. number of citations by other stakeholders;

2. how often the stakeholder is the source of relevant information for another stakeholder;

3. how much influence is given to a stakeholder by other important stakeholders on this topic.

This analysis showed that stakeholders covering Dell Hell relied heavily on Jarvis and four other bloggers closely associated with him. Bloggers seem to rely heavily on other bloggers for their news. Also, Jarvis was more than twice as authoritative as Dell on the issue of Dell's poor customer service. The paper describes this as the 'my story' phenomenon. If people report something that has happened to them, they are the most authoritative source. Bloggers rarely look at the other side of the story. In this case, this was exacerbated by Dell's failure to engage with the bloggers who were commenting on it.

Well-known blogger (and former Microsoft technology evangelist) Robert Scoble stresses the importance of trying to keep on top of consumer discussions in order to respond to false information: 'Somebody can post something totally false about you. But you can come to that story right away and answer it and kill a rumour before it turns into a *New York Times* article. Once it is printed in the *Times*, people think it must be true.'

EVALUATING WEBSITES AND ONLINE PRESS OFFICES

The online press room or press office has become a common element of the websites of organizations of any substance. They can vary from the posting of recently issued releases with archives of previous releases, to a fully fledged version with white papers, biographies of company spokespeople, FAQs, and even facilities for round table discussions and responding to press queries.

Whatever the precise format, common sense demands some sort of online press facility as the vast majority of journalists use the internet (as we all do) for basic background research on organizations they are interested in. It is also information that they can access around the clock, not being dependent on the availability of company spokespeople, which can be frustrating in different time zones. At the same time the organization in question can keep some element of control by being able to define the content and availability of posted information.

Although this seems common sense, there are indications that only a minority of organizations have clearly labelled online press rooms. Reber and Kim (2006: 317–18) state that: 'Although it would seem that websites are a natural location for organizations to connect with the media in a way that is easy for both the organization and the journalist, there is evidence that the Internet is not being used to its full advantage yet.' They go on to argue that although the internet is not the only element of a media relations programme, it is an important tool. Although Reber and Kim (2006: 329) were looking specifically at the websites of activist organizations, many of their conclusions are generally applicable. They found a lack of 'expert contact information, information request mechanism, and e-mail updates'. Their practical guidelines have been adapted to make them applicable across the board.

- Home pages should include a link to a press room; this frequently requires no more than organizing already available information in one place and linking to it.
- As part of the effort to build relationships, organizations should provide contact information for experts on news issues of relevance to the organization.
- A mechanism for responding to journalists' queries should be provided; this needs to be monitored and responded to in a timely manner.
- Regular e-mail updates to the media on relevant issues help build relationships.
- News releases and updates should be posted regularly, with an archive of dated releases.
- Online press rooms should also include position papers, backgrounders and other relevant publications.

Callison (2003: 31) summarized the opportunity provided to public relations practitioners by the internet and journalists' frustration with PR practitioners' response to that opportunity:

> the Web has the potential to be a key public relations tool but is not currently being used to its full potential in media relations. In fact, journalists do report turning to corporate Web sites when researching stories. But these same journalist [sic] also report often not finding what they are looking for on company sites, and a few have even suggested that their coverage of companies with poor Web presence is skewed negative, if they cover the companies at all.

Callison's research on Fortune 500 companies showed that only a minority (just over one third) centrally located and labelled materials that are of interest to the media. Companies with a higher Fortune 500 ranking were more likely to have an online press room. Although only two-thirds of sites with press rooms had links to those press rooms on the home page, 'buried' press rooms were generally easy to find, being able to be reached in an average of two clicks. The most commonly occurring items were press releases (unsurprisingly), executive biographies and executive photographs. However, 'seemingly useful items such as company logos for publication use, media kits, corporate profiles, and company backgrounders among others appeared in less than 25 per cent of press rooms' (Callison, 2003: 39).

The monitoring of online public relations is one of the 'black holes' in the evaluation lexicon. Because many practitioners were born well before the digital era, indeed started their professional careers before the digital era, they are not at ease with the internet environment. They monitor online coverage as if it were print media. Mark Prensky talks of a 'chasm between a younger generation of "digital natives" who have not known a world without computer games, and an older generation of "digital immigrants" forced to adapt to rapid changes in digital technology' (Cameron and Carroll, 2004). Readers will note the questionnaire responses by industry leaders on measurement of online media, such as: 'With great difficulty', 'Same way we evaluate print media – by gathering the clips, conducting content analysis, and logging them along with other media' and, 'Key message delivery, hits to sites'.

Others have developed specialist services in this field with web crawlers that track down messages and issues using key word searches. There are also free services from the major search engines, especially Google, and specialists like moreover.com. In areas of strong debate such as tobacco policy, advocacy groups have established daily news services. An example is tobacco.org, which has daily news scans from worldwide media that are presented in categories and supported by archives. It has proven very important in linking anti-smoking and public health advocacy groups around the world, but ironically provides a free service to tobacco manufacturers who can monitor their competitors and opponents.

A more difficult challenge is monitoring newsgroups and chat rooms. These can form and re-form very quickly. The evaluation of their credence and influence is demanding on resources and is not undertaken with the ease of daily or weekly monitoring of print or broadcast media. (For a more specialized view on this topic, see Phillips, 2001.)

These are key points from Phillips (2001: 85) about the reach of a website that indicate factors for DIY evaluation. They include:

● reference in newsgroups;
● hyperlinks to the site;

- ranking with search engines;
- online media awareness of the site;
- speed by which information is carried across the internet.

These factors will help construct a matrix view of both a corporate website (news group references, hyperlinks, search engine ranking) and message transmission/conflict messages (newsgroup reference, online media awareness and speed of transmission). Because the internet is constantly expanding, it is entirely possible to have messages lost in the clutter of sites and constantly changing search engine rankings. By monitoring the key points outlined by Phillips, online public relations activity can be tested for message reception on a daily basis. Only by building in response mechanisms can processing or acceptance be judged.

Phillips (2001: 77) also notes the internet search categories that media monitoring agencies use 'heavyweight search robots' to check daily. These are news sites and online e-zines, newsgroups and bulletin boards, and 'meta-search engines'. This final tool checks newly indexed, relevant content that has been added to the major search engines, which take up to six weeks to re-index their catalogues.

For consumer public relations, there are tracking tools that can be used. Professional Public Relations in Australia has one that can link internet enquiries directly to public relations activity. Director Clara Zawawi explains:

> We have a proprietary tool that allows us to monitor not only site activity but also where our hits come from and leave to go to. For example, if an Australian Tourism Commission story runs online in the *Auckland Herald* in New Zealand, we can track how many people jump from the *Herald* to the ATC site and then where they go to next, such as an airline site or travel agency site.

This enables the consultancy to measure the distribution and acceptance of messages and claim a Return on Investment (ROI) for its clients.

Another challenge in online public relations, especially in the corporate sector, is the rogue site, which has been established with 'the aim of damaging organizations' (Phillips, 2001: 203–05). These sites can be easily found, yet are not always accountable in terms of their accuracy, journalistic standards or editorial management:

> They have the potential to reach a mass international audience, which can be fascinated, entertained or easily led into believing half-

truths as fact or ranting as a legitimate concern... these sites can address legitimate concerns, highlight real failings or expose short-comings that need redress.

Almost all major world brands and transnational corporations have rogue sites monitoring and commenting on their activities. One of the best known sites is McSpotlight, which was set up to criticize the fast food company McDonald's. It became the subject of long-running litigation in the UK, ultimately with a finding against the two activists that operated it. However, this very large site had been mirrored in many countries and continues to operate.

By monitoring the online environment, public relations practitioners can track activist efforts. Once a rogue site is found, they need to evaluate its importance and decide how to respond online and offline. One problem they often face is that the critics are not identified or contactable, so negotiation and face-to-face discussion are not possible. Among the decisions to consider are whether to respond using the corporate website, and whether to take the company's case to mainstream media and stakeholders. A commonly used strategy is to include the rogue site's hyperlink on the corporate website, as this is considered to demonstrate transparency.

MEDIA EVALUATION AND THE NET

Niche and mainstream online media can supply monthly unique visits or impressions (or they can be easily tracked down). Similarly, while Google Trends tells you how many people are searching for something, what the demand is, blogpulse.com tells you what people are talking about. It won't tell you whether the exchanges are positive or negative, but it will tell you how often conversations are happening.

Although the internet and its Web 2.0 progeny (blogs and the like) pose particular problems for media evaluation and content analysis, there are advantages as well, owing to the nature of the medium itself. Blowers (2006: 21–22) gives the example of the BBC's 'news most popular now' feature, which indicates which stories on the site are the most popular:

> This is a classic example of online information 'leap-frogging' conventional media content analysis, going straight to media out-take (and one valuable step nearer to outcome). There are obvious shortcomings – the system lacks any metrics and is only a rank of

'relative' popularity. There is however some currency to it and it can be imagined that in future PR people will be saying their story was the second most read on the BBC website during a 24-hour period.

Looking at internet 'coverage' from a wider perspective, there is the benefit that would derive from looking at access data from more than one site. The aim would be to replicate the BBC's 'news most popular now' but covering a wider sample of sites and with the addition of the ability to sort the results by specific country, time-frame and using a measurable metric, then this would represent a powerful and authoritative measure of online users outtake.

Blowers believes that the fragmentation of the media is such that there is as much challenge in capturing relevant coverage as there is in analysing its content. He suggests that with the traditional media, there is a feeling that it can be delineated. In contrast, online (particularly blogging) is pervasive and anarchic so that a new skill will be understanding which of the coverage is significant to an organization's stakeholders.

Finally, Blowers (2006: 22–23) sees this as an area of concern for the current media evaluation industry. He sees the arrival of 'a new breed of online analysts who specifically aim to understand and represent web-players in a specific community or interest group'. With so much content around, the risk of analysts getting the sampling wrong and therefore getting the results wrong is very real:

> This has to be seen as a threat to the industry which could become very real if one of the large online software organizations decides to further develop one of the existing semi-intelligent text analysis programmes. This could easily result in a widely adopted, lower level (and low cost, if not free) online analysis package. All of a sudden a PR results system if [sic] available which is able to track key messages and favourability, and get 80 per cent right.

Blowers concludes that online media carry a host of challenges (and opportunities) for media evaluators. At the core of these challenges is the lack of valid audience data for the web, which means that using comparable metrics to present media impact from traditional and new media would yield incorrect data. There is, however, confidence that content analysis is independent of medium, and this will be able to be applied to analyse message usage and favourability.

A CYBERSPACE TOOLBOX

Paine (2002b) outlines half a dozen measurement devices as part of an ideal toolbox to 'measure your image or results in cyberspace'.

1. **A tool to find out what the cyber media is writing about you and what your constituencies are seeing about you (and your competition).** This type of tool is likened to press clipping services. The main challenge here is the handling of archived stories and 'dead' URLs.
2. **A tool to find out the size of the impact you are having.** This is an effort to come up with an online equivalent of circulation. The suggestion is that the best approach is the monthly 'unique audience': the number of different people that visit a site during a month. One problem is that small but influential sites may not be represented.
3. **A tool to find out what your constituencies are saying about you.** Here, chats and discussions in Usenet groups and other chat areas are monitored. The problem for the companies doing this type of monitoring is the volume of data that needs to be filtered. Then the postings need to be analysed and some indication of the impact of those postings made.
4. **A tool to determine what your constituencies think about you.** Here data is gathered from visitors, or they are surveyed through e-mail questionnaires.
5. **A tool to determine what action, if any, your constituencies are taking.** Customer transaction data can be tracked against web and PR data to determine the effect web activity has on customer purchase. Increasingly, market research companies are looking at web marketing results alongside other marketing activities.
6. **A tool to determine whether it's all worth it.** As with evaluation in general, there needs to be some examination of the costs of online PR and any information you have on the impact that the PR effort is having.

'Online PR is an integral part of the PR mix and I am not an advocate for pureplay online,' stresses Katy Howell. But she does feel that online needs to be taken very seriously. 'The circulation of the *Guardian* is nearly four times online as offline; the BBC news website gets 20 million visits a month.'

Howell is clear about there being two strong measures when evaluating online public relations: increases in online visibility (rankings in search engine, coverage in online publications, etc), and behavioural change (increases in search requests, visits to a website, etc). 'If you fill the first three pages in response to a web search, you are doing pretty well in terms of PR; search engines are a huge draw for the way we operate.' But she also feels that there is the potential to demonstrate behavioural change: 'If the noise is large enough and people are searching for it, you will see the searches for your brand increase.' However, the downside is the same as in the offline world. 'If there is a lot more going on than straight PR (banner advertising and search engine optimization, for example), how do you sort out which is having the effect, or what proportion of the effect?'

Howell points out that there is one way you can categorically determine where a website visit has come from. If your public relations activity is designed to drive traffic to a website, there are web analytic tools available that enable you to tell where the traffic has come from. For example, if a press release goes to a wire site (and has embedded links), you can prove a direct link between the enquiry and the press release. 'Much of the current success of online PR is about driving traffic to websites where it can have a huge impact. But there are wider implications for things like trust, image, sentiment and the like.' Here Howell still sees opportunities for effective evaluation. 'You can actually measure sentiment; you can tell whether people are talking about you positively or negatively. Monitoring companies discover the conversations and work out whether the buzz is positive or negative; they analyse whether people like you or not.

'There is too much attempting to force online into offline metrics and in particular the dreaded AVE. We ignore it. I want to see the trends going in the right direction on the website, online publishing sites and places like Google Trends. It can be much easier to see the impact online. Currently, online PR is all about an immediate call to action; it is the clicks that make it so powerful. If the BBC links to one of our clients, the impact can be seen immediately as website visits increase substantially. It's important to identify and then monitor the influencers; see what coverage they are giving you.' One key difference between online and offline is how often stories get picked up by others (particularly bloggers), and then viral into MySpace and other social networks. That doesn't tend to happen offline quite so quickly unless you are talking about a really negative or a really positive story.

Although other soft goals such as trust and positive image may have to rely on traditional market research, Howell still argues that it's possible to get a good indication of what's going on. 'If, for example, you are publishing a blog, you can look at the frequency of comments, how many people are engaging with you. If lots of people are talking to you, debating and discussing, then it is clear that you are generating awareness and building potential advocacy.' She also points out that online PR is still in its infancy and also tends to be project based. Consequently, it's much harder to benchmark norms because of the lack of historical data (the bedrock of effective econometric modelling).

But monitoring what is going on is key, as is rapid response. 'Stories and ideas can take off all by themselves and become, for example "blogswarms", where blog comments and posts swarm together over a topic. A prime example is the "Dell Hell" story where you can see the correlation between negative noise online and the share price starting to fall. Even if your board of directors does not take online seriously, they will soon start to take notice when it spins offline and does so dramatically.'

Katy Howell is Managing Director of immediate future ltd and advised on the preparation of this chapter

---

QUESTIONNAIRE RESPONSES

Q: How does your organization evaluate online media?

As a consultancy, we started a separate company specializing in new media, which has developed specialized tools and approaches to online media evaluation. **Dejan Verčič**

Key message delivery, hits to sites. **Alison Clarke**

Internal scanning. **Fran Hagon**

In the context of the objectives for each client programme. **Crispin Manners**

We use a media monitoring company and tend to pick a lot up ourselves. **Loretta Tobin**

We operate a media monitoring service that has, as part of the exercise, online extracts. **Ray Mawerera**

There is an assumption in the question that PR is equivalent to publicity. If an organization is going to effectively reach the public in a two-way programme, many elements will not involve publicity. Quite often publicity is used merely as an endorsement or awareness tool and is often not the core activity that makes the final impact. Online media is treated like any other element of the tactical campaign. **Annabelle Warren**

We would ordinarily work it out based on how much it would cost to advertise on that particular site times three. **Laurna O'Donnell**

We have a proprietary tool that allows us to monitor not only site activity but also where our hits come from and leave to go to. For example, if an Australian Tourism Commission story runs online in the *Auckland Herald* in New Zealand we can track how many people jump from the *Herald* to the ATC site and then where they go to next, such as an airline site or travel agency site. That's pretty effective. **Clara Zawawi**

With great difficulty! **Tom O'Donoghue**

In the same way as print, but the degree of sophistication is limited. **Mike Copland**

Same way we evaluate print media – by gathering the clips, conducting content analysis, and logging them along with other media. We try as much as possible not to use circulation as a measure of 'reach' because it's so subjective, but where clients insist, we make educated guesses. **Matt Kucharski**

It would be impossible on our slender resources. Monitoring coverage online is difficult enough. We check the online news services from the major outlets and any regional sites if we have a particular case. **Richard Offer**

The Association uses online media as a point of reference or as an information tool for lobbying. However, it does not actively evaluate online media, unless there is an issue specifically related to the Association, in which action may need to be taken. **Adam Connolly**

11

Future developments

Progress in solving the 'problem' of evaluation has been, at best, steady. Some would say that James Grunig's cri de coeur remains as valid today as when it was first issued two decades ago (see Chapter 3). The same people would be predicting the demise of the PR consultancy business with Quentin Bell's self-imposed deadline for clients to 'insist' on evaluation looming on the horizon.

However, they are beginning to become isolated pockets of resistance rather than representatives of the mainstream. Slowly – yes – but also surely, public relations practitioners are getting to grips with evaluation, and this chapter reports recent studies to support this assertion. This is not happening in isolation. It forms part of a broad effort to make public relations a professional and strategic discipline, one that can demonstrate, rather than simply claim, its business benefits.

This guarded optimism comes with a health warning. There will never be a time when the problems associated with evaluation of public relations activity will be completely solved. This is in the nature of the beast. It is both the joy and the curse of public relations that it is a broad church: a wide variety of practitioners, providing a wide range of services to a wide variety of organizations.

Public relations is also a complex discipline operating in a range of contexts. So, there is no Holy Grail, no magic bullet nor any simple solution. But there is gradual progress achieved on the back of a more sophisticated understanding of the complexities associated with public relations practice in general, and therefore its measurement and evaluation in particular.

DEVELOPING GOOD PRACTICE

The most recent major study into public relations practice was published at the end of 2003 in the UK. This was a project jointly funded by the UK's Institute of Public Relations (IPR) and the UK government's Department of Trade and Industry (DTI). The European Centre for Business Excellence was appointed to develop the project framework. The current issues identified in this report demonstrate how the problems and opportunities associated with evaluation are threaded through vast swathes of public relations practice.

- Increasing consensus as to the main purposes of PR and a fair degree of satisfaction as to the extent to which these purposes are achieved. Public relations must increasingly be seen in the context of longer-term strategic relationship management and engagement on emerging trends such as corporate social responsibility.
- Overlap between PR and other communications functions continues to be an issue.
- Lack of consensus among in-house PR practitioners as to the importance and effectiveness of audience research. Clearly more to be done to improve the application of research techniques to PR across the industry.
- Variations in approach to the role of communications strategy and the extent to which it supports overall business strategy.
- Organizations now outsourcing a broad range of PR activity to consultancies. But the commissioning process is identified as a major problem area, with PR consultancies believing the quality of the brief (PR objective setting) given by clients to be fairly poor.
- Need for greater training and development in the area of PR procurement and its management.

- Study reaffirms the need for PR practitioners to be more capable across a broad range of competency areas.
- The holding of formal qualifications in communications is by no means universal across the study sample.
- Less than 50 per cent of consultancies and in-house organizations appear to have formal training and development programmes for PR professionals. This suggests a need for real progress in education and training across the industry.
- PR evaluation was seen as moderately effective across a range of indicators, but both consultants and in-house practitioners felt their ability to benchmark performance between different providers of PR was relatively poor.

The report argues that if public relations practitioners are to become advisers (or counsellors) at strategic levels within their client or in-house organizations, then a major requirement will be their ability to quantify the value of the advice that they offer.

Turning to the issue of standard measures to evaluate PR, there does not seem to be any consistency in views on which measures are effective in assessing the impact of PR on the attitudes of target publics. While there is no particular preference, there is general approval of the measures available such as periodic surveys, individual feedback, and the use of (or sales of) products and services. So there does seem to be a consensus that there is no measure that is right for all circumstances, and that it depends on the 'issues, organizations and audiences involved'. Table 11.1 lists more detail on which parameters PR practitioners feel should be measured (DTI/IPR, 2003: 42).

The report implies criticism of practitioners (particularly those working in-house and in the private sector) for not understanding research and not taking it seriously. It points out that there is a tendency for practitioners to place research within marketing rather than it being an integral part of the public relations planning process. But the report is unequivocal in stating that research is intimately linked with evaluation and requires expertise in its delivery.

Moving to a broader perspective on evaluation, the DTI/IPR report confirms that consultancy practitioners, at least, are looking at evaluating the client relationships their public relations counsel is supporting, rather than simple concentrating on the process of public relations practice: '50% of respondents from PR consultancies stated they measure the quality of relationships with stakeholders/publics on behalf of their client organizations' (p 40). This thinking is extended into the comments the report makes on evaluation in

Table 11.1 *PR performance parameters that should be measured*

- Audience awareness, understanding, attitude and response were given as important PR performance measurements.
- This was supported by the general view that media KPIs are only indicators and not an end in themselves.
- However, some respondents did give quality, quantity and key messages in media coverage as important audience parameters.
- Relationships with journalists were also said to be an important measure.
- In addition to these, it was felt that activities achieved versus plan and timeliness should be measured.
- Contribution to business objectives was stated as an overall measure of performance, without specifying how the link to PR activities might be made.

general, where (among others) the strength of relationships over time is one of the points made, alongside stressing again the need for effective and well-resourced research capabilities.

- Approaches to PR evaluation need to be consistent with the nature of the organization's operations. Effective PR evaluation for a consumer goods company will be different from that of a public service provider, for example.
- Optimum use of performance measurement also depends on the organization's management culture, and good PR practitioners align their approach accordingly.
- Good PR evaluation is based on effective research capabilities, understanding changes in public perceptions over time. Effective research requires appropriate investment on the part of the organization.
- Good PR evaluation measures what is important rather than what is easy to measure. It is easy to measure PR outputs (such as coverage) rather than outcomes (such as changing public attitudes). However, impact on key individuals may be more important than overall coverage, and good PR should be making an impact on attitudes and the strength of relationships over time.
- The impact of PR is often indirect and so cause and effect cannot be proven. It may also be difficult to quantify the effects of good PR, such as the value of a brand being on television or placed in a major film. Good PR evaluation does

> not waste resources seeking to quantify the unquantifiable, but instead uses simple subjective measures of creativity, quality of work and main outcomes in these more difficult areas.
> ● Good PR evaluation allows space for unforeseen or unusual PR opportunities. An over-rigid evaluation framework may lead to opportunities being missed because they appear not to fit the measurement criteria.

Finally, the DTI/IPR (2003: 68) study reiterates the perspective of a future for PR practice, and therefore evaluation, which is concerned with facilitating, supporting and improving a complex web of stakeholder relationships:

> a future where PR will be concerned with managing multi-stakeholder interactions. PR practitioners will be involved in interactions with many different stakeholders, whether they are within the organization, customers or other immediate stakeholders, or one of many other publics. Within this multi-stakeholder environment, PR practitioners will need to become expert in assessing the interactions between different publics and how these affect the organization. They will need to understand what the organization and its actions mean to each stakeholder group.

More recently, Metrica Research Ltd conducted a study for the Institute of Public Relations and The Communication Directors' Forum (CDF), which was published in May 2004. First of all, this addresses the sloppy use of term 'ROI' in the context of PR evaluation:

> The actual definition of ROI is a ratio of how much profit or cost saving is realized from an activity against its total cost, which is often expressed as a percentage. In reality, few PR programmes can be measured in such a way because of the problems involved in putting a realistic and credible financial value to the results achieved. As a result, the term 'PR ROI' is often used very loosely. This is not only confusing but also misleading and helps explain why the PR industry has traditionally found it difficult to demonstrate meaningful success that links PR cause to PR effect.

Other commentators to criticize ROI include Lugbauer (2003) who argues: 'ROI is a very specific measure of the net income a firm earns with its total assets, one easier to apply to an enterprise than to a department.'

The IPR/CDF report argues that a considerably better alternative would be to speak of 'evidence-based PR', defined simply as the difference made as a result of PR activity. Given this broader definition, there is no question that excellent work is being conducted across the public relations industry to measure and report PR activities using sophisticated techniques. Examples of this include:

- Raising awareness among target audiences (eg to support sales).
- Increasing reach and frequency (eg to support branding).
- Increasing telephone calls to a helpline (eg to assist families).
- Driving x visitors to a website (eg to educate more people about…).
- Increasing number of direct sales enquiries by x (eg to improve the new business pipeline).
- Increasing message delivery to target audiences (eg to inform new target audiences of a particular service).

The recommendations of the IPR/CDF study reiterate the point already discussed about the true meaning of ROI, before addressing issues to do with making a business case for PR and pleading for a more sophisticated approach to evaluation, before raising important points about Advertising Value Equivalents (AVEs).

- The term 'PR ROI' is rarely used correctly and should in most instances be replaced with a more meaningful and accurate descriptive phrase, such as 'evidence-based PR'…. In order to avoid confusion, the term 'PR ROI' should only be used when a ratio of how much profit or cost saving can be directly attributed to specific PR activities.
- The cost of PR measurement should be considered against the business case of what PR programmes can achieve rather than against the budget of the programmes themselves. Viewed in this context – helping to make a strong business case – the cost of evaluation can be better justified.
- A significant change in the culture of the PR industry is required towards more sophisticated PR measurement as opposed to the 'magic bullet' approach that so many PR practitioners appear to desire.
- Many problems stem directly from an over-simplified view that 'PR is basically free advertising'. This leads to 'measures' such as AVEs, which continue to be used despite being completely discredited.

- When PR is compared with advertising, this should only be done using directly comparable measures, such as 'reach and frequency', 'cost per thousand', or changes in awareness and attitude measured through credible market research.
- The PR industry should place more emphasis on the technical understanding required to conduct proper planning, research and evaluation (PRE). On a long-term basis this should be encouraged through educational programmes that cover the technical aspects of PRE, particularly at degree level where courses are endorsed by the Institute of Public Relations. In the short term the IPR and other industry bodies, such as the PRCA and AMEC, should continue to work closely to address this problem.

RETURN ON INVESTMENT (ROI)

Over more than two decades, the terminology of public relations evaluation has been under discussion across the world. Lately, as the studies reported above indicate, the debate has been over the use of 'Return on Investment' or ROI in public relations. Is it convenient shorthand in business language for dealing with management, or the misuse of a financial measure that is out of place in communication terminology?

Watson (1997: 284) has commented that 'there is considerable confusion as to what the term "evaluation" means. For budget-holders, whether employers or clients, the judgements have a "bottom line" profit-related significance'. White (1991: 141) suggested that company managers have a special interest in the evaluation of public relations: 'Evaluation helps to answer the questions about the time, effort and resources to be invested in public relations activities: can the investment, and the costs involved, be justified?' Lindenmann, in Hon and Grunig (1999: 2), identifies 'value' as a key concept when he poses the question: 'How can PR practitioners begin to pinpoint and document for senior management the overall *value* of public relations to the organization as a whole?'

It would appear that the concept of demonstrating or proving value or organizational benefit is embedded in the language of public relations practice. It is a short step to the widespread use of business language in public relations. This has been called for by the evaluation commentator Jim Macnamara (2005). Watson and Simmons (2004: 2) noted that Macnamara had identified two failings that help explain why public relations lacks credibility in the eyes of management. The first was the failure of practitioners to undertake evaluation, and the second was failure to use the language of accountability preferred by management, such as MBO, TQM, QA, Benchmarking, etc. ROI could be, and often is, part of that language set.

Earlier, the role of procurement professionals in shaping the pricing, performance characteristics and reporting of public relations campaigns was described. The UK's Public Relations Consultants Association's guide for procurement professionals (*Purchasing Public Relations*) avoids the term 'ROI' and focuses on Key Performance Indicators (KPIs) in order to encourage the purchasers to focus on a range of objectives and outcomes, rather than a single ROI-type quotient on which performance is rewarded or penalized.

What Key Performance Indicators and what core deliverables do the consultancies envisage as being crucial to the success of the programme?

Which methods of measurement and evaluation do the consultancies believe are most suitable to the assignment? Have you set aside a separate budget for this function?

Another contrary view on ROI has been put forward by Murray and White (2004: 4–6) who undertook a qualitative study on UK CEOs' views about reputation management (see also Chapter 3). The main findings included the fact that CEOs did not consider that PR effectiveness is amenable to precise measurement, being long term and iterative in effect, or being an aid to avoiding surprises and mistakes. They also did not feel a great need to demonstrate a return on their investment in PR. Specifically, John Hancock, CEO of the MFI Group, rejected ROI: 'I don't believe there is a return on investment for public relations – it is a necessary cost. I can gauge how much I need to spend by comparing the cost of my PR resource with other costs and get a sense of what is appropriate.'

From Murray and White's qualitative research, it can be contended that the demand from business for evaluation language in its own terms may be over-stated, thus challenging industry proponents (such as the 2003 DTI/IPR report) for this terminology.

Despite these doubts over the validity of the use of ROI, it is widely used by practitioners. In Sweden, the term 'Return on Communication' was introduced in 1996 as a 'goal oriented, step-by-step process where communication performance measurements are linked with business relevant success factors' (Lautenbach, 2006: 2). This was influential in the creation of the Communication Value System developed by GPRA, the German PR consultancy body. In the UK, the Public Relations Consultants Association has introduced an online service – PR-Value.com – that can help clients and consultancies plan and then evaluate the business value of PR.

Although many in public relations practice use ROI, the validity of the term is not widely recognized by their customers and employers. It is increasingly being rejected by professional bodies as inaccurate and misleading. The debate over ROI also shows a very narrow view of public relations, essentially as a one-way marketing communications process. It ignores the broader discussion of two-way asymmetrical and symmetrical models and the capacity for public relations to create interactions and manage relationships.

However, trade press articles show that ROI is current terminology. An example comes from *PR Week*, US edition, 14 March 2005, which reviewed evaluation practice with the headline, 'The quest for ROI', and the first sentence of a 1,650-word article that read, 'Determining a return on investment for PR has never been easy'. The terms 'ROI' or 'return' was used 20 times.

Watson (2005) studied a wide range of public relations academic literature and found that there was almost no use of ROI and little demand for this term or recognition of it by employers and customers. What appears to be a convenient 'biz-speak' term could be another indication of the lack of confidence among PR practitioners (Watson and Simmons, 2004: 11) in explaining and promoting their strategies and methods of operation, and a form of ingratiation with purchasers of their services. By using current business language, they hope to be seen on the same level as sellers of capital equipment and direct-response services. By promising an ROI, they are pigeon-holing PR as publicity-function marketing communications.

The term 'return on investment' has become commonplace in discussions on public relations evaluation and effectiveness. However, as with all clichés, over-use has left it as a shell empty of meaning. Rather than its literal meaning (ratio of return to capital investment) it has become a vague term meaning something like 'the benefits arising from the PR effort'; it has lost its numerical connotation so this perceived benefit tends to be expressed in whatever terms suit. However, its hard-headed, numerical feel makes it a particularly attractive term when public relations operates in a marketing context.

Likely, Rockland and Weiner (2006) looked at the issue of ROI specifically in the context of the business value that can be derived from media coverage generated by public relations acting as part of a marketing effort. They suggest that most practitioners feel that such publicity has an effect on sales but there have been no methods to demonstrate this. Before addressing this point, they outline why pressures have arisen to demonstrate ROI (there are plenty of echoes with the drivers behind public relations and communications evaluation in general):

- Resources are limited, leading to pressure on budgets, so organizations will only invest in activities that directly contribute to increased revenues.
- Scrutiny is increasing so consultancies and in-house departments are under pressure to be accountable: not just generate coverage but demonstrate that business benefits accrue.
- Marketing is becoming more sophisticated and the suggestion is (together with other elements of the mix measuring ROI) that so should public relations.

In one sense, ROI is the holy grail. If taken literally, it is all about assigning a financial return to an investment in public relations. Likely, Rockland and Weiner (2006: 3) define it as 'a measure of the financial benefits of an activity against its associated costs'. They expand upon this definition in a communications context:

> Return on investment is the relation between overall expenditure on a communications activity and the benefits to the organization or one of its business units derived from the activity. Benefits can be expressed in many ways such as revenue generation, cost reduction, and cost-avoidance through risk reduction.

They stress that ROI is not restricted to the generation of revenue; it can also be based on the reduction of costs arising from a PR programme, or a PR effort that avoids costs in the first place by addressing a potential risk (eg negative legislation).

Four possible models are outlined by Likely, Rockland and Weiner (2006: 4) 'to calculate media relations publicity ROI'. They say that each has good and bad points, although as the fourth is based on AVEs, many would argue that this model – at least – has more bad than good.

1. Return on impressions model

This approach is based, first, on the assumption that media coverage drives behaviour. It then assumes that a set number of media 'impressions', each carrying the appropriate message, is required to make one person aware of the product or service. Note that 'impressions' is an alternative term for 'opportunity to see' (OTS). The third assumption is that once a number of people are aware, a proportion of those made aware will purchase the good or service that has been publicized.

Here is a hypothetical example based on the methodology presented by Likely, Rockland and Weiner (2006):

- A publicity campaign for a product costs £50,000 and generates 500,000 impressions.
- Previous studies have shown that for this sort of campaign, 10 impressions are required to make one person aware (this figure is for illustrative purposes only). So we estimate that 50,000 have been made aware of our product.
- We know that 5,000 people have purchased the product (the desired behaviour). So, we estimate that 10 per cent of those made aware have purchased the product. (One problem is that although we know 5,000 people bought the product, we don't know that they were all made aware by the media relations publicity campaign.)
- The profit on sales of 5,000 units is £100,000 (£20 per unit). The ROI is profit generated divided by campaign cost and is therefore 2:1 (100,000/50,000) or 200 per cent.

There are a number of concerns with this approach. First, there are the assumptions that have to be made. In the spirit of econometrics, it is suggested that these assumptions are based on historical data: that is, data on impressions obtained and sales achieved is available from previous campaigns, which are then projected forward. It also assumes – as is often the case when PR evaluation looks simple and clear cut – that there are no other communications effects. Even if the media publicity campaign were the only formal marketing communications effort, people still talk to each other, obtain further information from the internet, take into account previous experience with the brand or retailer, and the like. The authors argue that 'this is a ballpark approach where one uses existing data on the ratios of impressions to awareness to behaviour to get a general sense of ROI' (Likely, Rockland and Weiner, 2006: 6). It may be the case that this approach does generate numerical data (subject to the availability of historical benchmarks), but there remains a concern that the credibility of that data is suspect.

2. Return on media impact model

Here media coverage is analysed as traditionally associated with media evaluation (tone, message delivery, prominence, publication, third-party comment, etc). Coverage might be scored out of 100, where allocation of scores will probably depend on the objectives of the campaign, and (as is standard practice) this is tracked over time. Sales are tracked over time, as are other independent variables such as price and advertising. Statistical analysis is then undertaken to determine the effect on sales of changes in the media relations score and/or different elements of the quality (eg tone) or quantity (eg impressions/OTS) elements of the media evaluation score. Likely, Rockland and Weiner (2006: 7) point out the issues associated with this approach:

● Media relations publicity and other forms of marketing communications such as advertising often affect sales over time, and estimating the lag effects can be quite complicated.
● Unless every factor affecting sales can be defined, the model is incomplete. There are likely to be extraneous variables that are driving sales, which makes the model less precise.
● If advertising or other aspects of marketing communications have much greater resources than publicity, it may be difficult to isolate perturbations that are due to media relations publicity.

Perhaps one key point to add is that elements of the marketing communications mix do not necessarily act independently or represent alternative means of achieving the same ends. For example, publicity might raise awareness and then sales promotion prompt the sale (behaviour).

3. Return on target influence model

While the two models discussed above tend to be in the spirit of econometrics, this third approach is more like market research used for direct measurement. The aim is to bridge the gap between the input (media coverage) and the effect (normally behaviour change). Surveys are conducted among a sample of the target public. The aim is to establish whether the message contained in the media impressions generated had an effect on the target audience. The questionnaire looks at whether respondents were exposed to the media coverage and what they took from it. The type of result expected is that likelihood of purchase is greater (by a defined amount) if a media impression is seen.

The problems that Likely, Rockland and Weiner (2006: 8) identify with this approach include the frequent inability of respondents to remember exactly when and where they received the message, making it difficult to distinguish between advertising and media impressions. They also repeat their point that 'media relations publicity, more times than not, has a delayed effect as do other marcom efforts'.

4. Return on earned media model

This again is a method for deriving an ROI figure, but is based on AVEs (discussed below), which the authors accept is a 'much-debated issue'. They even admit: 'The three authors of this document disagree on the appropriateness of AVEs' (Likely, Rockland and Weiner 2006: 9).

ECONOMETRICS

As has been indicated, at least some of these attempts to establish a true return on investment for public relations activity (or at least, publicity-seeking media relations) are in the spirit of econometrics. Here is the Holy Grail, at least for commercial communications, if you believe financial return to be the ultimate measure of communications effectiveness. Econometric modelling is arguably the ultimate evaluation tool. It can disentangle the effects of a campaign from all the other factors in play. But of course, it is not that simple: it is a complex, specialized technique that requires expertise, big budgets and historical data.

Econometrics is normally applied in a marketing context and therefore is concerned with sales. The PRCA's best practice guide to evaluation explains that 'There are two ways of approaching an evaluation, the old way and the best practice way.' Say there is a burst of communications activity (which might well be public relations) and after the communications activity, sales react. The 'old way' was to measure the sales blip (and claim credit for it). But the problem is that this makes an assumption: that without any communications activity, sales would have remained constant.

With no communications activity at all, sales would probably degrade over a period of time. The best practice approach is to ask what would have happened to sales if there had been no communications. This includes the blip but also takes into account other factors that would have depressed sales with no communications support. Of course, the assumed degradation in sales is hypothetical and therefore an estimate. There are three ways of making this estimate (ideally all three are used):

1. A **time-series** analysis, which looks at periods when the brand had less communications support, or even none at all.
2. A **regional** analysis, which looks at sales in those regions where the brand has less communications support, or even none at all (in advertising parlance known as a 'quiet region').
3. A **competitive comparison**, which looks at what happens to sales of other brands that get less communications support, or even none at all.

There still remains an uncomfortable element to this discussion: communications activity was undertaken, sales went up, therefore the former caused the latter. Here, econometrics, which uses statistical techniques to disaggregate sales data, can help establish the causal link between communications and sales. It attempts to look at all the factors that affect sales in an effort to disentangle their different effects.

The output from an econometric analysis is a model that enables a prediction to be made as to what would have happened if the communications campaign had not taken place. As – in theory, at least – everything else that might also have an effect is taken into account, then the communications effect is simply the difference between actual and predicted sales. Econometrics is a specialist service and the PRCA's best practice guide to evaluation advises how to get the most from it.

1. Econometrics is a highly technical and specialized discipline: use a properly qualified econometrician.
2. Allow plenty of time: a thorough analysis may take 6–12 weeks.
3. Brief your econometrician well: set clear research objectives and prioritize them.
4. Be prepared to supply lots of data and information.
5. Garbage in, garbage out: make sure your data is complete and accurate.
6. The model is thoroughly tested.
7. Ensure the econometrician explains the findings clearly.
8. Use the model once you've got it; it is useful for planning future campaigns as well as evaluating the past.
9. Monitor how well the model forecasts.
10. Update your model regularly.

ADVERTISING VALUE EQUIVALENTS (AVEs)

Advertising Value Equivalents (AVEs), also known as Advertising Value Equivalency (AVE), is a concept that has been in existence for some time; once plunging the depths of being referred to as Advertising Costs Avoided. The extent to which it is derided by many senior practitioners and researchers is perhaps only matched by its widespread use, particularly by consultancies responding to client pressures for hard data. The attractiveness of the concept is that it places a financial value on media coverage. Its problems are legion, not least that even those willing to embrace it accept that it as flawed.

Jeffries-Fox (2007: 2) defines AVEs as follows:

> AVEs are calculated by measuring the column inches (in the case of print), or seconds (in the case of broadcast media) and multiplying these figures by the respective medium's advertising rates (per inch or per second). The resulting number is what it would have cost to place an advertisement of that size in that medium.

Not least among the problems with AVEs is that many people then go further and apply a multiplier to the AVE figure to take account of media coverage's (supposed) enhanced credibility – and therefore persuasiveness – over advertising. A multiplier of 3 is perhaps most common, but virtually any number under 10 is used; none of them with any apparent justification. Lindenmann (2003) quotes 2, 3, 5 and 8, while Jeffries-Fox (2007) suggest a range from 1.5 to 6. To compound this confusion, there has also been a suggestion that rather than a multiplier, a divisor should be used to account for the inherent control associated with placing advertising messages.

This multiplier is sometimes referred to as 'PR Value'. This is based on the assumption that 'public relations is more credible and carries more impact than advertising and therefore deserves a higher weight than straight circulation and audience' (Weiner and Bartholomew, 2006: 6).

However, Lindenmann (2003) has serious reservations about the concept:

> Most reputable researchers view such arbitrary 'weighting' schemes aimed at enhancing the alleged value of editorial coverage as unethical, dishonest, and not at all supported by the research literature. Although some studies have, at times, shown that editorial coverage is sometimes more credible or believable than is advertising coverage, other studies have shown the direct opposite, and there is, as yet, no clearly established consensus in the communications field

on what is truly more effective: publicity or advertising. In reality, it depends on an endless number of factors.

Weiner and Bartholomew (2006: 6) conclude their discussion of multipliers by calling for a standard definition of impressions (or OTS) that 'does not include any inflammatory elements including the use of a multiplier of audited circulation or audience numbers, or multiplier to account for added value'. They call for all practitioners to use the best available data so that results are consistent.

Likely, Rockland and Weiner (2006) have developed the concept of AVEs and integrated it with the concept of ROI with their fourth media relations publicity ROI model. This is known as the 'Return on Earned Media' model. 'Earned media' is a term to describe editorial coverage in the same way that advertising is referred to as 'paid media'. Once the AVE has been calculated it is adjusted by a multiplier, although 'This adjustment can be altogether subjective and arbitrary – with many PR consulting and research firms applying different and so-called "proprietary" earned media multipliers' (Likely, Rockland and Weiner, 2006: 9).

In order to address at least some of the severe limitations of AVEs discussed below, this model then uses a divisor (described as an algorithm). This divisor is to take account of what percentage of a perfect placement is actually delivered: 'media relations publicity is often not able to deliver the full set of messages to the right people at the right time in the way that advertising can'. How one judges what percentage of perfection is delivered by a particularly press clipping or item of broadcast coverage is not made clear.

Finally, the ROI (according to this model) is calculated in the normal fashion: incremental gain divided by the cost of the publicity effort. Likely, Rockland and Weiner (2006: 10) accept that this model is imperfect but argue that: 'there are many marketers who need to decide on the relative efficacy of advertising and media relations publicity, and in the absence of other ways to derive the answer, AVEs can provide helpful guidance'.

Jeffries-Fox (2007) starts to outline some of the reservations about AVEs. He points out that the credibility of the news media is declining and varies from topic to topic. He also argues that public relations practitioners, on occasions, are trying to achieve an absence of coverage. Finally, he points out that news and advertising operate differently: 'we don't know how to compare the relatively diverse set of messages delivered by news coverage to the relatively homogeneous messages delivered by advertising'.

The logistical issues identified by Jeffries-Fox (2007) include the problems of publishers and broadcasters who do not accept advertisements in certain sections (such as front pages), or do not accept advertisements at all (for example, the BBC). Other issues include the treatment of negative or simply neutral stories, and a news story that covers a number of topics with a passing mention of your particular organization.

However, many practitioners continue to use AVEs under pressure from clients and managers, even when the practitioners themselves share some – or all – of these concerns. The suggestion is that as AVEs are based on circulation and media credibility (a more prestigious publication may be able to charge relatively high advertising rates), then they may be considered some sort of indication of the prominence of editorial coverage. This may be particularly appropriate when comparing different time periods or doing a competitive analysis.

PAYMENT BY RESULTS

Another influence on terminology has been the emergence in the mid-1990s of payment-by-results (PBR) and performance-based fees (PBF) for public relations consultancy services. This has been driven by the introduction of procurement professionals into negotiations for the supply of professional services to major organizations, both governmental and commercial. These focus on achievement of Key Performance Indicators, negotiate 'value for money' and do not necessarily seek long-term relationships with professional advisers. The outcomes for procurement operatives are the subject of strict contractual terms and are determined by financial or sales figures, or media output indicators. (This emphasis on business language excludes the very important governmental and not-for-profit sectors whose communication objectives may be entirely non-financial or non-sales in content.)

A key – if not essential – element of PBR is deciding on the criteria by which the achievement of results is assessed, ie evaluation. PBR has come to the fore for a number of reasons: pressure on budgets, demand for justification of PR spend and, maybe, confidence among public relations consultancies in the value of the services they offer. In a sense, consultancies have always been paid by results in that clients will not continue to employ them (and therefore pay them) unless they are satisfied with the 'results' that the consultancy delivers.

PBR is more specific than the obvious point of clients only continuing to employ providers who provide a satisfactory level of service. It is normally associated with a 'bonus' being paid for exceptional performance. In return for a possible bonus the base payment is lower than the consultancy's normal day rate. It appears, therefore, that PBR schemes are coalescing around a guaranteed reduced payment in exchange for a bonus if defined targets are met. There are no standards, but one suggestion is that the guaranteed payment is in the region of 80 per cent of the normal rate; common sense would indicate that if the relevant criteria are met, then the bonus would result in a payment of 120 per cent, an uplift of a fifth on the consultancy's standard rate.

It does seem that PBR has gained a toe-hold as a means of consultancy remuneration. There is also some indication that it suits two – very different – types of client. For the first-time user of PR it has the potential to offer some reassurance. Intrinsically, services cannot be fully assessed prior to consumption, so the clients with limited public relations experience might be attracted to the reassurance associated with payment by results. At the other end of the scale, experienced users of public relations services may have the sophisticated understanding of PR evaluation required to establish the criteria on which the results are going to be assessed. Naturally, a workable PBR scheme is completely dependent on clear criteria and measurement.

Somewhere between a third and a half of PR consultancies in the UK offer a PBR scheme. Opinion is almost equally divided between it being consultancy-initiated, client-initiated or a joint decision. Some consultancies even see it as an important means of attracting new business, even if once discussions between consultancy and potential client are held, the relationship is established on a more traditional basis. Even when new relationships are established using a PBR scheme, it is common for the client-consultancy relationship to move on to a more traditional basis quite quickly. This is not because of any problems with PBR, but it is no longer necessary once an effective relationship has been established.

However, PBR is not without problems and there are indications that, in the UK at least, the initial growth of PBR schemes has stalled at fairly low levels. One reason is the difficulty for an effective evaluation system to be reasonably simple; deriving a scheme that is both simple and fair can be challenging.

Also, impact measures may well only be appropriate if PR is the only communications tool to be used, and even then major external events may well reduce or negate the impact of PR activities, however skilfully deployed. In the more common situations of PR being one element in a mix of activities, then measures of media coverage could also be used, but our old friend the substitution game rears its ugly head.

Even if the adoption of a full-blown PBR scheme is not appropriate, the discussion of such an approach can be useful in itself. This is not limited to persuading first-time users of PR to dip a toe in the water, but can help prompt an objective-led approach to developing public relations strategies without the need for a formal PR scheme. This approach can be summarized as one that focuses on the client and its business strategy, rather than the PR process.

The PRCA's best practice guide to agency remuneration summarizes the advantages and disadvantages of payment by results schemes.

Advantages

- The increasing focus on accountability makes it highly desirable that agencies are rewarded – at least in part – on the basis of performance and deliverables.
- It is very helpful, in new relationships especially, and after a precise scope of work has been agreed, for 'success' to be defined – and some part of the agency's reward to be related to it.
- In a relentlessly competitive market for agency services PBR schemes give incumbent agencies the opportunity to demonstrate on an ongoing basis the contribution they make – and to benefit from their efforts.

Disadvantages

- It is often difficult to isolate the effect of marketing communications on sales and commercial goals. This can lead to protracted negotiations on the exact mechanics of PBR arrangements.
- PBR schemes can sometimes be constructed in too complicated a way, leading to an extended 'How much is the agency entitled to?' debate.
- Clients do need to provide for at least the possibility of the agency winning the full incentive. Failure to do so can lead to damage to the relationship.
- PBR, which is meant to be motivating for agencies, can work the other way if the agency consistently fails to earn the level of incentives it feels it deserves.

MANAGEMENT OVERVIEW

It has almost become a cliché to say that communications and public relations objectives need to be related to marketing/corporate objectives if the public relations function is going to be taken seriously and sit at the top table as part of the management coalition. It is a theme of this book that, while this aspiration is wholly appropriate and therefore should be sought assiduously, it is rarely simple. This is because public relations effects are normally but a subset of communications effects in general, and they – in turn – are but some of the influences that affect the attainment of corporate objectives.

One effort to link communications and business objectives is represented by an online resource called the PR Value Cycle (www.pr-value.com), provided by the UK's PRCA. It claims that it 'is designed to support the assessment of PR's effectiveness well beyond the traditional media coverage level'. It comprises four stages:

1. **Business Value Planner:** Defines the strategic goals for the PR and sets the objectives at both a communication level and at a business/organizational level.
2. **Evaluation Planner:** Specifies the desired responses from the PR and establishes what evidence is needed to determine whether or not those responses were achieved.
3. **Evaluation Execution:** How will this information be gathered, by whom and what precise 'success threshold' will be used?
4. **Evaluation Review:** Given the strategic goals, objectives, desired responses and measured responses, what business value is the project concluded to have generated?

It is difficult to criticize what PR Value sets out to achieve. It is also laced with elements of realism with considerations such as how success will be perceived by different people within the organization, managing expectations, taking into account internal and external factors, the role of PR among other communications activities, and looking at both 'end' audiences and 'influencer' audiences. It also offers a systematic and repeatable approach.

The worry remains, however, that there will be plenty of occasions when it will not be possible to answer the questions posed to make the tool a practical one. The requirement to answer the question, 'How will the PR contribute to business value?' (eg sales, reputation) is one – important – example. Evaluation becomes relatively trivial if this question can be answered easily, and it is interesting to note that there is a tendency with the case studies provided on pr-value.com for them to be the relatively rare instances when public relations is the only (or certainly the major) communications activity.

Nonetheless, the thinking that goes behind PR Value is sound, it provides helpful advice, and it offers a systematic approach to thinking about public relations evaluation. Although packaged for use by public relations consultancies, its thinking is directly transferable to an in-house environment.

It might also be the case that the level of detail suggested by PR Value is appropriate for the PR practitioner's day-to-day work. It would then simply need the headlines to be extracted for management reporting (client or in-house). It is this issue that Macnamara (2006) has addressed with his concept of 'two-tier evaluation'. He suggests that senior management is frequently under time pressures and may not understand the complexities of public relations practice. The result is that they look for simple data, and that PR practitioners need to respond to this demand for simplicity.

The challenge is to meet this demand without providing data that is misleading or invalid. So the suggestion is that rather than try to satisfy everybody with the same set of reports, a two-tier approach is used. On the one hand, public relations practitioners should carry out the most in-depth research possible given the resource and time constraints they operate under. On the other, 'recognizing the needs of management for condensed reports and brief information, once reliable data has been gathered, the most salient data should be selected for presentation to management' (Macnamara, 2006: 4).

This two-tier approach has many echoes with the formative/summative or process/impact guises of public relations evaluation. Indeed, much of media evaluation falls into the category of formative evaluation and frequently there is no need to share it in detail with clients or managers, not because it is a closely guarded secret, but because its role is feedback to guide the day-to-day actions of the practitioner rather than make a summative judgement as to whether the campaign has been an overall success or not.

An example Macnamara (2006) gives concerns reputation measurement. Such studies usually involve detailed research that generates significant amounts of data. The detail is valuable to practitioners for planning and tracking progress. However, management will not have the time (or the interest) to review reams of data. So, to provide this top tier of data, it is condensed to give an overall score (on a scale of 1 to 10), which enables comparison between different time periods. There may also be the need to identify where the corporate reputation varies between different stakeholder groups. 'With a two-tier approach, practitioners can enjoy the benefits of comprehensive data to guide their work in which they can have confidence, while having simple metrics to satisfy management demands in reporting.'

MOVING EVALUATION FORWARD

Evaluation of public relations is a complex issue that varies considerably according to a variety of factors. Here are the principles that lie behind the thinking on evaluation we have espoused in this book.

There is no simple solution to the 'problem' of evaluation. There is no magic bullet, Holy Grail or an effortless way out. We are talking about a sophisticated process that requires sophisticated thinking:

- Effective evaluation starts with effective objective setting. At its simplest, PR evaluation is simply checking that the objectives set have been met. It is because objective setting in public relations is not straightforward (SMART objectives are an ideal and rarely achievable) that PR evaluation is not straightforward.

- Evaluation is a research-based discipline; evaluation is research, research is evaluation. All professional public relations practitioners need to have some understanding of research methods so they can understand, commission and analyse appropriate research to support the programmes they plan and implement.

- Evaluation focuses on the process of public relations activity because the more effective the process, the more likely (but not certainly) the impacts sought will be achieved. Process evaluation is an automatic part of professional practice that need not be shared with – but is not a secret from – clients and colleagues or employers.

- Evaluation focuses on the impact of public relations activity because the ultimate purpose of public relations activity is not the outputs from the public relations process. It is the impact of that process on the publics/stakeholders being addressed.

- Evaluation is a short-term activity because many public relations campaigns – usually of a publicity-seeking, awareness-raising nature – have short-term effects. These are normally based on media relations, and media evaluation may be some indicator of their effectiveness.

- Evaluation is a long-term activity because many public relations campaigns – normally involved with changing attitudes and behaviours – have long-term effects. Here, media relations is frequently only part of the mix and direct measurement needs to be part of the evaluation effort.

- Evaluation is user-dependent because public relations efficacy will be judged on those criteria important to the client or the employer. We may wish to educate them to be more rounded in their approach to what PR can achieve, but their current criteria are the starting point.

- Evaluation is situation-dependent because the range of contexts that public relations operates in needs to be matched by the range of approaches used for evaluation. Evaluation for a national campaign to launch an FMCG product will be very different from that associated with an international public affairs effort.
- Evaluation is realistic because public relations is a pragmatic discipline operating in the real world. Resources should not be wasted on trying – and failing – to achieve the ideal when the more easily achieved possible gives some indication of what is probably going right, and what might be going slightly wrong.

TOP TIPS FOR EVALUATING PUBLIC RELATIONS

1. We have to do more than just evaluate media coverage, because media coverage, while frequently a key driver of effectiveness, does not in itself define effectiveness.
2. Recognize that much media coverage assesses the **efficiency** of PR activity; measuring audience reach, OTS and AVEs, etc tells us how well we have deployed a given budget. They do not tell us about the effect on target audiences.
3. Effectiveness means a result or outcome that impacts an organization's business objective(s). Therefore it is essential to identify the business objective that PR is required to support, and from there to anticipate the type and level of audience response which, if achieved, will be evidence of real effectiveness.
4. PR is diverse in its techniques and target audiences. As a result PR is required to address a wide spectrum of business objectives (though not necessarily at the same time). Sales effectiveness is often the ultimate goal of many marketing PR programmes, but for other areas of PR the contribution to share price, costs and corporate reputation is the business rationale for investing in PR.
5. Establish the expected 'influencing pathway'. PR works by influencing audiences, often in multiple combinations, in order to achieve desired responses (such as interest to buy, investment advice or regulatory/legislative orientation, etc).

6. One important dimension is evaluating the cost of 'getting things wrong'. This is particularly relevant in the area of crisis and issues management.
7. Where PR is one component in the marketing activity mix, think about PR's special role and how this can be reflected in the way messaging and audiences can be differentiated from other media. In this way, audience responses can be more readily attributed to the effect of PR.

(PRCA Best Practice Guide to Evaluation)

When asked why evaluation is important, Crispin Manners is unequivocal: 'Smart organizations already recognize that good communications are essential to organizational success. Effective evaluation can tell the board what is working – or not – with sufficient insight and speed that communications efforts and investment can be directed where they will have the greatest influence on corporate objectives.'

Manners argues that to do this, you must know what qualifies as good communications and be able to demonstrate a causal relationship with the desired outcomes. 'Evaluation that illuminates this relationship in the context of what the boardroom values will give the board confidence to invest in communications. The challenge is to create benchmarks that resonate with the financial director and managing director, not just the communications director.

'We haven't proved our value to the extent that we should because evaluation hasn't been designed in from the outset – at the beginning of the planning process.'

Manners believes much more rigorous work needs to be done with business leaders to really understand how communications can impact on the business objectives they are trying to achieve. Through the planning process, milestones along the way to meeting those objectives can be identified. Easy-to-understand – and measure – benchmarks, which link back to communications activity undertaken, can then be established. He adds: 'The evaluation conundrum is solved through better planning, but PR as a discipline has been fairly slow to come to the planning table at the level it needs to.'

At the same time, Manners is clear that the focus of evaluation has to change significantly in response to the introduction of new technology. 'There is an urgent requirement for evaluation to move away from being a historic measurement of what you have done, to a current measurement of what you are doing. Traditional channels of influence are no longer the only ways to reach out to your stakeholders. The internet and broadband enable you to have a much more direct engagement with them and you need real-time feedback to guide that dialogue.' He suggests that public relations needs to re-learn one of its primary skills when it began as a discipline: its listening ability.

So how does the public relations industry need to react? 'First, there has to be a complete attitude change. We have to change from being "tell" wordsmiths, to people who are so tuned in to what's being said out there that we can provide advice with such currency that it needs to be listened to. Second, we need to recognize that the shift away from traditional sources of information is permanent. Even the most respected journalists now monitor what is being said by influential consumers and use what they are saying to drive their editorial agenda.'

Manners stresses that public relations people are over-reliant on traditional sources of influence. 'Influential consumers need to be communicated with in exactly the same way that we used to communicate with the news editor of the *FT*. Indeed, when individuals are regarded as an authority on a category, they are trusted even more than journalists, and certainly more than commercial organizations. Increasingly, they have to become our first port of call.' He argues that practitioners have to change the scale and breadth of how they monitor who says what, and recognize that influence now has global reach. 'It's category interest that matters: somebody based in India or Indiana – or even Ipswich – can share the same category interest. We need to continue to work with traditional sources of influence, but also embrace new channels.'

Active monitoring is required of the online communication between communities that share a common interest, or are trying to persuade each other of the merits of their own interest. 'This would enable us to arrive in the boardroom with information of value; of value because we are providing a current assessment of continuing challenges, not appearing to be simply trying to prove our worth after the fact.' Manners is concerned that, currently, public relations is still seen as too much of a 'tell' channel with not enough listening going on. But, there is a real opportunity for public relations to be the communications discipline that brings a listening channel back to communications. 'With the right type of listening, the sort of evaluation that proves the value of PR becomes very easy to identity and to link to outcomes.'

Manners feels that, as a consequence, there is a significant change going on in the evaluation profession itself, with a split developing between those that recognize the need for immediacy and those still trying to do it the 'old' way. Smart services are being developed that monitor current reactions to enable campaigns to change direction if they are not working. 'It is that kind of immediacy that PR as a discipline needs to bring to the table because it's the sort of value that the board will sit up and take notice of.'

Crispin Manners is CEO of Kaizo, a Fellow of the CIPR and a former Chairman of the UK's Public Relations Consultants Association (PRCA).

QUESTIONNAIRE RESPONSES

Q: How will evaluation of public relations activity develop over the coming decade?

Today, public relations is still a soft profession. The majority of people working in it have an educational background in humanities or social sciences – ie they are weak in their research training. As public relations is becoming socially (and commercially) ever more important, more people with a harder research-based background will enter the profession and numbers will become as important for public relations practice as words are. **Dejan Verčič**

It will increasingly be a requirement and practitioners who don't will fall behind. That will result in being less likely to win business for consultants and less likely to get funding for in-house practitioners. **Alison Clarke**

1. More evidence-based.
2. Needs to inform budgets.
3. If done well, will give credibility and increase our areas of core responsibility and organizational integration (corporate governance, funding strategies, risk management, high-level government and political relations, etc). **Fran Hagon**

It will switch from today's position of justifying one's existence after the fact to designing in success before the fact. In other words, there will be a demonstrable switch from an emphasis on evaluation to one on more effective planning. **Crispin Manners**

It will become an in-house function of PR agencies – most will have a department dedicated to it and we will have to carry the cost because clients will still refuse to pay for it! **Loretta Tobin**

It is going to become more important in coming years to demonstrate the effectiveness of PR as companies become more demanding in terms of tangible results. I see IT playing a major role, with technological evaluation techniques developing and close focus spotlighting PR activity as an inherent part of business strategy in an increasingly globalized world. **Ray Mawerera**

Hopefully it will lose the 'bogey-man' status and become part of everyday language in our industry. It should be like oxygen – something used constantly for life but not actually discussed in medical terms every day. **Annabelle Warren**

I believe it will be instrumental to campaigns. I also believe that there is a market for a more sophisticated evaluation software package that does it all for you – feed in one end and it comes out with a full analysis at the other end. **Laurna O'Donnell**

I think it will become an expectation by clients. **Clara Zawawi**

Ever-increasing effectiveness of computer-based software and tools along with more sharply defined demographic data. The downside will be a public over-researched, over-consulted, over-surveyed, resulting in low meaningful participation and questionable results. Also, the accelerating use by marketing/sales organizations to approach the public under the guise of 'research' can be expected to further degrade meaningful quality participation. **Tom O'Donoghue**

Make it credible – because answerable to the board for its role. It will also result in a shift towards media neutral planning as real measurement of all disciplines will raise the right questions about which tools should be used where and when, and in combination with which other tools. **Mike Copland**

The tools for evaluation will continue to come down in price and become more sophisticated, but unfortunately that doesn't make the measurement any more accurate or conclusive. We're measuring changes in behaviour here – whether it's perceptions or actions – and until we can break our programmes down to target 'publics of one', truly conclusive evaluation will be difficult to achieve. That, however, doesn't mean we shouldn't try – because the sheer exercise of benchmarking audiences, developing clear objectives and measuring on the back end will result in a stronger programme. **Matt Kucharski**

If I really knew, I'd set up an evaluation company! The future may lie online. Just as advertisers can get instant figures on how many people watched a particular advert online and can interrogate the data on their PCs, perhaps campaigns will be evaluated online. YouGov [a UK online research service] is already interviewing this way and producing opinion polls. Perhaps evaluation will go the same way. **Richard Offer**

Public Relations is a relative new concept and over the last two decades it has developed considerably. Evaluation has not typically been a focus for PR campaigns, yet the benefits received from evaluating campaigns will ensure that the coming decade will see evaluation techniques advance, hence becoming an essential component of any PR activity carried out. It will develop to give an organization control over the campaign, to have increased response rates with higher conversion rates. **Adam Connolly**

It can only get better. **John Bliss**

References

Anderson, F and Hadley, L (1999) Guidelines for setting measurable objectives, available from www.instituteforpr.com

Austin, E and Pinkleton, B (2001) *Strategic Public Relations Management*, Lawrence Erlbaum, Mahwah, NJ

Baerns, B (1993) Understanding and development of public relations in Germany, East and West, in *Proceedings of the 2nd European seminar for Teachers, Practitioners and Researchers*, Prague

Baerns, B (2005) 'Modelling and evaluating public relations measures and campaigns by German professionals – final report', 12th International Public Relations Research Symposium, Bled, Slovenia

Bell, Q (1992) Evaluating PR, in *Institute of Public Relations Handbook*, Kogan Page, London

Blaxter, L, Hughes, C and Tight, M (1996) *How to Research*, Open University Press, Buckingham

Blissland, J (1990) Accountability gap: Evaluation practices show improvement, *Public Relations Review*, **16** (2)

Blissland, J in Wilcox, D *et al* (2000) *Public Relations Strategies and Tactics*, 6th edn, Longman, Harlow

Blowers, M (2006) Cracking content – a guide to measuring the media, present and future, available at www.mediaevaluation. eu

Botan, C and Hazleton, V (1989) *Public Relations Theory*, Lawrence Erlbaum, Hillside, NJ

Broom, G and Dozier, D (1990) *Using Research in Public Relations*, Prentice Hall International, Englewood Cliffs, NJ

Bruning, S D and Ledingham, J A (1999) Relationships between organizations and publics: Development of a multi-dimensional organization-public relationship scale, *Public Relations Review*, **25** (2), 157–70

Bruning, S D, Castle, J D and Schrepfer, E (2004) Building relationships between organizations and publics: Examining the linkage between organization-public relations, evaluations of satisfaction, and behavioral intent, *Communication Studies*, **55** (3), 435–46

Callison, C (2003) Media relations and the internet: how Fortune 500 company websites assist journalists in news gathering, *Public Relations Review*, **29**, 29–41

Cameron, D and Carroll, J (2004) 'The Story So Far...'. *The Researcher as a Player in Game Analysis*, Media International Australia, No.100, pp 62–72

Crabble, R and Vibbert, S (1986) *Public Relations as Communication Management*, Bellwether Press, Edina, MN

Cutlip, S, Center, A and Broom, G (2006) Effective Public Relations, 9th edn, Pearson Education, NJ

Daymon, C and Holloway, I (2002) *Qualitative Research Methods in Public Relations and Marketing Communications*, Routledge, London

Dearstyne, B W (2005) Blogs: The New Information Revolution?, *Information Management Journal*, **39** (5)

Denscombe, M (2003) *The Good Research Guide*, 2nd edn, Open University Press, Maidenhead

Department of Trade and Industry and the Institute of Public Relations (2003) *Unlocking the Potential of Public Relations: Developing good practice*, IPR, London

Doyle, P (2002) *Marketing Management and Strategy*, 3rd edn, Pearson Education Ltd, Harlow

Dozier, D (1984) The evolution of evaluation methods among public relations practitioners, *Paper presented to the Educators Academy, International Association of Business Communicators*, Montreal

Dozier, D (1985) Planning and evaluation in public relations practice, *Public Relations Review* **11**, Summer

Dozier, D (1988) Organic structure and managerial environment sensitivity as predictors of practitioner membership of the dominant coalition, *Paper presented to the Public Relations Division, Association for Educators in Journalism and Mass Communications Conference*, Portland, Oregon

Dozier, D and Ehling, W (1992) Evaluation of public relations programs: What the literature tells us about their effects, in *Excellence in Public Relations and Communication Management*, ed JE Grunig, Lawrence Erlbaum Associates, NJ

Dozier, D and Repper, F (1992) Research firms and public relations practices, in *Excellence in Public Relations and Communication Management*, ed JE Grunig, Lawrence Erlbaum Associates, NJ

Fairchild, M (2002) Evaluation: An opportunity to raise the standing of PR, *Journal of Communication Management*, **6** (4)

Festinger, L (1957) *A Theory of Cognitive Dissonance*, Stanford University Press, Stanford CA

Fill, C (2005) Marketing Communications: Contexts, Strategies and Applications, 4th edn, Pearson Education, Harlow

FitzGibbon, CT and Morris, LL (1978) *How to Design a Programme Evaluation*, Sage Publications, Beverley Hills, CA

Fleisher, C S and Mahaffy, D (1997) A balanced scorecard approach to public relations management assessment, *Public Relations Review*, **23** (2), pp 117–42

Gaunt, R and Wright, D (2004) PR measurement, available at www.bench point.com/Download/Download.asp

Gregory, A and Edwards, L (2004) *Pattern of PR in Britain's 'Most Admired' Companies*, Leeds Business School for Eloqui Public Relations

Gregory, A, Morgan, L and Kelly, D (2005) *Patterns of PR in Britain's 'Most Admired' Companies and Public Sector Organisations*, Leeds Business School for Eloqui Public Relations

Grunig, J (1984) Organizations, environments and models of public relations, *Public Relations Research & Education*, **1**

Grunig, J (ed) (1992) *Excellence in Public Relations and Communication Management*, Lawrence Erlbaum, Mahwah, NJ

Grunig, J (1994) A situational theory of publics: Conceptual history, recent challenges and new research. Paper presented to the International Public Relations Research Symposium, Bled, Slovenia, July 1994

Grunig, J E (2002) Qualitative methods for assessing relationships between organizations and publics, available at wwwinstituteforpr.org

Grunig, JE and Hon, L (1999) *Guidelines for Measuring Relationships in Public Relations*, The Institute for Public Relations, Gainesville, FL

Grunig, J and Hunt, T (1984) *Managing Public Relations*, Holt, Rinehart & Winston, New York

Hallahan, K (1999) Content class as a contextual cue in the cognitive processing of publicity versus advertising, *Journal of Public Relations Research*, 11 (4), pp 293–320

Hering, R, Schuppener, B and Sommerhalder, M (2004) *Die communication scorecard: Eine neue methode des Kommunikations managements*, Hering Schuppener, Stuttgart

Hibbert, Z and Simmons, P (2006) War reporting and Australian defence public relations, an exchange, *PRism* online public relations journal, available at praxis.massey.ac.nz/evaluation.html

Hiebert, R and Devine, CM (1985) Government's research and evaluation gap, *Public Relations Review*, 11 (Fall)

Hodgson, B (2006) Media Relations Rating Points (MRP) in action… So what next? (20 June), available at blogs.hillandknowlton.com/bligs/brendan-hodgson

Hon, L C and Grunig, J E (1999) Guidelines for measuring relationships in Public Relations, available at wwwinstituteforpr.org

Hyman, HH and Sheatsley, PB (1947) Some reasons why information campaigns fail, *Public Opinion Quarterly*, 11, pp 412–23

Institute of Public Relations (2003) *IPR Toolkit: Media evaluation edition*, IPR London

Institute of Public Relations and Communications Directors' Forum (2004) *Best Practice in the Measurement and Reporting of Public Relations and ROI*, IPR, London

International Public Relations Association (1994) *Public Relations Evaluation: Professional accountability*, International Public Relations Association. Gold Paper Number 11, IPRA, Geneva

Jeffries-Fox, B A (2007) *Discussion of Advertising Value Equivalency*, available at wwwinstituteforpr.org

Jo, S, Hon, L C and Brunner, B R (2004) Organisation-public relationships: Measurement validation in a university setting, *Journal of Communication Management*, 9 (1), pp 14–27

Johnson, J J and Kaye, B K (2004) Wag the Blog: How reliance on traditional media and the internet influence credibility perceptions of weblogs among blog users, *Journalism and Mass Communication Quarterly*, 81 (3)

Judd, LR (1990) Importance and use of formal research and evaluation, *Public Relations Review*, 16 (4)

Kane, E and O'Reilly-de Brun, M (2001) *Doing Your Own Research*, Marion Boyars, London

Kaplan, R and Norton, D (1996) *The Balanced Scorecard: Translating strategy into action*, Harvard Business School Press, Boston

Kotler, P and Keller, K L (2006) *Marketing Management*, 12th edn, Pearson Education/Prentice Hall, NJ

Lautenbach, C (2006) Seven steps to the board room seat – a communications performance management system developed by Germany's PR association GPRA, *PRism* online public relations journal, available at praxis.massey.ac.nz/evaluation.html

Lazarsfeld, PF, Berelson, B and Gaudet, H (1948) *The People's Choice*, Columbia University Press, New York

Ledingham, J A (2003) Explicating relationship management as a general theory of public relations, *Journal of Public Relations Research*, **15**, pp 181–98

Likely, F, Rockland, D and Weiner, M (2006) Perspectives on ROI of media relations publicity efforts, available from www.instituteforpr.org

Lindenmann, W (1990) Research, evaluation and measurement – a national perspective, *Public Relations Review*, **16** (2)

Lindenmann, W (1993) An 'Effectiveness Yardstick' to measure public relations success, *Public Relations Quarterly*, **38** (1), pp 7–9

Lindenmann, W (2006) Public Relations Research for Planning and Evaluation, available at www.instituteforpr.org

Lindenmann, W and Likely, F (2003) Guidelines for measuring the effectiveness of programs and activities, available at www.instituteforpr.org

Lugbauer, C (2003) What now? New attitudes and approaches to communications measurement, *Public Relations Strategist*, **9** (4), p 37

MacManus, T and Moss, D (1994) Bled hears clash of (research) cultures, *IPR Journal*, **13** (4)

Macnamara, J (1992) Evaluation of public relations: The Achilles' heel of the PR profession, *International Public Relations Review*, **15** (24), pp 17–31

Macnamara, J (1999) Research in public relations: A review of the use of evaluation and formative research, *Asia-Pacific Public Relations Journal*, Winter

Macnamara, J (2000) The 'Ad Value' of PR, *Asia Pacific Public Relations Journal*, **1** (2), pp 99–103

Macnamara, J (2002) Research and evaluation, in *The New Australian and New Zealand Public Relations Manual*, ed C Tymson, P Lazar and R Lazar, Tymson Communications, Sydney

Macnamara, J (2005) *Jim Macnamara's Public Relations Handbook*, Archipelago Press, Sydney

Macnamara, J (2006) Two-tier evaluation can help corporate communicators gain management support, *Prism* online public relations journal, available at praxis.massey.ac.nz/evaluation.html

McCoy, M and Hargie, O (2003) Implications of mass communication theory for asymmetric public relations evaluation, *Journal of Communication Management*, **7** (4), pp 304–16

McElreath, M (1997) *Managing Systematic and Ethical Public Relations Campaigns*, 2nd edn, Brown & Benchmark, Madison, WI

McElreath, M P and Blamphin, J M (1994) Partial answers to priority research questions – and gaps – found in the Public Relations Society of America's Body of Knowledge, *Journal of Public Relations Research*, **6** (2), pp 69–103

McGuire, WJ (1984) Attitudes and attitude change, in *Handbook of Social Psychology*, II, 3rd edn, ed GG Lindzey and E Aronson, Random House, NY

Market Sentinel, Onalytica and Immediate Future (2005) Measuring the influence of bloggers on corporate reputation, available at www.immediatefuture.co.uk

Mercer Human Resource Consulting (2003) Developing a picture of the communication profession: Key findings, Unpublished report of a survey conducted online through the Public Relations Institute of Australia and International Association of Business Communicators

Mullins, L (2005) Management and Organisational Behaviour, 7th edn, Prentice Hall, Harlow

Murray, K and White, J (2004) CEO views on reputation management, available at http://www.insightmkt.com/ceo_pr_briefing/

Noble, P (1994) A proper role for media evaluation, *International Public Relations Research Symposium*, Bled, Slovenia, July

Noble, P (1999) Towards an inclusive evaluation methodology, *Corporate Communications: An International Journal* **4** (1)

Owen, R (2002), Payment by results – an option for today's PR industry? www.blackandwhitecommunications.com

Paine, K (2002a) How to measure your results in a crisis, www.instituteforpr.com

Paine, K D (2002b) Measures of success for Cyberspace, available at www.instituteforpr.org

Paine, K D (2006) Designing and implementing your communications dashboard: Lessons learned, available at www.instituteforpr.org

Patton, MQ (1982) *Practical Evaluation*, Sage, Thousand Oaks, CA

Pavlik, JV (1987) *Public Relations: What research tells us*, Sage, Newbury Park, CA

Phillips, D (2001) *Online Public Relations*, Kogan Page, London

Philips, D (2005) A Bibliographical Resource of Works about Public Relations Media Measurement Research and Evaluation, available from the author, dphillips@netreputation.co.uk

Pickton, D and Broderick, A (2001) *Integrated Marketing Communications*, Prentice Hall, Harlow

Public Relations Consultants Association (PRCA) (1998) *Agency Remuneration: A best practice guide on how to pay agencies*, PRCA, London

PRCA (2004), *Evaluation: A best practice guide to evaluating the effects of your campaign*, PRCA, London

PRCA (2006), *Purchasing Public Relations: A guide for procurement professionals*, PRCA, London

PR Value Cycle, available at www.pr-value.com

Prensky, M (2002) *Digital Game-Based Learning*, McGraw Hill, New York

Putt, G and Van der Waldt, D L R (2005) 'A quantitative matrix model for strategic management of stakeholder/issues relationships', 12th International Public Relations Research Symposium, Bled, Slovenia

Reber, B H and Kim, J K (2006) How activist groups use websites in media relations: evaluating online press rooms, *Journal of Public Relations Research*, **18** (4), pp 313–33

Ridgway, J (1996) *Practical Media Relations*, Gower, Aldershot

Rossi, PH and Freeman, HE (1982) *Evaluation – a Systematic Approach*, Sage, Thousand Oaks, CA

Ruhl, M (1992) Stepping stones towards a theory of public relations, in *European Public Relations – Data Review*, 2, ed C Scherpereel, CERP Education, Brussels

Sennott, R (1990), in *Using Research in Public Relations*, ed GD Broom and DM Dozier, Englewood Cliffs, NJ, Prentice Hall

Simmons, P and Watson, D (2005) Public relations evaluation in Australia – practices and attitudes across sectors and employment status, *Asia Pacific Public Relations Journal*, 2005 (2), available from www.deakin.edu.au/arts/apprj/articles/simmons_30%20Nov%20051.pdf

Simon, R (1984) *Public Relations Concepts and Practices*, 3rd edn, Macmillan, New York

Sinickas, A (2004) Five good reasons not to measure, *Strategic Communication Management*, **8** (5) available from http://www.sinicom.com/Sub Pages/pubs/articles/article70.pdf

Smith, P (1998) *Marketing Communications: An integrated approach*, 2nd edn, Kogan Page, London

Smith, R (2005) *Strategic Planning for Public Relations*, 2nd edn, Lawrence Erlbaum Associates, Mahwah, NJ

Stacks, D (2002) *Primer of Public Relations Research*, Guildford Press, New York

Stacks, D W (ed) (2007) Dictionary of Public Relations Measurement and Research, available at www.instituteforpr.org

Steiner, CJ and Black, L (2000) The role of public relations professionals in corporate strategic planning in Australia: Educational implications, *Asia Pacific Public Relations Journal*, **2** (1), pp 63–82

Swinehart, JW (1979) Evaluating public relations, *Public Relations Journal*, **35** (July)

Thellusson, J (2003) Measuring PR's value, *Admap*, February, Issue 436, WARC (World Advertising Research Center), Henley on Thames

Thomlinson, D T (2000) An interpersonal primer with implications for public relations, in (eds) J A Ledingham and S D Brunning, *Public Relations as Relationship Management*, Lawrence Erlbaum Associates, Mahwah, NJ, pp 177–203

Thurstone, L L and Chave, E J (1929) *The Measurement of Attitude*, University of Chicago Press, Chicago

Tixier, M (1995) Appraising communication: Reality or utopia?, *International Public Relations Review*, **18** (3)

VanLeuven, J *et al* (1988) Effects-based planning for public relations campaigns, presented to PR Division, Association for Education in Journalism and Mass Communications, Portland, OR, July

van Ruler, B (1992) Response to Professor Dr M Ruhl, in *European Public Relations – Data Review*, 2, ed C Scherpereel, CERP Education, Brussels

Vos, R and Schoemaker, H (2004) *Accountability of Communication management: A balanced scorecard approach for communication quality*, LEMMA, Utrecht

Walker, G (1994) Communicating public relations research, *Journal of Public Relations Research*, **6** (3)

Walker, G (1997) Public relations practitioners' use of research, measurement and evaluation, *Australian Journal of Communication*, **24** (2)

Watson, T (1992) Evaluation: Public relations' biggest issue, *International Public Relations Review*, **15** (3)

Watson, T (1994) Public relations evaluation: Nationwide survey of practice in the United Kingdom, *International Public Relations Research Symposium*, Bled, Slovenia, July

Watson, T (1995) Evaluating Public Relations: The creation and validation of models of measurement for public relations practice, Unpublished PhD thesis, Nottingham Trent University (Southampton Institute)

Watson, T (1996) Public relations evaluation: The second nationwide survey of practice in the United Kingdom, Unpublished, Winchester, UK

Watson, T (1997) Measuring the success rate: Evaluating the PR process and PR programmes, in *Principles and Practice of Public Relations*, ed PJ Kitchen, Chapman and Hall, London

Watson, T (2001) Integrating planning and evaluation: Evaluating public relations practice and public relations programmes, in *Handbook of Public Relations*, ed R Heath, Sage Publications, Thousand Oaks, CA

Watson, T (2005) ROI or evidence-based PR: the language of public relations evaluation, *Prism* 3, available at: http://praxis.massex.ac.nz

Watson, T and Simmons, P (2004) Public relations evaluation – survey of Australian practitioners, Proceedings of the ANZCA 04 Conference, Sydney, July

Weiner, M and Bartholomew, D (2006) Dispelling the myth of PR multipliers and other inflationary audience measures, available at www.institureforpr.org

Weiss, C (1977) *Evaluation Research – Methods of assessing program effectiveness*, Prentice Hall, Englewood Cliffs, NJ

White, J (1991) *How to Understand and Manage Public Relations*, Business Books, London

White, J (2002) Fee setting in public relations consultancies: A study of consultancy and client views of current practice in the UK, *Journal of Communication Management*, **6** (4), June

White, J and Blamphin, J (1994) *Priorities for Research in Public Relations Practice in the United Kingdom*, London City University/Rapier Research, London

Wilcox, D *et al* (2000) *Public Relations Strategies and Tactics*, 6th edn, Longman, Harlow

Wylie, F in Wilcox, D *et al* (2000) *Public Relations Strategies and Tactics*, 6th edn, Longman, Harlow

Xavier, R, Johnston, K, Patel, A, Watson, T and Simmons, P (2005) Using evaluation techniques and performance claims to demonstrate public relations impact: an Australian perspective, *Public Relations Review*, **31** (3), pp 417–24

Xavier, R, Patel, A and Johnston, K (2004) Are we really making a difference: The gap between outcomes and evaluation research in public relations campaigns, *Proceedings of the ANZCA 04 Conference*, Sydney, July

Zerfass, A (2005) 'The corporate communication scorecard: a framework for managing and evaluating communication strategies', 12th International Public Relations Research Symposium, Bled, Slovenia

FURTHER READING FROM KOGAN PAGE

Creativity in Public Relations, 3rd edn, 2007, Andy Green

Effective Internal Communications, 2005, Lyn Smith

Effective Media Relations, 3rd edn, 2005, Michael Bland, David Wragg and Alison Theaker

Effective Personal Communication Skills for Public Relations, 2006, Andy Green

Effective Writing Skills for Public Relations, 3rd edn, 2005, John Foster

Managing Activism: A guide to dealing with activists and pressure groups, 2001, Denise Deegan

Online Public Relations, 2001, David Phillips

Planning and Managing Public Relations Campaigns, 2nd edn, 2000, Anne Gregory

Public Affairs in Practice, 2007, Stuart Thomson and Steve John

Public Relations: A practical guide to the basics, 2nd edn, 2003, Philip Henslowe

Public Relations in Practice, 2nd edn, 2003, Anne Gregory

Public Relations Strategy, 2nd edn, 2007, Sandra Oliver

Risk Issues and Crisis Management: A casebook of best practice, 3rd edn, 2005, Michael Regester and Judy Larkin

Running a Public Relations Department, 2nd edn, 2001, Mike Beard

Index